CANCUN

COZUMEL
& THE
RIVIERA MAYA
ALIVE!

2nd Edition

Bruce & June Conord

HUNTER

Hunter Publishing, Inc.
130 Campus Drive, Edison, NJ 08818
732-225-1900 / 800-255-0343 / fax 732-417-1744
e-mail: comments@hunterpublishing.com
www.hunterpublishing.com

In Canada
Ulysses Travel Publications
4176 Saint-Denis, Montréal, Québec
Canada H2W 2M5
514-843-9882, ext. 2232 / fax 514-843-9448

In the UK
Windsor Books International
The Boundary, Wheatley Road, Garsington
Oxford, OX44 9EJ England
01865-361122 / fax 01865-361133

ISBN 1-58843-123-1
© 2002 Bruce & June Conord

This and other Hunter travel guides are also available as e-books in a variety of digital formats through our online partners, including Amazon.com, BarnesandNoble.com and eBooks.com.

Maps by Kim André & Kim Foley MacKinnon
© 2002 Hunter Publishing, Inc.
Index by Elite Indexing

Dedication

To Beatrice "Billy" Bilton, with undying love.

Acknowledgments

The authors would like to thank the Mexican Tourist Board, the Cancún Convention & Visitors Bureau and the local tourism officials in the state of Quintana Roo for their cooperation in researching this guidebook. Additional thanks go to Julie Fernandez of YP&B Public Relations, and the Cozumel Hotel Association for their assistance on Cozumel. Our Mexico travel haircuts are provided by Peggy and Sylvia, who always ask about our trips. Last, but not least, we want to acknowledge the inspired help of our editors, Kim André and Kim MacKinnon.

www.hunterpublishing.com

You can view Hunter's extensive range of travel guides online at our exciting website. Now you can read excerpts from books that interest you, as well as view the table of contents *before* you buy! We also post comments from other readers and reviewers, allowing you to get a real feel for each book. All transactions are processed through our secure server.

We have guidebooks for every type of traveler, no matter the budget, lifestyle or idea of fun. From dive guides and hiking books to volumes that inspire romantic weekend escapes!

Our top-selling guides in the **ALIVE!** series include: *The Cayman Islands Alive!; Martinique & Guadeloupe Alive!; Dominica & St. Lucia Alive!; Miami & the Florida Keys Alive!* and *Aruba, Bonaire & Curaçao Alive!* Click on "Alive Guides" on the website and you'll see all the other exciting destinations covered in this series.

Active travelers should be sure to check out our ***Adventure Guides***, a series aimed at the independent traveler with a focus on outdoor activities. Adventures can be as mild as beachcombing on a deserted shore or hiking a rugged hill, or as wild as parasailing, hot-air ballooning or diving among shipwrecks. All books in this signature series offer solid travel information, including where to stay and eat, transportation, sightseeing, attractions, culture, history and more.

Log on to www.hunterpublishing.com to learn about our other series – *Hunter-Rivages Hotel Guides, Landmark Visitors Guides, Romantic Weekends, Nelles Guidebooks* and *Travel Packs* and more.

About the Authors

Bruce & June Conord have been travel hounds for years, but Mexico kept luring them back with its charm and beauty. They drew on their knowledge and travel experience in the area for this book and its companion, *Adventure Guide to the Yucatán, Cancún & Cozumel*, now in its second edition.

Both Conords collaborate on a monthly travel column and Bruce has written numerous magazine articles as well as three biographies for children and young adults. He graduated from Rutgers University and studied Spanish at Forester Instituto in Costa Rica, a country the Conords also love. Their *Adventure Guide to Costa Rica* will be published in 2002.

June was born in Plymouth, England and spent part of her childhood in a picturesque village in Cornwall. She attended Plymouth Art College before emigrating to the States. Her travel articles and photographs have been published in magazines, newspapers and on the web.

Together, their journeys have taken them to 15 countries around the world but, when work is done, they head for the Yucatán to relax.

About the Alive Guides

Reliable, detailed and personally researched by knowl-edgeable authors, the *ALIVE!* series was founded by Arnold and Harriet Greenberg.

Arnold has co-authored *South America on $40 A Day*, as well as *St. Martin & St. Barts Alive!; Aruba, Bonaire & Curaçao Alive!* and *Buenos Aires & the Best of Argentina Alive!*

Harriet has co-authored *The US Virgin Islands Alive!* and *St. Martin & St. Barts Alive!* She is currently re-searching *The British Virgin Islands Alive!* and *Puerto Rico Alive!*

This accomplished travel-writing team also operates a re-nowned bookstore, **The Complete Traveller**, at 199 Madison Avenue in New York City.

We Love to Get Mail

This book has been carefully researched to bring you current, accurate information. But no place is un-changing. We welcome your comments for future edi-tions. Please write to us at:

Cancún, Cozumel & The Riviera Maya Alive!
c/o Hunter Publishing
130 Campus Drive
Edison, NJ 08818

You can also e-mail us at: comments@hunterpublishing.com.

Contents

Introduction

Americans have always been eager for travel, that being how they got to the New World in the first place.

Otto Friedrich, *Time* magazine, April 22, 1985

From ancient ruins to white tropical beaches, magnificent hotels to rustic getaways, Cancún, Cozumel, and the Riviera Maya offer fabulous vacations on exotic beach island settings enhanced by modern comforts and conveniences. It's hard to imagine a destination more richly endowed with cultural and natural wonders – or better weather. Plus, you don't have to speak Spanish to enjoy the superb delights of Mexico's Yucatán Peninsula – English is welcome everywhere! That alone may explain why Cancún is now the number one Latin American destination for North Americans, with over 2½ million visitors a year.

We know of few places that provide more all-around pleasure. Whether your definition of holiday fun is lying on a beach sipping margaritas, dancing the night away, snorkeling among brilliantly colored schools of fish, or exploring the spectacular ruins of the lost Maya civilization – the Cancún/Cozumel area has it all!

This region has a very different culture than the rest of Mexico. It's very safe – there's less crime in Cancún and Cozumel than in most small cities across the United States.

This book will give you inside information on the best values in lodging, meals, recreation and shopping. We offer thorough, first-hand evaluations of dozens of hotels and restaurants so you can find the perfect match for your vacation. We also tell where to find incredible gifts and handicrafts at unbeatable prices!

The Attractions

With this book you can enjoy the best of the glitz and glamour of the area's resorts – all at a price that emphasizes value. Sit and enjoy a delicious dinner of fresh-caught fish under the shade of a palapa at a hard-to-find seaside restaurant where only insiders go. Stay in a romantic Spanish Colonial-style hotel or an all-inclusive luxury resort just built this year. Perhaps you'd like to sleep in a beachfront bungalow so close to the Caribbean that the waves lap gently against the front porch. Roam white sandy beaches and swim turquoise seas, or look out onto miles and miles of unbroken rain forest.

It's a region whose legacy is intricately involved with the past, offering magnificent ruined Maya cities with temples, ballcourts and giant pyramids where humans were once sacrificed. Take a trip to deserted antiquarian sites and climb above the jungle canopy on imposing stone pyramids with only the ghosts of warrior kings to keep you company.

Snorkel to a spectacular reef alive with exotic fish that are as curious about you as you are about them. Or pilot a boat to an island bird sanctuary with Captain Ricardo aboard the last wooden boat built on Isla Mujeres.

UNITED STATES OF AMERICA

N

MEXICO

Gulf of Mexico

Mexico City

Mérida • • Cancún

Caribbean Sea

Pacific Ocean

BELIZE

GUATEMALA

© 2001 HUNTER PUBLISHING, INC

At night, dance in the discos to rock and roll and salsa, or take a party boat for a moonlit cruise. Lay back and admire the southern night sky – bright enough to read by and streaked with the traces of falling stars. Shop in local *mercados* for traditional crafts such as hammocks, wood carvings and pottery. Rub shoulders (if you're very short) with Maya women in their ancestral *huipil* dresses. All this and more you'll find here in our new *Cancún, Cozumel & the Riviera Maya Alive!*

We hope you enjoy it.

If you're tempted to explore more of the countryside, pick up a copy of our other best-selling book by Hunter Publishing: ***Adventure Guide to the Yucatán, Cancún & Cozumel, 2nd Edition***. The Mexico Ministry of Tourism praised it, saying, "This in-depth travel guide opens the doors to our enchanted Yucatán. *Bienvenido a Mexico*."

How to Use This Book

If you don't know where you are going, you will probably end up somewhere else.
Lawrence Johnston Peter, 1919-1990

After a bit of local history we offer handy hints about what to expect in Mexico and the culture and customs. For specific locations, we arranged the book by geography and popularity: Cancún and Isla Mujeres first, then Cozumel, Playa del Carmen, and finally we retrace direction down the coast of Riviera Maya. In each case we list our evaluations of the hotels and restaurants right up front. We follow with best bets in shopping, what to do from *Dawn to Dusk*, where to find the nightlife, and lastly, an A-Z list of handy local info. Places to go on day-trips, such as Xcaret or Chichén Itzá ruins, are listed in the *Field Trips* section. You should refer to this section even if you're staying on the Riviera Maya because the sights are easily accessible from the entire coast. We hope this proves helpful and that you have your best vacation ever. If you have any suggestions, corrections or criticisms, please send us an e-mail at junioc@aol.com or brucewrite@aol.com.

Top Five Things to Do & See

Are we there yet?
– every kid in America at one time or another

1. TULUM RUINS

Set up on a bluff over the turquoise Caribbean, the view and the feeling you get from it are memorably spectacular. See page 265.

2. CHICHEN ITZA RUINS

The ancient Maya abandoned this most interesting city at the height of their civilization. Now excavated, its buildings are magnificent. See page 278.

3. SNORKEL/DIVE COZUMEL

The undersea world of the reef that runs down the coast is breathtakingly beautiful – and easily accessible. See page 214.

4. AKTUN CHEN CAVES

A tour of fascinating stalactites and stalagmites in a large underground labyrinth. The ancient Maya held the underground as sacred. Deep, sparkling green cenote (underground lake). See page 263.

5. XCARET, XEL-HA, TRES RIOS, XPU-HA

These water parks offer a full day of fun and activities in a natural setting. See pages 258-263.

Alive Guide Ratings

There is no wealth but life.
John Ruskin, 1819-1900

Nearly everyone who comes to Cancún, Cozumel, Playa del Carmen and the Riviera Maya loves it. What's not to love? Your vacation can be a stay at an exclusive resort, a backpacking exploration on foot or anything in between. In addition to the resort hotels, there are clean, good-value lodgings in town for those on a tighter budget.

If you enjoy a slower lifestyle, check out Isla Mujeres, the "Island of Women," which lies across the bay from the Cancún hotel zone and offers inexpensive lodging. Then there's Playa del Carmen, a bohemian beachside town across the strait from Cozumel that mingles the deluxe resorts of Playacar with the funky small European hotels in the older part of town.

Cozumel itself is an island so fantastic that huge cruise ships jockey for dock space so their passengers can enjoy this world-class diving and snorkeling paradise.

Our varied accommodation listings are not in any particular order so you should probably read through all profiles before making a choice. Although we have made every effort to be as accurate as possible, things change in Mexico – sometimes rapidly.

The prices we give in dollars are approximate, subject to change. Hotel and restaurant rates change faster than anything. Here's how to use the Alive pricing scales:

Alive Price Scale – Restaurants
(per person, not including beverage)

Inexpensive . . . . less than US $6
Moderate. . . . . US $6-$13
Expensive . . . . over US $13

A Note about All-Inclusives

Prices are based on two people per room, per night. So that you may compare apples and oranges, we have priced all-inclusive resorts for double occupancy. Despite the fact that this type of establishment generally costs more than a regular hotel, remember that you get a whole lot more for your money. Meals, amenities, activities and sometimes drinks are provided without additional cost.

Seasonal Considerations

It is self-evident that the high season brings higher prices. But even within that season, prices slide according to the occupancy rate. The per-person price at Royal Solaris Caribe, for example, was $195 in December, but only $110 in March. We rated hotels at their average high-season price in December, January and February.

Alive Price Scale – Accommodations
(per night/two people per room)

Prices do not include a 12% tax.

Inexpensive. . . . . under US $40
Moderate. . . . . US $40-$100
Expensive . . . . US $101-$200
Deluxe. . . . . US $201-$300
Super. . . . . US $301-$400
Ultra . . . . over US $400

Happy trails to you.
Roy Rogers and Dale Evans

Land of the Maya

One touch of nature makes the whole world kin.
Troilus & Cressida, William Shakespeare

Geography

The Yucatán Peninsula sticks out into the Gulf of Mexico like a huge hitchhiking thumb. Its broad width provides a natural division between the warm waters of the Gulf and those of the Caribbean Sea. Because it borders the Central American countries of Guatemala and Belize, many people think of the region as being Mexico's most southern point, but the whole area is actually farther north than Acapulco. The peninsula is comprised of three Mexican states: **Campeche**, **Yucatán** and **Quintana Roo**, which includes Cancún and Cozumel. The Caribbean coastline of Quintana Roo was christened the **"Riviera Maya"** as a publicity link to Mexico's Pacific coast, known as the Mexican Riviera. Unfortunately, the government didn't restrict the development to boutique or small hotels – for which the magnificent coast is ideally suited. That lack of regulation resulted in a few properties that bulldozed down mangroves and built hotel rooms by filling in wetlands. Also, several huge all-inclusive resorts duplicate what you can get in Cancún – at an environmental cost. We don't include these on principle.

Environment

For a relatively small geographic area, the mostly dry-forested Yucatán Peninsula has an amazing variety of ecosystems that nurture a multiplicity of plant and animal life. Major tracts of wilderness are now dedicated for preservation: In the state of Quintana Roo, there's **Sian Ka'an Biosphere**, south of Tulum; Cozumel offers the **Chankanaab Lagoon National Park**; and near Cancún you'll find the **Isla Contoy Bird Sanctuary**. The state of Yucatán boasts **Rio Lagartos** and **Celestún** national parks. These are bird sanctuaries renowned for their fabulous flamingos.

Forests

In the north, the flat Yucatán landscape grows a scrub mixture of thorny leguminous trees and cactus. Greenery is subdued in the dry season (winter), but the landscape comes alive in spring and summer. If you are visiting during this lush season, you'll see a display of flaming orange-red flowering trees lining many sidewalks. These are the beautiful **royal poinciana.** The profusion of flowers encourages domesticated bee-keeping. If you have a sweet tooth, don't go home without a bottle of Yucatecan honey.

The southern part of the peninsula, along the Belize and Guatemala borders, sports a wilderness of seasonal rain forest. Thankfully, the value of the staggering biodiversity in the southern rain forest is no longer being ignored and conservation

Honey or miel (me-EL) has been a vital food source & an important crop since pre-Columbian times. The Maya even have a "Bee God."

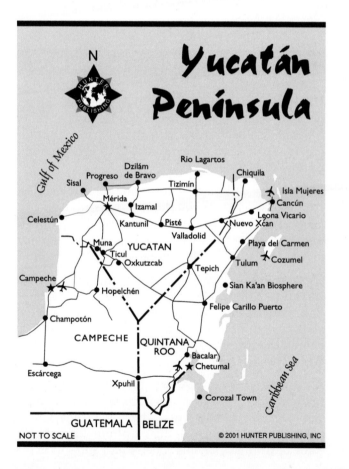

© 2001 HUNTER PUBLISHING, INC

One jungle plant (chechem) causes a skin rash. The plant that cures the rash (chacah) usually can be found nearby.

efforts are now making inroads. In addition to the biospheres of **Sian Ka'an** (1.5 million acres), **Rio Lagartos** (118,000 acres) and **Celestún** (15,000 acres), nearly two million acres of evergreen jungle forest were set aside in the extreme south of Quintana Roo and Campeche as the Calakmul Biosphere Reserve. Flowing into neighboring Guatemala, it's the largest rain forest park in all North America.

Flowers, Fruit & Fragrances

Bananas, oranges, coconuts and limes are the important produce of the countryside. Limes, called *limones* (lee-MON-ehz), are an important ingredient in Yucatecan cooking and give the cuisine a unique flavor.

One in a hundred planted coconut seeds will grow into two trees. It's considered good luck if this happens.

Despite the yellowing disease that has devastated coconut groves throughout Central America, Florida and Mexico, **coconuts** are still plentiful and cold coconut juice (*cocos frios*) is a popular drink. It's sold like lemonade at roadside stands.

Oranges are especially sweet and juicy in the Yucatán. Known as *naranjas* (na-RAHN-hass) in Spanish, they are often sold on the street with the skin peeled. For an incomparable experience, eat one as the locals do – dipped in red chili powder. Wow! Sweet and hot.

A must-stop on any *Alive* guide itinerary is the town *mercado* (market), where you may sample some of the regional fruits and vegetables. Check out the red radishes as big as plums, carrots the color of orange crayons, beans and nuts of every

Quintana Roo

N

Chiquila
Contoy
Isla Mujeres
Kantunilkín
Cancún
Leona Vicario
Puerto Morelos
Chemax 180 Nuevo Xcan
Valladolid
307 San Miguel
Cobá Playa del Carmen
Xcaret Paamul Cozumel
Puerto Aventuras
Akumal
YUCATAN Tulum
Tepich
Tihosuco Boca Paila
To Mérida 295 307
Señor Punta Allen
Dziuché José María Morelos Sian Ka'an Biosphere
Polyuc Felipe Carillo Puerto
Laguna Kana
Punta Herrero
Petcacab Nohblec
QUINTANA 293 Limones
ROO
Lázaro Cárdenas
Kinichná
Bacalar Majahual
Dzibanché Calderitas
Sergio Butrón 307
Chetumal
Nicólas Kohunlich Xcalak
Bravo
Caribbean Sea

BELIZE

© 2001 HUNTER PUBLISHING, INC   NOT TO SCALE

Land of the Maya

size and description, and big bunches of bright fresh flowers. Try *jícama* (HE-cama), a delicious root vegetable that tastes like a cross between an apple and potato. It's peeled and eaten raw sprinkled with lime juice, chili and salt. You'll also find it sliced in plastic cups and sold by vendors in the square or on the streets.

Animals

A wonderful bird is the pelican,
His bill will hold more than his belican.
He can take in his beak
Food enough for a week,
But I'm damned if I see how the helican.
The Pelican by Dixon Lanier Merritt, 1879-1954

The "land of the turkey and deer," as the Maya call the peninsula, features such exotic natives as peccaries, tapirs, manatees, iguanas and jaguars. And a large number of animals use the Yucatán as the tourists do – it is a prime spot for migrating birds and butterflies to winter over in this diverse tropical land. All told, 147 species of vertebrates, not including fish, are native to the Yucatán. If you appreciate nature, visit now – Quintana Roo's shoreline has been renamed the "Riviera Maya" by the tourist board, which forebodes rapid development of the coast south from Cancún.

Flamingos

The biospheres at Celestún, near Mérida on the Yucatan, and Río Lagartos are home to huge flocks of pink flamingos. These large wading birds have long spindly backward-bending legs and thin curved necks and beaks. Their colors run from a soft pinkish-white to a stunning salmon-pink. Guides take tourists out in boats to the feeding areas. It's breathtaking to see a huge flock, which can number more than 25,000 bright pink birds.

★ DID YOU KNOW?

It's the mineral salt content of the muddy water that affects the coloring of the birds. The higher the salt content, the brighter the birds' colorings – and the Yucatán's salts make for spectacular colors.

Flamingos feed standing on the mud banks of estuaries and in lagoon shallows. They force muddy water through the serrated edges of their bill, straining animal and vegetable matter for consumption.

Life Undersea

> *The sea has many voices.*
> T.S. Eliot, *The Dry Salvages*, 1888-1965

Reels

South from Isla Mujeres, a sliver of an island just off Cancún, the second longest coral reef in the world stretches down to the Bay of Honduras, over 156 miles away (250 km). The entire peninsula is one gigantic limestone reef forced up from the bottom of the sea as tectonic plates crashed together.

◎ TIP

Mexican laws severely restrict the harvesting of sea turtles. If you see a sea turtle dish offered on a restaurant menu, please don't order it.

The reefs provide the perfect habitat for hundreds of types of fish, shellfish, invertebrates, reptiles and amphibians. The beaches are breeding grounds for sea turtles, who come ashore to lay their eggs in the sand. With so many predators – seagulls, fish, raccoons, foxes and human poachers – only about 4 or 5% of the young turtles reach maturity. Isla Mujeres has a turtle research station that makes for a pleasant and educational visit.

 ## Fish

When most people think of the sea they think "fish." So if it's fish you want – to see or to eat – then you've found a home along the Caribbean coast. Put on a snorkel and mask and join the excitement below the waves. Spanish grunts, French grunts, yellowjacks, barracuda, queen triggerfish, blue tangs, red snappers, banded butterfish, groupers, damselfish, sergeant majors, angelfish and spotted drums are just a few of the colorful, edible inhabitants found here.

All men are equal before fish.
Herbert Hoover, 1874-1964

People of the Yucatán

The forces of the past live on and exert influence on us, though we may not be consciously aware of this... we are all imbedded in the flux of generations, whose legacy of thought and feeling we irrevocably carry along with us.
Gods, Graves & Scholars by Kurt W. Marek

The Yucatán is home to some of the friendliest folks in the world. Whether you're dining in Cancún's lively restaurants downtown, tooling around Cozumel on motorscooters, climbing ancient Maya ruins, laying back in a hammock, or shopping in Valladolid's *mercado*, you can be sure of a warm welcome.

The history of the people is fascinating. Tragedy, peace, bloodlust, sacrifice, war, gore, romance, glory, pain, triumph, love, ignorance, enlightenment, lost opportunities, treachery, greed, friendship and intrigue fill the chronicle of Mexico's Yucatán.

The Maya

The essence of tragedy is to know the end.
Charles W. Ferguson

Astronomers, mathematicians, agronomists, philosophers, artists, architects, sculptors and warriors – the Maya of old were a rich, complex society. They built a glorious civilization that stretched from the Yucatán Peninsula into the Mexican states of Tabasco and Chiapas and the countries of Guatemala, Belize, El Salvador and Honduras.

Their stunning accomplishments are still evident. It was the Maya who first domesticated chocolate, chili peppers, vanilla, and papayas. It was they who built causeways and reservoirs, created great works of sculpture and art, carved fantastic jade masks and wove rich colorful textiles. The Maya also developed sophisticated mathematical systems; complex, accurate calendars; and perfectly proportioned buildings of immense size and beauty. Many of these accomplishments took place while Europe remained in the Dark Ages.

However, by the time of its "discovery" by Europeans, Maya civilization had risen and fallen several times. Magnificent classic Maya cities once inhabited by thousands of people were suddenly abandoned, forfeited to the encroaching jungle.

The great mystery is why. That question lured the Yucatán's first tourist, John Lloyd Stephens, a self-taught American archeologist, to explore the ruins of southern Mexico in the early 1840s.

Stephens described his first sight of the great Maya civilization: *"... emerging suddenly from the woods, to my astonishment came at once upon a large open field strewed with mounds of ruins and vast buildings on terraces and pyramidal structures, grand and in good preservation, richly ornamented, without a brush to obstruct the view, in picturesque effect almost equal to the ruins of Thebes."*

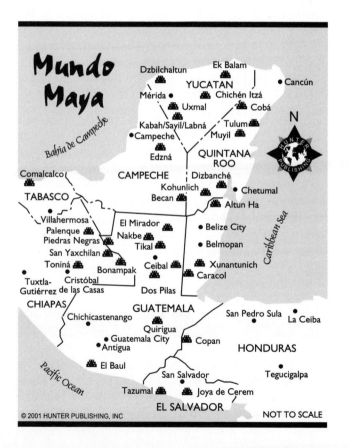

Mundo Maya

Dzbilchaltun
Ek Balam
YUCATAN
Cancún
Mérida
Chichén Itzá
Uxmal
Cobá
Kabah/Sayil/Labná
Tulum
Campeche
Muyil
Bahía de Campeche
Edzná
QUINTANA ROO
N
Comalcalco
CAMPECHE
Dizbanché
Kohunlich
Chetumal
TABASCO
Becan
Altun Ha
Villahermosa
El Mirador
Belize City
Palenque
Nakbe
Piedras Negras
Tikal
Belmopan
San Yaxchilan
Caribbean Sea
Toniná
Ceibal
Xunantunich
Bonampak
Caracol
Tuxtla-Gutiérrez
Cristóbal de las Casas
Dos Pilas
CHIAPAS
GUATEMALA
San Pedro Sula
La Ceiba
Chichicastenango
Quirigua
Guatemala City
Copan
Antigua
HONDURAS
El Baul
Tegucigalpa
Pacific Ocean
San Salvador
Tazumal
Joya de Cerem
EL SALVADOR
© 2001 HUNTER PUBLISHING, INC
NOT TO SCALE

Land of the Maya

Spanish Conquest

In 1519, a well-armed expedition led by **Hernán Cortéz** landed on the island of Cozumel, a religious and trading center for the Maya. But hostile indigenous warriors twice repelled him from the rest of the peninsula so, sailing around to the Gulf, Cortéz and his men disembarked near the present-day city of Veracruz. Residents here believed the Spanish to be gods and promptly surrendered. It was in Veracruz that Cortéz learned of Mexico's strongest empire – who were at the height of their civilization – the Aztec. The Aztec ruled all of central Mexico from their floating capital city, Tenochtitlán.

The first Mexican Indian people Columbus encountered on the Yucatán coast in 1502 were the Maya, who were the last Indian civilization to be conquered.

Cortéz's small band of battle-hardened soldiers began a quick, two-year conquest of the powerful Aztec empire. Superior steel weapons, horses and invaluable alliances with rivals of the Aztecs – combined with a prophecy that predicted the Aztec downfall at the hands of an avenging god – allowed Cortéz, a consummate warrior and ruthless tactician, to succeed. In a very short time, a thousand-year-old civilization of millions fell to a force of barely 500 men.

New Spain

The Yucatán Peninsula, however, proved to be more difficult to subjugate than the rest of Mexico. Cortéz handed that task over to his lieutenant, Francisco de Montejo. Montejo and his son led a bloody, cruel, and bitter conquest that lasted over 20 years.

Even then, Spanish control over the land and its people was incomplete, and sporadic warfare continued for centuries. In some sense, the resistance didn't end until the 1930s when Quintana Roo's Cruzob Maya finally made peace with the Mexican government. The Maya lamented their loss in the book *Chilam Balam de Chumayel,* in which they cried:

> *"There was no sin...*
> *No illness afflicted man,*
> *Aches did not hurt the bones,*
> *Fevers were unknown,*
> *There was no smallpox...*
> *All that ended with the dzules [strangers]*
> *They taught fear... "*

Colonial Days

[The conquest] was neither a victory nor a defeat; it was the painful birth of the Mexican nation, the Mexico of today.

Inscription placed in 1964 on Tlatelolco Square,
Mexico City

Dirty Business

Almost immediately, the Yucatán became a Colonial backwater compared to the rest of Mexico and South America. To the great disappointment of the Spanish conquerors, there was no gold in its limestone flatlands. The precious metal ornaments they saw when they first landed at Cozumel were all imported from the highlands. The only exploitable economic resource was the land, so Montejo gave large parcels of it away to his soldiers in exchange for loyal service in battle. As a result, a feudal nobility of prominent families came to control large cattle ranches and farms called *haciendas*. The labor pool was the Maya, who were exploited mercilessly. The haciendas grew to become the financial, political and social base for the privileged class in the Yucatán and remained in that role until well into the 20th century.

On September 28, 1821, three centuries of Spanish Colonial rule ended and Mexico, the nation, was born. Powerful hacienda families in the Yucatán – unhappy with a centralized government and federally imposed land reforms – declared their independence from Mexico. But that made little difference to the Indian community – either way its people were still under the yoke of oppression. Consequently, in early 1847, while the federal government was preoccupied with the Mexican-American War and Yucatecans were bickering over independence, the Maya rebelled.

Blood from a Stone

The **War of the Castes** began in 1847 (so called because of the complex racial levels, or "castes," that the Spanish had developed to differentiate the mixed bloodline of the Mexican people). Very quickly the Maya armies forced the Yucatecan population inside the defensive walls of the cities of Mérida and Campeche. Historians estimate the Maya were within a week of driving them into the sea.

What happened next can be explained only by the religious significance of the land – and *maize* – to the Maya. On the verge of victory, the entire army packed up and went home – to plant corn. In Maya religion and philosophy, life and time were – and still are – cycles, and the cycle indicated it was time for crop-planting.

The Yucatecans used the reprieve to reinforce themselves with federal soldiers, offered in exchange for their renewed support of a united Mexico. Barbarous counterattacks on the dispersed Maya regained much of the land the Yucatecans had lost. Many captured Maya were sold as slaves to the sugar barons of Cuba ($45 for men, $25 for women, children free).

Land of the Maya

Whenever I hear anyone arguing for slavery,
I feel a strong impulse to see it tried
on him personally.

Abraham Lincoln, 1809-1865

Shortly thereafter, sisal (*henequen*) production provided a new source of wealth and stability to the Yucatecans in the north. But anarchy still reigned in the east, well past the official end of the Caste War in 1855. Skirmishing continued off and on until the very early 1900s, when the Maya were finally subdued by repeating rifles and years of starvation and disease. In 1901, the frontier became the Federal Territory of Quintana Roo and official statehood finally came in 1974, just in time to build Cancún.

New Age

The Yucatán's past – desperate and bloody, rich and grand, glorious and shameful – has been replaced with a present that offers much promise. Between the 1930s and the 1970s, socialism had a strong voice in federal government and the worst of the Indian abuses were addressed. During this time the Maya gradually converted their economy from a barter system to one which has a monetary base. Changes accelerated in the 1970s with improved roads, the development of Cancún and the statehood of Quintana Roo, all of which boosted the peninsula's economy.

The people of the Yucatán are hardworking and peace loving. We love to stop in small towns and chat with the locals, who are always pleased to meet us and giggle at our bad Spanish and even worse Mayan. In fact, everyone we meet in the Yucatán welcomes us with genuine hospitality and are eager to show the very best of the land they call home.

The area is a treasure trove of attractions – historical and contemporary, natural and phenomenal. So put away any fears of *banditos*, or getting lost in the wilderness or being eaten by wild animals. Come down for the vacation of a lifetime.

> *... life, liberty and the pursuit of happiness.*
> The American Declaration of Independence,
> July 4, 1776

Land of the Maya

Getting Ready

Pack up your troubles in your old kit bag and smile, smile, smile.

popular song during World War I

Details, Details

The **high season** in the Yucatán occurs during the dry winter months (December through April), with peaks at Christmas and Spring Break. **Hurricane season** runs from August through October, with September the most likely month for the unpredictable storms. The weather is comfortably warm year-round, with an average temperature of 80°F (27°C).

Money Matters

The Mexican currency is the **peso**, sometimes called the new peso after a drastic devaluation late in 1994. It floats against the dollar at the rate of around eight pesos to the dollar, as of this writing. The more pesos per dollar, the better the rate of exchange for you.

The US dollar can be exchanged at banks or change booths (*casitas de cambio*). Although dollars are accepted almost everywhere (at a variable exchange rate), it's a good idea to bring traveler's checks to convert at a bank or change booth – you should have a passport for ID. Many restaurants add a 10% tip to the bill. Leave more if the service is good.

Most prices in the shops (written as NP$ or N$) are quoted in pesos – but make sure beforehand. Hotel prices are generally in dollars.

Bring lots of dollar bills for tips. It's easier than figuring out the exchange rate.

★ A WAKE-UP CALL

A careless businessman took one of the glamorous suites in Casa Turquesa in Cancún thinking that the 3,200 price was in pesos. The next day he was presented with a bill for 24,000 new pesos, the equivalent of US $3,200! Have a nice day, Señor.

Credit Cards, Traveler's Checks

Only hotels, larger shops and restaurants accept credit cards. Banks exchange cash or traveler's checks, without commission, during limited hours.

In Cancún, Playa del Carmen, Tulum and Cozumel, exchange booths are open longer hours and will change cash or traveler's checks. You'll need a copy of your passport and sometimes another form of ID in order to make the exchange.

Shop around. The rates vary between change booths and even banks – and they change daily.

The worst place to convert spending money is your hotel in the hotel zone, where the rates are generally lower than anywhere else. The change booths with the best rates in Cancún are downtown. The best rates are usually found at one of the three cambios located on Av. Cobá, just before you get to Av. Tulum.

ATMs

ATMs are located inside shopping malls and banks. Any credit card charges or ATM withdrawals go through at the official exchange rate. We've found it more convenient to use ATMs when we travel than to bring much cash or traveler's checks.

Passports & Visas

No visas are required for travel in the Yucatán, but tourist cards are a must (you'll be given one on the plane). Stays can be extended for up to 180 days, but you are given only 30 days when you arrive. Applications for extensions should be made at the **Immigration Office** in Cancún, at the corner of Av. Uxmal and Nader (☎ 9/884-1658 or 884-2892).

To enter Mexico, Americans and Canadians need proof of citizenship, such as a passport or birth certificate and a photo ID. (Canadians may use a Canadian Identification Card as proof of citizenship; UK citizens need a passport.)

Passport applications for United States citizens can be obtained from regional or federal authorities at major post offices, courthouses or federal passport agencies in major cities. You can also download an application online at http://travel. state.gov. If you lose your tourist card, the Cancún Immigration Office can replace it.

A passport carries hefty weight with bureaucratic Mexican officials, so it pays to have one.

What to Bring

Pack light. The Yucatán offers a warm-weather climate with only occasional rain or cool temperatures. Dress styles are relatively casual in most restaurants and clubs, even in the evening. Plus you can always buy clothes there, especially T-shirts and sportswear. In-town laundromats offer inexpensive drop-off, wash and fold services.

Electrical appliances such as blowdryers and electric shavers will not present a problem: electricity is the same as in the States.

Fair Air Fare

One way to save money is to check your newspaper's travel section for package trips that include airfare and choice of accommodations from luxury to moderate. Large package vacation companies with service to Cancún include **Apple Vacations** (www.applevacations.com) and **Funjet** (www. funjet.com). Ask your travel agent to check for specials, or check on the Internet.

> ## ⊚ TIP
>
> Ask your travel agent to check the bucket shops or wholesalers for airfare-only deals. We once flew Apple Vacations air-only on a Mexicana flight at a substantial discount. Use this book to find a hotel that you like and get a good travel agent to make reservations and find the lowest airfare.

Direct flights are now offered from the US to Cozumel, or you must connect through Cancún International (CUN).

Regional airlines that fly from Cancún to Cozumel, Chichén Itzá or Mérida include **Aero-Cancún** (☎ 9/886-0224) and **Aerocaribe Aerocozumel** (☎ 9/848-2000 or 886-0162).

Flight Times to Cancún (hours)

New York 3½
Miami 1½
Los Angeles 4½
Vancouver BC 6
Toronto 4½
Denver 4
Europe 12

Getting Ready

Health & Safety

 No shots are required. However, we recommend that all travelers get a **hepatitis B** shot no matter where in the world they are going. Most hotels and restaurants offer purified tap water, but drink bottled water (*agua purificada*) or seltzer water (*agua mineral*) to be sure. Qualified English-speaking doctors are available for health emergencies.

Be sure to wash your hands every chance you get, especially at meal times. If you do get sick it's usually the scary but not serious ***tourista***. *Tourista's* symptoms, which mimic those of salmonella poisoning, may include any or all the following: nausea, diarrhea, vomiting, stomach cramps and raging fever.

◎ TIP

If we're in one of our budget hotels, the first thing we do when we start feeling bad (and it does come on very quickly) is upgrade to a hotel with air conditioning – maybe cable TV – and a comfortable bed.

A couple of aspirin and plenty of sleep is called for. If you're suffering with diarrhea and stomach cramps, take the recommended dose of Imodium AD. It's necessary to drink plenty of bottled water or Coca Cola with lime. In severe cases, you should drink rehydration fluids such as

Pedialyte, available at local drugstores. We also drink *manzanilla* (chamomile) tea with honey, a helpful and pleasant folk remedy. We repeat the Imodium if the diarrhea returns.

In about 24 hours we're usually feeling well enough to get back out and enjoy the sunshine – with some reservations. If you've had a bout, you may still feel a little weak: Take it easy and don't overexert. For a few days you may also experience mild stomach cramps after eating. Eat light and cut out liquor and hot spices.

Sun poisoning, even sunburn, is a serious consequence of trying to get a quick tan (and there is no such thing). Use sunscreen with a strength of 30 or higher and you'll still get a tan within the week. Wear a hat. Children are particularly susceptible. Keep them well protected.

Sunscreen is not effective until 30 minutes after it has been applied to your skin.

Crime

Most crime in the Yucatán is limited to a rare pick-pocketing or over-charging. Use common sense and normal precautions, especially in crowded areas, and you should have no problems.

Health Clubs

Most larger hotels have their own health clubs open exclusively to hotel guests. However, there are two public gyms in Cancún. **Gold's Gym** (☎ 9/ 883-2933) is open Monday through Friday, 7 am-

Getting Ready

Cancún's marathon in December has a maximum of 10,000 runners. To enter, ☎ 525/536-7148; fax 687-4912.

9 pm and Sunday from 9 am-9 pm. It's at the Plaza Flamingo in the hotel zone. **Michaels' Gym** (☎ 9/884-2394) is on Av. Sayil No. 66, near the bullring. There is also a small gym, **Isleño's**, on Isla Mujeres. Additionally, the Cancún hotel zone has a walking/biking path nearly 16 km (10 miles) long.

Smoking

Two excellent Mexican cigars are Santa Clara's Los Aromas de San Andrés and Cruz Real.

There's far too much. Cuban cigar smokers will be pleased: what's considered the ultimate smoke is legal here. You can even take a quick junket to Havana from here, but don't tell the US State Department. Among the best-known Cuban brands (illegal to bring back to the States) are Partagas, Punch, Romeo y Julieta, Cohiba, Hoyo de Monterrey, Montecristo and H. Upmann.

◎ TIP

Look for the word "Cubana" or "Habana" on the label because some Cuban brand names are made in other countries as well.

Telephones

To call Mexico, dial 011 for an international line, then 52 for Mexico, followed by the number listed in the text. We've given the area or city code first, separated from the phone number by a slash (/).

Calls between different areas in Mexico are preceded by 019. However, *local calls do not need the area code*. If you're in Cancún, for example, and the number we list is 9/888-8888, simply drop the 9 when you dial.

Calls Home

If you call home from your hotel room, make sure surcharges and rates aren't exorbitant. You can call through Telemex and charge it to an AT&T card, but it's a little more costly than dealing direct with a USA-based server. Reach a direct line to the major American telephone companies from a hotel that offers its guests access to long-distance calling.

95 is the country code for the US.

Public Telephones

Public telephones marked *"Ladatel"* can also be used to charge a call to your calling card or to call the States directly. The only way to reach the operator or a direct service from a pay phone is by using a Ladatel or Ladaphone phone card, which may be purchased from any of the many vendors that display the blue and yellow Ladatel logo. The cards, commonly sold in values of 30, 50 or 100 pesos, will allow you to dial direct. Ladatel cards have a computer chip that tracks the time on line. With Ladaphone cards you punch in a code before dialing. To reach your US long distance carrier for calling card calls, see "Collect & Charge" below.

Getting Ready

N WARNING

Avoid calling home on phones
that offer calls to the US or Canada by punching *01, or a similar prefix, to charge the call on a
major credit card. These phones
are everywhere in Cancún and,
although convenient, charges
are upwards of US $25 for the
first minute! It's a rip-off aimed
at young vacationers who might
not have major phone company
cards.

Collect & Charge Calls

Call collect or charge your AT&T credit card by dialing 090 and speaking with the operator. To
reach **AT&T Direct Service**, dial ☎ 001/800/
462-4240. For **MCI WorldPhone**, ☎ 001/800/
674-7000. **Sprint International** is at ☎ 001/800/
877-8000. Good luck!

Internet & E-mail

Internet cafés are the main resource for local people to send & receive e-mail. Every town has one
or more, so just go in and sign on. It costs about $5
an hour.

Things to Buy

Silver and gold jewelry, pottery, hammocks, honey, embroidered dresses, T-shirts, folk art, Panama hats, men's guayabera shirts, wood carvings, pewter, and blankets.

Mexico leads the world in silver (plata) production.

Tipping

Many restaurants often add a 10% tip, *propina*, to your bill. If you have received good service, don't hesitate to leave another 10% on the table. Tips are the major source of income for service workers, as their salaries are well below North American standards and sometimes even below Mexican standards. Maid service in rooms should be tipped at least US $2 per night.

Customs Allowances

Customs stops on the way in and out of Mexico are fairly simple. Don't have drugs or firearms, period. Drug possession penalties in Mexico (even for the smallest amount) include harsh prison terms and the embassy can do little to help you. It's just not worth it. The Yucatán is making a serious effort to curb drug trafficking. If you drive in the countryside you can expect to be stopped occasionally by the Army's anti-drug patrols.

Getting Ready

You can carry into Mexico two bottles of any liquor and two cartons of your favorite coffin nails. There's a green light/red light Customs system. You punch a button at inbound Customs and, if the traffic light goes green, you can pass through unhindered. If it flashes red, you are subject to either a cursory or complete luggage search. On your return to the United States you can bring in up to US $400 per person of duty-free goods, including one liter of alcohol. Canadians are allowed $300 with a written exemption, or $100 without.

Driving/Car Rental

 Rental cars are relatively expensive and you should buy all the insurance on offer. Unlike the United States, rental drivers are liable for 10% of the car's value, so we strongly advise taking zero deductible policies. Roads are in excellent condition, but night driving in the countryside is very dangerous for a variety of reasons.

⚠ WARNING

Be cautious when you drive in Mexico, as left turns are made from the right lane. On Cozumel's four-lane northern road, for example, in order to make a left turn, pull into the right lane and wait until the traffic passes before you turn. Yikes!

Buses are a good alternative and very reasonably priced. The hotel zone in Cancún offers frequent bus service along the main drag and into downtown for just 60¢. The bus station for long-distance service is downtown at Av. Uxmal & Tulum.

More Information

To get information and brochures about Cancún, Cozumel and Mexico in general, call the **Mexico Hotline**. In the US, ☎ 800/44-MEXICO (800/446-3942); in Canada, ☎ 800/2MEXICO (800/263-9426). Online info is available at www.Cancun. com; e-mail welcome@cancun.com.

Numerous tourist information booths at the airport and in downtown Cancún advertise free trips to Isla Mujeres, discounted tours or car rentals, gifts, free Jungle Tours, etc. These are mostly time-share promotions that require what is euphemistically called "an hour" of your time. Unless you're an old pro or are thinking seriously of joining an interval ownership group, your best bet is to just say no.

Your best bet is to pick up a copy of the *Cancún Tips* magazine – free – and go.

Getting Ready

Metric Conversions

GENERAL MEASUREMENTS

1 kilometer	=	.6124 miles
1 mile	=	1.6093 kilometers
1 foot	=	.304 meters
1 inch	=	2.54 centimeters
1 square mile	=	2.59 square kilometers
1 pound	=	.4536 kilograms
1 ounce	=	28.35 grams
1 imperial gallon	=	4.5459 liters
1 US gallon	=	3.7854 liters
1 quart	=	.94635 liters

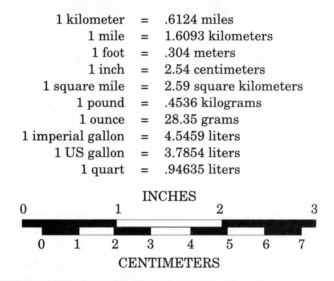

TEMPERATURES

For Fahrenheit: Multiply Centigrade figure by 1.8 and add 32. **For Centigrade:** Subtract 32 from Fahrenheit figure and divide by 1.8.

CENTIGRADE		FAHRENHEIT
40°	=	104°
35°	=	95°
30°	=	86°
25°	=	77°
20°	=	64°
15°	=	59°
10°	=	50°

Time & Measurements

As of now, the Yucatán remains on Central Standard Time. Weights, measures and temperatures are given in metric. Gasoline is sold by the liter and distances are measured by kilometers. Dates are expressed with the day first, followed by the month (Christmas Day is written 25/12).

Culture & Customs

If you reject the food, ignore the customs,
fear the religion and avoid the people
– you'd better stay home.
James A. Michener

What to Expect

The *siesta* is still a part of the Mexican lifestyle. It's not as common in Cancún or Cozumel as it is in rural Mexico due to the overwhelming influence of North American culture.

People speak **English** everywhere and the city's hotels, stores, restaurants and workers cater to American tastes.

It's definitely not acceptable to **sunbathe topless** on beaches that are used by local families. Nor should you wear revealing clothes or bathing suits in the shopping malls, on the bus, or in the streets downtown.

Getting Ready

The majority of Mexicans are Catholic and conservative, but they can party with the best of them too. We'd like to think that users of this guide would be sensitive to local mores and want to present only the best of themselves.

Sports

Bullfight critics row on row
Crowd the vast arena full
But only one man's there who knows
And he's the man who fights the bull
Frederico Garíca Lorca Spanish poet, 1899-1936

The ancient Maya played a kind of basketball/soccer game in which the players could not touch the ball with their hands or feet, but propelled it instead with their hips. You'll see stone rings that were goals on the ceremonial ballcourt at Chichén Itzá. Losers were sacrificed.

Today's Yucatecans enjoy organized sports such as baseball, basketball and soccer. **Bullfighting** goes on year-round in Cancún every Wednesday in the bullring downtown. Be forewarned that they slay bulls in the course of the fight. Cost is around US $35.

The resort sport activities available here include diving, snorkeling, windsurfing and swimming. Cancún has an international marathon race in December, attracting world-class runners as well as amateurs. There are several fishing tournaments and, if you feel like trying your luck, you can charter a fishing boat any day of the week from Cancún, Cozumel or Isla Mujeres.

Weather

*There is really no such thing as bad weather,
only different kinds of good weather.*

John Ruskin, 1819-1900

Seasonal Temperatures in Cancún

Month	High (°F/°C)	Low (°F/°C)
Jan	80/27	64/18
Feb	86/30	68/20
Mar	90/32	72/22
Apr	95/35	77/25
May	99/37	81/25
Jun	99/37	77/25
Jul	99/37	77/25
Aug	99/37	77/25
Sep	91/35	73/23
Oct	95/35	73/23
Nov	88/31	72/22
Dec	80/27	65/19

Getting Ready

Holidays & Festivals

*To many people holidays are not voyages of
discovery, but rituals of reassurance.*

Philip Andrew Adams, Australian

Most of Mexico's festivals and holidays have religious significance. In the Yucatán, these aren't solemn occasions but spirited celebrations that, in some cases, blend Maya rituals and culture with the Catholic religion. Local people dress up and enjoy dancing, music, feasts and fireworks. For more details on any of these events, you can call the Mexico Government Tourist Office, ☎ 800-44-MEXICO.

☆ JANUARY

1 Jan: **New Year's Day**.

6 Jan: **Día de los Reyes Magos**: Day of The Three Kings. Gifts are often exchanged this day instead of Christmas.

☆ FEBRUARY

2 Feb: **Candeleria** (religious holiday).

5 Feb: **Flag Day/Constitution Day** (legal holiday).

Feb/March: **Carnival**. This is especially festive on Cozumel.

☆ MARCH

Around 21 March: **Vernal Spring Equinox**. The shadow of a serpent appears to undulate down the steps of the pyramid of Kukulcán at Chichén Itzá.

21 March: **Birthday of Benito Juárez**.

March/Apr: **Easter Sunday**. Perhaps the most holy day in Mexico. The week preceding is **La Semana Santa** (Holy Week).

☆ APRIL

End of Apr/beginning of May: **International Yacht Races**, Isla Mujeres.

El Cedral Fair, Cozumel.

☆ MAY

1 May: **Labor Day** (legal holiday).

2-3 May: **International Deep-Sea Fishing Tournament**, Cozumel.

5 May: **Cinco de Mayo**. This holiday commemorates the Battle of the Puebla (1862), in which the Mexican Army defeated invading French troops.

17-27 May: **Jazz Festival**, Cancún.

☆ JUNE

4 June: **Festivities**, Valladolid.

24 June-9 Aug: **Saints Peter & Paul**, Cozumel.

☆ JULY

25 July: **Saint James the Apostle**, Rio Lagartos.

☆ AUGUST

17 Aug: **Cruz de la Bahia** celebrates the founding of Isla Mujeres in 1854. A bronze cross weighing approximately one ton, 39 feet in height and 9¾ feet wide, was planted into the Manchones Reef between Isla Mujeres and the coastline in 1994.

Getting Ready

The "Cross of the Bay" is the island's tribute to all the men and women of the sea. Scuba divers celebrate with a mass dive.

☆ SEPTEMBER

15 Sept: **Independence Day** (legal holiday).

ca. 23 Sept: **Autumnal Fall Equinox**, Chichén Itzá.

29 Sept-9 Oct: **Saint Miguel Archangel**, Cozumel.

☆ OCTOBER

2nd weekend Oct: **Music Festival**, Isla Mujeres.

12 Oct: **Columbus Day** (legal holiday).

31 Oct: **All Souls' Eve**. Boo!

☆ NOVEMBER

1-2 Nov: **All Souls' Day/All Saint's Day/Day of the Dead**. Graveside and church ceremonies honor the memory of departed loved ones. Instead of a somber occasion, the Day of the Dead is a happy celebration with a fiesta atmosphere. As well as sugar skulls and candy skeletons, a family meal is eaten at the gravesites and favorite food is left for the departed souls. A haunting experience.

12 Nov: **Cozumel Marathon Race**. The 26.2-mile race attracts runners from the US and Mexico.

End of November-beginning of December: **Expo-Cancún**. Arts and crafts, exhibits and folk dancing.

☆ DECEMBER

8 Dec: **Feast of the Immaculate Conception**.

12 Dec: **Our Lady of Guadalupe**. A big holiday in honor of Mexico's patron saint.

15 Dec: **International Marathon Cancún**. Begun in 1996.

25 Dec: **Christmas Day**.

31 Dec: **New Year's Eve**. Party time.

Honeymoons & Weddings

An archeologist is the best husband any woman can have: The older she gets, the more interested he is in her.
Agatha Christie, 1890-1976

Mexico is now the number one foreign destination for honeymooning couples. It's no wonder, explains Geri Bain, travel editor of *Modern Bride Magazine*: "Couples nowadays are looking for more than just a nice beach location and good weather. [They] want a romantic and relaxing setting combined with adventure and outdoor activity. Mexico amply satisfies these criteria."

Call your travel agent for honeymoon packages. Many resorts also offer wedding deals, allowing for a romantic tropical affair at your hotel. You can arrange your own idyllic marriage ceremony anywhere. It's easy to plan a civil or religious ceremony in Mexico. The legal requirements and regulations are minimal and mirror what a couple would need to provide in the United States.

Lots of companies can help with wedding arrangements, from the Justice of the Peace to flowers
and cake. **Weddings on the Move** is one. Call
☎ 800/444-6967. **Cancún Weddings** (☎ 9/884-
9522) arrange nuptials in the ever-popular honeymoon resort town of Cancún.

Required Marriage Documents

- ❏ *Tourist card*
- ❏ *Birth certificate*
- ❏ *Blood test certificate*
- ❏ *Valid passport or driving license*
- ❏ *Divorce certificate (if applicable)*
- ❏ *Marriage Application form*
- ❏ *Four witnesses*

Eat, Drink & Shop

Food

*In a foreign café, three Englishwomen
walked in wearing the most outlandish
holiday clothes and Panama hats, with
lots of raincoats and cameras and
walking sticks and rucksacks.
They stood about looking for a waiter
and one said in a loud voice,
"How do we attract attention?"*
1956 letter, Elizabeth Taylor, novelist.

Yucatán cooking is unique. One great specialty
(*Yucateca*) offers seafood or meat flavored

with a spicy, but not hot, anchiote paste. Another, *pibil*, features meat marinated in a rich sauce, then steam-baked in an earthen pit.

Despite having a habanero pepper 20 times hotter than the jalapeño of northern Mexico, Yucatecans prefer their heat on the side, rather than cooked into the food.

The region's native pepper is the habanero. This lantern-shaped fireball comes in green, red or yellow. On Caribbean islands it is known as the Scotch bonnet.

TIP

Always ask if the dish of salsa offered contains habanero before scooping some up on a chip. You might get an unpleasant surprise if you don't like it hot.

Each Yucatecan state has its own culinary claim to fame – as well as the old Mexican standby of tacos and burritos. *Poc chuc*, a dish made famous by Los Almendros restaurants, is thinly sliced pork marinated in sour orange and vinegar. The strips are then grilled and the dish is served topped by pickled onion.

Sopa de limon is a chicken soup with tortillas and a squeeze of lime juice; *cochinita pibil* and *pollo pibil* are flaky tender pieces of pork or chicken spiced and marinated in a rich pibil sauce and baked in banana leaves; and anything that includes "*à la Yucateca*" in its title is spiced in a wonderfully tasty anchiote paste and grilled to perfection.

Cancún also boasts some of the best international cooking around.

Getting Ready

Drink

National drinks include margaritas and tequila. Unless you specify, you can assume the liquor in your mixed drink will be of the lowest quality.

You can buy German or American beer in bars, but why would you? Mexico's beers are excellent. **Sol**, **Dos Equis** and **Corona** brands may be familiar to you, while **Superior** and **Victoria** are two lesser-known but excellent Mexican beers. Two great Yucatecan brews are *Montejo* (our all-time favorite) and **Leon Negra**, a dark amber. A refreshing light-alcohol drink is *chelada*, a glass of lemon-lime soda with a little beer added.

Tequila is a hard liquor distilled from the blue agave henequen plant. If you're drinking it straight, try don Julio Reposado or Herradura Reposado. For a complex taste, ask for any brand that is *añejo* (aged), such as Centenaro Añejo.

Licuados, fresh fruit juice drinks, are available plain or mixed with milk. Our favorite is *horchata*, a refreshing rice drink. It's made from rice and milk, then flavored with cinnamon and cane sugar. Or try *Jamaica* (ah-MY-ka), a fresh juice drink made from flowers.

Shopping & Bargaining

There are plenty of designer clothes and gift stores in the large shopping malls of the Cancún hotel zone and on Cozumel. Prices are lower in downtown Cancún, where three indoor flea markets can be found on Av. Tulum.

"Señora, Señor, where are you from?" "Best price, cheaper than Kmart," vendors call out to entice you into their stalls. This constant come-on is an irritation to many North Americans who are used to begging for sales help at home.

Most of the vendors can't afford to stock the stalls they sell from. Consequently, they have their goods on consignment. Anyone who has ever worked for commissions knows how tough that can be, especially in a country where the wage averages only US $25 per week. Please don't take their constant pleas personally or be offended. Usually a smile and a firm, "no, gracias" discourages further patter.

Markets generally open about 10 am and close as late as 11 pm.

Best Buys

A seasoned negotiator offers about half of the asking price and settles for a price somewhere in between. There are some unique gift items we usually can't pass up.

Silver and gold jewelry are cheaper in Mexico, so we always look for the unusual.

Pewter objects are always a good buy.

Large hand-woven string **hammocks** are the traditional bed, couch and crib in the Yucatán. Made of nylon, cotton, silk or sisal, they are extremely comfortable once you get used to sleeping in them.

The brightly colored earthernware you see is called Talavera de Puebla. *It is named for the town of Puebla, where it is made.*

Pottery is a good bet – the Maya were known for their skills, as are other indigenous people in Mexico.

Also check out **hand-painted laquerware, blankets** and **woven baskets**.

Once you leave Cancún you will see Maya women dressed in traditional white cotton shift dresses called *huipiles* (WE-peels). Colorful embroidery adorns the square neckline and hem. A white cotton lace-trimmed underskirt (*ternos*) peeks out demurely below the hemline. The embroidery on the *huipiles* of Quintana Roo's Maya is geometric and abstract. In Yucatán state it is done in a cross-stitched floral style. Each village has a distinctive pattern as well. Silk or cotton shawls (*rebozos*) are also part of the traditional dress.

Men's business dress includes short-sleeved embroidered and pleated light cotton, rayon, or silk shirts called *guayaberas* (gwi-ya-BEARas), which are worn outside the pants. This traditional shirt is common throughout the Hispanic Americas, where it's generally too warm to wear ties and jackets. Guayaberas come in soft pastel colors and bright white.

Quality **Panama hats** are made in the state of Campeche from the fibers of the jipijapa palm. They offer excellent protection against the strong Mexican sun and their fibers breathe, allowing the air to keep your head cool. Size of fiber, closeness of weave and suppleness determine three general qualities. The best are known as *fino* – with a fine weave of thin palm fibers. Buy the best you can afford for both comfort and longevity.

Cancún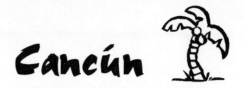

I never expected to see the day when girls would get sunburned in the places they do now.

Will Rogers, American humorist, 1879-1935

The sandy strip of Cancún's hotel zone forms the shape of a lucky number seven, wedged between the turquoise surf of the Caribbean and the calm waters of the Nichupté Lagoon. Luxury hotels pack the shoreline. The word Cancún in Mayan means "golden snake," and it aptly describes the long sliver of powdery white sand beaches. Squeezed along the 23½-mile (27 km) causeway, 25,000-plus hotel rooms, in a mix of architectural styles, welcome sunworshippers and vacationers from all over the world. Last year, nearly three million visitors arrived at the international airport here, most bound for the luxury and pampering of the famous hotel zone.

Unlike Acapulco or Puerto Vallarta, which were idyllic little villages until tourism replaced fishing as the major source of income, Cancún (pop. 300,000 plus) is a made-to-order resort, built specifically for tourism in an area where the wild jungle once met a deserted shore.

Inland from the waterfront is the other side to Cancún, the Mexican town that sprang up to supply housing and community for the hospitality workers in the hotel zone. While much of it is not of particular interest to the visitor, the downtown

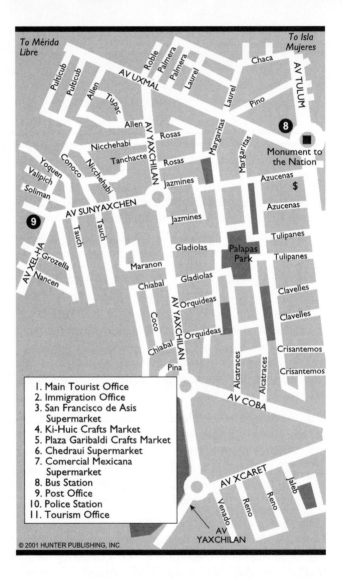

To Mérida Libre

To Isla Mujeres

AV UXMAL

AV TULUM

Roble
Palmera
Palmera
Laurel
Chaca
Pulticub
Pulticub
Allen
Tupac
Allen
Laurel
Pino
Nicchehabi
AV YAXCHILAN
Rosas
Margaritas
Margaritas

8

Monument to the Nation

Yoquen
Valipich
Conoco
Tanchacte
Nicchehabi
Rosas
Jazmines
Azucenas

$

Soliman
AV SUNYAXCHEN
Jazmines
Azucenas

9

Tauch
Tauch
Gladiolas
Palapas Park
Tulipanes
Tulipanes

AV XEL-HA
Grozella
Nancen
Maranon
Chiabal
Gladiolas
Clavelles
Clavelles

Coco
AV YAXCHILAN
Orquideas
Orquideas
Alcatraces
Alcatraces
Crisantemos
Crisantemos

Chiabal
Pina

1. Main Tourist Office
2. Immigration Office
3. San Francisco de Asis Supermarket
4. Ki-Huic Crafts Market
5. Plaza Garibaldi Crafts Market
6. Chedraui Supermarket
7. Comercial Mexicana Supermarket
8. Bus Station
9. Post Office
10. Police Station
11. Tourism Office

AV COBA

AV XCARET

Jaleb
Reno
Reno
Venado

AV YAXCHILAN

© 2001 HUNTER PUBLISHING, INC

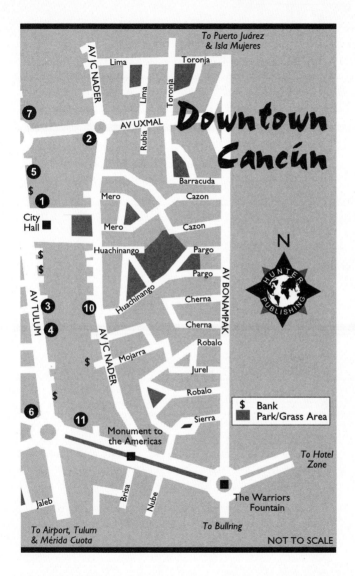

Downtown Cancún

To Puerto Juárez & Isla Mujeres

AV JC NADER

Lima
Toronja

Lima
Toronja

AV UXMAL

Rubia

⑦
②
⑤
$ ①

City Hall

Barracuda
Mero   Cazon
Mero   Cazon

Huachinango   Pargo
Pargo

$
$

AV TULUM

③
④

⑩

Huachinango

Cherna
Cherna

Robalo

AV JC NADER

Mojarra

$

Jurel

Robalo

$

⑥

Sierra

⑪

AV BONAMPAK

N

HUNTER PUBLISHING

$ Bank
Park/Grass Area

Monument to the Americas

To Hotel Zone

Jaleb

Brisa
Nube

The Warriors Fountain

To Bullring

To Airport, Tulum & Mérida Cuota

NOT TO SCALE

strip (*El Centro*) has taken on a life and personality all its own. We suspect that if the resorts in the hotel zone sank into the sea, Cancún downtown would stay on, living and working much as it does now – a gumbo of Yucatecan, Maya, Mexican and North American lifestyles. It's a pleasant and lively place to visit or stay. And you don't feel like you're in Kansas anymore.

Whatever your vacation needs, between the two Cancúns you'll be satisfied. Get-away-and-relax-on-the-beach vacationers will find Cancún is all it's cracked up to be. More adventuresome, lower-budget travelers can find the best of both worlds downtown or on Isla Mujeres.

Finding Your Way

The international airport is situated outside the city in the dry jungle. To get to your hotel, you must buy tickets for the *colectivo* buses, which are sold from a central booth in the airport. Just tell the driver which hotel you're staying at: prices are fixed. If you don't relish the thought of being stuffed into a VW minivan, pay extra for a taxi. If you're going budget by staying downtown, there is a public bus service to Av. Tulum (US $6), found across the parking lot of the main terminal.

If you have come in on a charter, you probably landed at the "South" terminal. The same transportation choices apply. There is a free shuttle bus back and forth between here and the main terminal. Just ask.

ISLA MUJERES

Mujeres Bay

Playa Las Perlas
Playa Juventud
Playa Linda
Playa Langosta
Playa Tortugas
Xcaret Terminal
Punta Cancún

Kukulcán Blvd

Cancún City

Gas Station	5 km/3 miles
Downtown	2 km/1.25 miles
Puerto Juárez	6 km/3.75 miles
Punta Sam	8 km/5 miles
Mérida	325 km/202 miles

Playa Ganiota Azul
Playa Chac Mol

Pok-Ta-Pok

Bolórquez Lagoon

Cancún's Hotel Zone

Yamil Lu'um

Playa Marlin

Playa Bellenas

N

Nichupté Lagoon

Kukulcán Blvd

San Miguelito

🏛	Archeological Zone
🌴	Beach
$	Bank
S	Shopping Plaza

Ruinas del Rey
Playa Delfines

2 km

2 miles

Rio Inglés Lagoon

Punta Nizuc

Airport	5 km/3 miles
Xcaret	72 km/44.75 miles
Xel-Há	118 km/73 miles
Tulum	131 km/81.5 miles
Chetumal	384 km/238.75 miles

Airport

Cancún

© 2001 HUNTER PUBLISHING, INC

The Hotel Zone

The hotel zone sits alongside the clear waters of the Caribbean and is the "Cancún" you see in all the brochures and ads. The beaches on the windward side (the top part of the number seven) are better for swimming. The leeward beaches are more picturesque, with broad stretches of sand, warm waters and strong surf.

All beaches in Mexico are open to the public at no charge, and you can use any hotel's beach – if you can reach it. There are several excellent public beaches scattered along the strip.

To get along the 17-km **Kukulcán Boulevard** that bisects the narrow island, you can take local taxis, public buses (less than US 70¢), or the new water taxi service that plies the lagoon. Every hour the **Aqua Bus** (☎ 9/883-5649) picks up and drops off passengers at various stops at the lagoon's marinas and restaurants. It is a fun way to get around. A weekly pass is about US $35, daily costs US $15, and one-ways are approximately US $3.

The Paseo Kukulcán connects the hotel zone with the downtown where it becomes **Av. Cobá**. The main drag downtown is **Av. Tulum**, which runs north and south perpendicular to Av. Cobá. Taxis back and forth from the hotel zone are available day or night.

Bus service is available 24 hours a day. Buses marked *Zona Hoteles, Ruta* (Route) 1 or 2, take you to town and back (*Ruta* 1 turns up Av. Tulum,

Ruta 2 continues across it). Most of the downtown attractions – stores, hotels, restaurants – are clustered around three parallel avenues of Nader, Tulum and Yaxchilán. The bus station is behind the circle of Av. Tulum and Av. Uxmal.

Before you leave the airport be sure to pick up free copies of *Cancún Tips* (two separate editions in two sizes) and the *Hotel Guide*, if available. These magazines have discounts and special offers that are well worth searching out. Examples include a $25 discount on an Avis rental and discounts for the Isla Mujeres shuttle.

Leaving Town

When you are going back to the airports at either Cancún or Cozumel, you must take a taxi, there is no bus service. Or your hotel may offer a shuttle service. Ask at the hotel's front desk for the current fare and don't be shy about negotiating. *¡Buen viaje!*

Best Places to Stay

God bless the man who invented sleep.
Miguel de Cervantes, 1547-1616

Cancún

With over 25,000 hotel rooms, Cancún is the largest resort area in Mexico and one of the largest in the world. When you compare hotel and restaurant prices in Cancún's hotel zone with those in major North American metropolitan areas you can see what a bargain Mexico is. Not because it's so much cheaper in Cancún – because you'll pay about the same price as you would in, say, the New York area – but when you walk out the door you're on a magnificent beach. Plus, you're on vacation!

Official Hotel Ratings

The Mexico Tourism Office has developed their own star hotel-rating system (which we repeat here by showing stars like this ☆), with a super-special category called "Gran Turismo" (indicated throughout this book by a ❀), their highest ranking.

Stars are awarded not necessarily on perceived class or elegance, but on location and amenities. Cancún's hotel zone boasts more than 55 hotels and 15,000 hotel rooms in the top two categories: "**Five-Star**" and "**Gran Turismo**."

These establishments include: beachfront location (Caribbean or bay); cable and/or satellite TV; a/c; laundry and dry cleaning service; mini-bars; combination baths (tub and shower); banquet and convention facilities; travel agency; car rental; gift shop; and watersports facilities.

Many hotel properties are converting to an all-inclusive format in response to increasing demand. All-inclusive generally means that all your meals and drinks are included in your room price. Sometimes non-motorized watersports are added. Other organized activities for guests, such as games or aerobics, are also free. These arrangements have their advantages as well as disadvantages. We've had vacations both ways and enjoyed them both for different reasons.

If you're going all-inclusive only because you're concerned about personal safety, getting ripped off, or you're worried about the quality of food in local restaurants, put your fears aside. Tourists' safety and comfort are a priority in all hotels.

◎ *TIP*

Regardless of whether you are staying downtown or in the hotel zone, it pays to see the room first. If you are not happy with the one you have been given, ask for a better room. Can't hurt.

If you are shopping for weekly stays in villas or condos try calling: **Mexico Accommodations**, ☎ 800/262-4500, or **Condo World**, ☎ 800/521-2980. Prices vary.

Alive Price Scale – Accommodations
(per night/two people per room)

Inexpensive	under US $40
Moderate	US $40-$100
Expensive	US $101-$200
Deluxe	US $201-$300
Super	US $301-$400
Ultra	over US $400

Cancún

Remember that the government adds a 12% room tax.

Hotel Zone

❦ CASA TURQUESA
Kukulcán, Km 13.5
☎ 9/885-2924, fax 9/885-2922
www.casaturquesa.com
Deluxe

Casa Turquesa is listed as one of the Small Luxury Hotels of the World.

As you walk to your room along a warren of marble-floor hallways and sitting areas, past original works of art, you may just run into Bruce Willis, or perhaps Sly Stallone or Reba McEntire. The Casa's small number of opulent suites and renowned (but somewhat pricey) restaurant – appropriately named Celebrity – attract notables (including the President of Mexico) who cherish their privacy and comfort.

Each of the 31 suites is very large, with king-size beds, full couch, cocktail table, dining table with chairs and private balcony or patio facing the beach – complete with a two-person hot tub and built-in daybed.

The honeymoon suite sits high above the hotel with panoramic private balconies. Casa's amenities include a big pool, cable TV, two restaurants, tennis court, fitness center, safe, mini-bar, wet bar, massage, free in-room musical CDs and VCR movies.

HOTEL FLAMINGO ☆☆☆☆
Kukulcán, Km 11
US, ☎ 800/544-3005; Mexico, 9/883-1544
Fax 9/883-1029
www.flamingo.hotels-cancun.com
Expensive

220 rooms, junior suites, two pools, balconies, safe, restaurant, wet bar.

The Flamingo is ideally located on a white Caribbean beach in the center of the *Zona Hoteles*, about midway from the airport to the center of town. The comfortable rooms all have balconies and air conditioning.

The poolside restaurant, La Frente, has sliding glass windows that overlook the sea. An all-you-can-eat buffet features a different theme every night: Yucatecan, Mexican, Italian, International, etc. It costs about US $10 per person.

Hotel Flamingo is opposite the Flamingo shopping mall.

Relax near the pool with an American masseuse who helps get the kinks out for US $10. Across the street, the Flamingo Plaza is a good place to shop and is a source of inexpensive hotel zone food, with a Sanborns, TCBY, McDonalds and our Mexican fast-food favorite, *Checándole*.

CALINDA BEACH ☆☆☆☆☆
Kukulcán, Km 8.5
☎ 800/228-5151
www.calinda.hotels-cancun.com
Moderate/Expensive
470 rooms with air conditioning, telephones, pool, hot tub, restaurant, watersports, TV.

This Quality Hotel property, one of two in the hotel zone, is situated on one of the area's prettiest and best swimming beaches, adjacent to the inlet of the lagoon. Several sailing vessels that offer cruises dock right here at the lagoon's marina, including a colorful pirate ship.

The attractive medium-size rooms in its pyramid-shaped building all have views of the soft surf. A

Cancún

As you look out across the bay from Calinda, you see the twinkling lights on Isla Mujeres, Island of Women.

recent remodeling features bright white tile, floral fabrics, oak furniture and marble baths.

CLUB LAS VELAS ☆☆☆☆☆
Kukulcán, Km 5.8
☎ 9/883-1111, fax 9/883-4959
www.afwpi.com/clublasvelas.html
Deluxe – All-Inclusive
285 rooms with air conditioning, two restaurants, nautical center, TV.

Club Las Velas is especially popular with English travelers.

An all-inclusive resort facing the picturesque Laguna Nichupté. The rooms and two-level suites here are located in white adobe-style buildings scattered around colorful garden-filled courtyards. The effect is pleasantly reminiscent of a Colonial Mexican village. One courtyard, surrounded by cool plants and shade trees, boasts a huge green pond with several freshwater giant turtles and many fish. Another is like a central village square and features nightly entertainment. Las Velas, which means "sails" in Spanish, has a sandy beach on the lagoon. For those who prefer the ocean, the resort's own boat ferries guests to seaside beaches, or you can walk across the road to a public beach. Some rooms could use a few more comforts (such as table/reading lamps) in the en suite sitting areas. It is quiet and secluded – a real taste of Mexico.

EL PUEBLITO BEACH HOTEL ☆☆☆☆
Kukulcán, Km 17.5
☎ 9/885-0422, fax 9/885-0731
www.elpueblito.com
Deluxe – All-Inclusive
240 rooms with air conditioning, three restaurants, five pools, safe, TV, tennis court.

A few all-inclusive hotels in the zone try to create their own Mexican atmosphere and El Pueblito – which means "small village" – does that very well. Twenty-one multi-unit guest houses clustered around green, flowery courtyards overlook a fine sand Caribbean beach. The reception and dining area are housed in a Colonial-styled hacienda. The rooms are large, with simple furnishings that invoke an "Old Mexico" feeling. Small enchanting terraced pools cascade down to the seafront. Recently renovated, it's located on the quieter, southern end of the hotel zone, across from El Rey Maya ruins. A good buy, especially if you are not into the pressed flesh of larger resorts.

El Pueblito is popular with both Europeans and South Americans.

ROYAL SOLARIS CARIBE ☆☆☆☆☆
Kukulcán, Km 20.5
☎ 9/885-0100, fax 9/885-0975
www.clubsolaris.com
Ultra – All-Inclusive

There is a lot of Internet chatter about this extremely popular beachfront property housed in two towers. Each of the two complexes, adjacent to each other, has its own ambience: the Royal Tower has a modern décor with a hustle-and-bustle atmosphere; the Caribe Tower is smaller, sporting a Spanish Moorish design. All 500 rooms, mid-size but attractive and very clean, feature one king-size or two double beds. One hundred rooms offer balconies and all have a view of either the ocean or lagoon. There are eight restaurants, five snack bars, four swimming pools, tennis courts, hot tub and a kids' mini-club – plus a bright white beach below the seawall.

Cancún

SOLYMAR ☆☆☆☆
Kukulcán, Km 18.7
☎ 9/885-1811, fax 9/885-1689
Moderate/Expensive
245 rooms and suites, TV, two pools, restaurants, bars.

This hotel, where Apple Vacations literally owns most of the rooms, has an appealing, unpretentious atmosphere. Ocean-view rooms overlook a central courtyard garden with two large square pools, and the pristine white sands of the Caribbean. There are also some individual villas available, right on the beach. The medium-size standard rooms all feature balconies and kitchenettes. Their décor consists of white walls, warm mahogany wood trim, stone tile in the bathrooms and colorful drapes and fabrics.

⚜ CAMINO REAL CANCÚN
Punta Cancún
US, ☎ 800/528-8300; Mexico, 9/883-0100
Fax 9/883-1730; www.caminoreal.com
Deluxe
381 rooms and suites, hairdryers, TVs, telephones, turn-down service, tennis courts.

Without a doubt this property has the best location for both ocean views and swimming beaches. Straddling the island's easternmost point and rimmed by water on three sides, the Camino Real enjoys a reputation as one of Mexico's best resort hotels. Accommodations are in either of two distinctive white buildings that make up its hotel section. Original rooms are in a sloping, three-story pyramid structure whose western face overlooks a natural saltwater lagoon (home to fish and sea turtles). The eastern side looks out over a seawall to a lighthouse and the blue Caribbean. Between the east and west wings an interior garden grows. The newer, 18-story tower has all ocean-view deluxe rooms with amenities similar to a concierge club, including breakfast. The hotel boasts three beaches. One is located on the calm, shallow Bahia Mujeres, with excellent swimming and a watersports pier. A second beach lies just over the sand bar and under the palm trees at the lagoon. The third is a white sand beach in front of the tower on the Caribbean. Guest rooms have bright décor, rattan furniture, marble floors, tiled baths and balconies or terraces. There's a large pool with a swim-up bar, plus four restaurants, including the Maria Bonita, which offers a gourmet Mexican menu of regional specialties.

❦ **FIESTA AMERICANA CANCÚN**
Kukulcán, Km 8.5
☎ 800/343-7821; in Mexico 9/883-1400
Fax 9/883-2502; www.fiestamericana.com
Super – All-Inclusive
261 rooms, 15 suites, three restaurants, bars.

Wrought iron balconies and soft pastel colors against burnt orange give this archetypical Mexican resort it's not-so-typical charm. The courtyard in the center of this horseshoe-shaped five-story hotel – built to resemble a Mexican hacienda – is filled with tropical landscaping and a beautiful odd-shaped pool, complete with swim-up bar. A small terraced beach, ideal for swimming, faces the languid waters of the sheltered bay.

Rooms feature attractive Mexican tile flooring and soft furnishings with a casual Mexican feel. Attached streetside is L.F. Caliente, a nightclub/restaurant and sports betting bar (it's legal here).

Cancún

Across the street from the Maya Fair shopping Plaza. They also offer a rate that includes breakfast.

❧ **SHERATON RESORT AND TOWERS**
Kukulcán, Km 12.5
☎ 800/325-3535; in Mexico, 9/883-1988
Fax 9/885-0974; www.sheraton.com
Deluxe

Near the Sheraton is the ruin. Yamil Lu'um. Its Temple of the Hand was so named because a handprint of a man was discovered in the stucco of an inside wall. An impression of the tail and backside of a cat are also there.

The older Sheraton, comprised of a pyramid-style building and an adjacent tower, is located next to some small Maya ruins on a bluff above a good beach. It's super-clean inside. Set back from the road, the hotel features several acres of manicured jungle gardens in the middle of which is a huge figure-eight-shaped pool. The large, L-shaped lobby has a cool fountain garden under a skylight. Medium-size rooms have stone tile bathrooms and either two double beds or one king-size. Standard oceanfront rooms have wonderful views, but no balconies. Tower rooms, which include breakfast, have private balconies and ocean views. Oceanfront and garden suites have a large balcony with hot tub and two bathrooms. There are two swimming pools with swim-up bars (one oceanfront), two wading pools, tennis courts, playground, a great gym and mini-golf.

❧ **FIESTA AMERICANA CORAL BEACH**
Kukulcán, Km 9.5
☎ 800/343-7821; in Mexico, 9/883-2900
Fax 9/883-3084
www.fiestacoralbeach.hotels-cancun.com
Super/Ultra

The majestic pink Fiesta Americana, winner of a recent AAA Five-Diamond Award, dominates the corner of Kukulcán Blvd. at Punta Cancún, opposite the convention center. This location is the center of social and shopping activities in the hotel zone. In fact, many vacationers think this corner, at the top of the number "7," is downtown Cancún (it is not).

The 602 suites are located in two tall curved wings, and all have ocean views. The massive hotel sits on a beautiful calm Caribbean beach facing Isla Mujeres. Guest rooms, with split-level sitting areas, have marble floors with throw rugs, pastel fabrics, original artwork, large balconies and elegant combination bathrooms with double sinks in curved marble. Facilities include four restaurants, four bars (one is a swim-up, another is a video bar), health club and spa, fabulous undulating free-form pool complete with slides and an island, three indoor Astroturf tennis courts and a kid's club. Very elegant, it is arguably Cancún's most magnificent property, and certainly boasts the most prestigious address.

❧ HYATT REGENCY
Kukulcán, Km 9.5
☎ 800/233-1234; in Mexico, 9/883-1234
Fax 9/883-1349; www.hyatt.com
Expensive/Deluxe
300 rooms, three restaurants, bars, two pools, health club.

The popular Hyatt has a 14-story tower that features a huge circular glass atrium and open-air lobby with plants hanging down from above. The building is sandwiched between the Camino Real and the Krystal hotels on Punta Cancún. With rooms that boast beautiful multicolor marble tile floors, light wood and rattan furnishings and com-

Cancún

bination baths, the Hyatt is also convenient to shopping and nightlife. The hotel has a quiet, exclusive feel. An inviting split-level pool with cushioned lounge chairs and a jungle-like waterfall is a big plus, because the hotel has no ocean beach to speak of. Although it is hard against the Caribbean, the rocky shore will come as a disappointment to some. The hotel offers a free shuttle service several times a day to the Hyatt Caribe further down the hotel zone, which does have a good beach. Regency Club rooms with added amenities are on the top two floors and there is a Camp Hyatt kids' club available. There's live entertainment every evening.

⚓ HILTON BEACH & GOLF RESORT
Kukulcán, Km 17
☎ 800/445-8667; in Mexico, 9/881-8000
Fax 9/881-8080; www.hilton.com
Super

The Hilton, formerly Caesar's Park, rises majestically on a wide sand beach near the bottom of the island's long "7" shape. It commands a spectacular unobstructed view of the Caribbean and Playa Delfines. It has its own 18-hole championship golf course next to the lagoon.

This property occupies the largest piece of land of any Cancún property (250 acres). The pyramid-shaped hotel offers 426 ocean-view rooms with computer ports, dual jacks on phone lines and voice-mail. Rooms have a soft beige and pink décor with marble tiles, pastel Mexican cotton bedding, pottery lamps, light wood and rattan furnishings and large combination bathrooms. Very small balconies. On the side of the main building, lovely low-rise villas, called Royal Suites, weave their way down to a perfect white beach. These suites are considerably larger than regular suites and boast amenities equivalent to concierge floors, including continental breakfast, hors d'oeuvres and separate desk for check-in. There are numerous sizeable swimming pools, a fully equipped health club, five restaurants, swim-up bar, lighted tennis courts and an on-site water sports center.

Ask about their golf packages and specials. Hilton also offers a Red Cross-certified child care program (US $36 extra) and an on-premises doctor. Fancy and very elegant, the Hilton is impressive.

⚜ MARRIOTT CASA MAGNA
Kukulcán, Km 16.5
☎ 800/223-6388; in Mexico, 9/881-2000
Fax 9/881-2085; www.marriotthotels.com
Super – breakfast included

The Casa Magna was named in the top 100 hotels in Travel & Leisure's *annual survey. The same magazine called our* Adventure Guide to the Yucatán *"a great new resource."*

This Marriott property is another of the impressively-sized, hard-to-miss hotels in the zone. A huge beige-and-white six-story modern Mediterranean structure, its architectural décor features domes, arches, statues and stone planters. Inside, 450 rooms and suites are decorated in a tropical style with marble floors covered by colorful area rugs and combination baths. For the bored they offer cable TV with on-demand video. The "Club Amigos" children's activity center offers interactive computer video games. An excellent restaurant, Mikado, serves Japanese and Thai cuisine. Typical Marriott quality.

Cancún

✴ RITZ CARLTON-CANCÚN
Kukulcán, Km 15
☎ 800/241-3333; Mexico 9/881-0808
Fax 9/881-0815; www.ritzcarlton.com
Deluxe/Super/Ultra
369 rooms and suites.

Built in 1993 and facing 1,200 feet of pristine beach, the Ritz Carlton is one of the most upscale properties. Each large guest room offers dramatic ocean views, private balconies, thick carpeting, Drexel wood furniture, overstuffed chairs and marble combination baths with twin sinks. The atrium at the center of the W-shaped, five-story, Mediterranean-style hotel is crowned by a regal stained-glass dome custom-made by an artist from Puebla, Mexico. The lobby and lounges have spectacular views. Amenities include three restaurants, two bars, two pools, spa and fitness center and a sandy beach manned by a lifeguard. This property has garnered the AAA Five Diamond Award as well as numerous other quality awards. This is a resort that lives up to the Ritz name.

PALACE RESORTS ☆☆☆☆☆
☎ 800/346-8225
www.palaceresorts.com
Super – All-Inclusive

There are four all-inclusive Palace hotel resorts in the Cancún area: **Beach Palace, Sun Palace** and **Cancún Palace**, all in the hotel zone, and **Moon Palace**, a few miles south along the coast. Each has its own personality, but they all offer fine facilities and great locations. Very popular with American vacationers. The Palace resorts have a twist on time-share ownership. Instead of selling a piece of one single room or a certain week, they offer club memberships good for all their Cancún resorts, providing discounts year-round. We're sure they'll tell you all about it.

PRESIDENTE INTER-CONTINTENTAL
Kukulkán Km 7.5
☎ 800-327-0200; in Mexico, 9/883-0200
Fax 9/883-2515
www.interconti.com
299 rooms, 2 pools, 4 restaurants, tennis, air, cable TV, kids club.

The Presidente is the grand old dame of Cancún – it was one of the (if not *the*) – first hotel built in the hotel zone. But not to worry, all the rooms were tastefully remodeled in 1999. The lobby's reflecting pool is particularly intriguing and the lobby bar features nightly live entertainment. The comfortable rooms feature king-size or two queen beds, dining table and chairs, and tiled bathrooms. They face either the lagoon or the beach and are in the tall tower or the lower wing. The breakfast buffet is outrageously good, plus they offer free greens fees at Pok-Ta-Pok golf course.

Downtown

The downtown area of Cancún provides the best opportunity for bargains in hotels and restaurants – but without the beach. Unfortunately, too many tourists believe the rumors – retold by unethical individuals – about dangers and rip-offs outside the protected cocoon of the hotel zone. These are untrue. Crime is no more prevalent here (and is probably less common) than in many

US cities. We've selected a series of hotels in safe areas downtown with reputations for customer satisfaction.

Alive Price Scale — Accommodations
(per night/two people per room)

Inexpensive. . . . . under US $40
Moderate. . . . . US $40-$100
Expensive . . . . US $101-$200
Deluxe. . . . . US $201-$300
Super. . . . . US $301-$400
Ultra . . . . over US $400

Remember that the stars assigned by the Mexico Tourism Office relate to certain amenities and location only. Consequently, we might stay in a two-star over a three-star, or even a one-star over a three, simply because it offers what we're after at the price we need.

Cleanliness, ambiance, value and security are what we look for. The downtown hotels we selected below are all decent and worthwhile accommodations.

⊚ TIP

Find a little freebie called the *Hotel Guide* (☎ 9/880-1645) or the *Cancún Tips* magazine and look for some good discount coupons.

NOVOTEL ☆☆
Av. Tulum
☎ 9/884-2999, fax 9/884-3162
www.novotelcancun.com
Inexpensive/Moderate
41 rooms with air conditioning or fans, TV, restaurant, pool.

Located at the circle of Av. Tulum and Uxmal, the modern Novotel is reminiscent of an old Colonial building. There's heavy wood furniture in the sitting area and an indoor courtyard garden. The "superior" rooms are in the main building and are so-called because they offer cable TV, air conditioning and a small balcony. Out back, next to the tiny pool, there are two Caribbean-style wooden buildings that house the "standard" rooms. Except for the lack of television and the ceiling fans instead of air conditioning, these rooms have the same amenities and are even slightly larger than the superiors. We think these quieter rooms are the better buy if you are willing to forgo TV and air conditioning.

INN EL PATIO
Av. Bonhampak #51, at corner of Cereza
☎ 9/884-3500, fax 9/884-3540
www.cancun-suites.com
Moderate

Enter through the heavy black wrought iron gate (secured after dark) into a small, pleasant, Mexican tiled courtyard with patio furniture nestled among the greenery. The upper rooms are accessed through an outside stairs that has an additional small sitting area built in. A communal kitchenette with refrigerator, sink, hot water maker, and purified water is located on the second floor. Each comfortable room has either a queen or two twin beds, and super-clean bathrooms. The furnishings are strictly Spanish with carved wood armoires and leather chairs. The owners succeed in delivering a different, more authentic, Cancún experience.

MARIA DE LOURDES HOTEL ☆☆
Av. Yaxchilan
☎ 9/884-4744, fax 9/884-1242
Inexpensive/Moderate
51 rooms with air conditioning, TV, phones, pool.

The Maria is a perennial good value and very popular "close-to-it-all" downtown hotel. Pleasant and friendly, it has an outdoor patio, pool and small restaurant open Monday-Saturday from 7-11 am for *desayuno* (breakfast) and 4-8 pm for *cena* (dinner). Each respectably sized room has two twin beds and a clean bathroom. This hotel understands its clientele – budget-minded travelers who enjoy cultural interaction as part of their vacation – and caters to them. Always gets a good review.

HOTEL HACIENDA ☆☆☆
Av. Sunyaxchen
☎ 9/884-3672, fax 9/884-1208
Inexpensive/Moderate
35 rooms with air conditioning, pool, restaurant, TV.

We met some Americans at the Hotel Hacienda who liked the place so much they stayed for several months.

This family-owned hotel has a small restaurant for breakfast and lunch next to a sparkling swimming pool in a serene center courtyard. Located on a quiet street only two blocks from downtown. Some rooms are higher priced because, according to the manager, the mattresses are newer and more comfortable and the TV is larger and comes with a remote control (the channels are all in Spanish). Otherwise, all the rooms are identical. Limited private parking in front.

VILLA MAYA CANCUN ☆☆
Av. Uxmal No. 20 at the corner of Rubia
☎ 9/884-2829, fax 9/884-1762
Inexpensive
13 rooms with air conditioning, TV, pool.

Nestled on the corner of a dead-end street (Rubia) and across from the Howard Johnson, the Villa Maya is quiet and clean with comfortable rooms and a friendly staff. This is a good choice for an inexpensive stay in town without sacrificing comfort or cleanliness. Upstairs rooms are brighter. It has a very helpful travel agency in the lobby. A sentimental favorite.

HOLIDAY INN ☆☆☆☆
Av. Nader No 1
US, ☎ 800/465-4329; in Mexico, 9/887-4455
Fax 884-7954
Moderate

The Holiday Inn is a little out of the way, one block north of Av. Uxmal on Av. Nader, but it is the downtown's premier hotel. Next to a school, on a bend in the road of a quasi-residential neighborhood, it is quiet and secure. The atrium lobby has overstuffed furniture to relax in and through its glass doors is the central courtyard containing the long irregularly shaped blue pool, with a waterfall at one end, and an inviting snack palapa bar. The four-story colonial-styled wings, whose well apportioned comfortably-sized rooms feature two matrimonial beds and tile bath, surround the

Cancún

sunny courtyard. When there is business done in Cancún, it's usually done here – in comfort.

HOTEL ANTILLANO ✩✩
Av. Tulum and Claveles
☎ 9/884-1532 or 884-1132
Fax 9/884-1878; www.hotelantillano
Moderate
48 rooms, air conditioning, TV, pool, phones.

Antillano's will store your gear – as do many hotels – while you wander the peninsula.

The well-known Antillano is as bright and fresh and spotlessly clean as it was the first time we stayed here many years ago. This perennial favorite of travelers is an excellent choice in downtown. The floors are all polished terra-cotta tile and the rooms are stucco-white with rosewood trim. In larger rooms the feeling is intimate, with curved walls and bathrooms and closets set back into niches. Smaller rooms are a little close. Perhaps the best-looking of the downtown hotels.

EL REY DEL CARIBE ✩
Av. Uxmal near the corner of Nader
☎ 9/884-2028, fax 9/884-9857
www.reycaribe.com
Moderate
25 rooms with air conditioning, pool, hot tub, parking, TV, kitchenettes.

There are seven rooms at the back of El Rey that don't face the street.

The Rey del Caribe is a white hacienda-styled building with a green central courtyard garden and terra-cotta tile floors. Just off the busiest part of town, the Rey is the best value in moderate hotels. All the clean and bright rooms have something of a Colonial feel and are modern and well equipped with kitchenettes. A hot tub and tiny pool are nestled among the flowering plants.

Number 25 offers the best of both worlds with size and brightness. On the third floor front are two very appealing rooms if you're not carrying a lot of luggage. One is a single and the other, #18, has a balcony with a good city view.

HOWARD JOHNSON
KOKAI CANCUN ☆☆☆☆
Av. Uxmal #26
☎ 800/446-4656; in Mexico, 9/884-3218
Fax 9/884-4335
www.howardjohnsonkokai.com.mx
Moderate – includes breakfast
48 rooms, roof garden, free beach shuttle, bar with live entertainment, roof garden, restaurants, pool.

We list three hotels in a cluster in a residential area of Av. Uxmal, including this Howard Johnson (for those who need a familiar name). It could use a remodeling, but it is still a comfortable, if not predictable, Ho-Jo. Surprisingly low price includes a generous continental breakfast.

Best Places to Eat

Part of the secret of success in life is to eat what you like and let the food fight it out inside.
Mark Twain, 1835-1910

What's a vacation for, if not to dine out? In Cancún, there's a whole range of choices – Mexican, continental, Italian, Chinese, Japanese, steak, seafood, fast food, barbeque – it's all there and in every price range. We skipped the obvious

American chains – such as TGI Friday's, KFC and McDonalds – in favor of new dining experiences.

Like North Americans, Mexicans love to dine out. Consequently, every street corner seems to sprout an eatery. Naturally, the hotel zone prices are higher than those in downtown. The service and ambiance may be better too. But even if we're staying in the hotel zone, we still find ourselves eating downtown several times a week.

> ### ◎ NOTE
>
> Although we rate US $15 for a dinner as expensive, remember this is compared to restaurant prices that are low to begin with. In that price range you're eating a complete meal of fresh lobster or succulent steak. That same fine food, service and ambiance in a metropolitan area of the United States would cost significantly more. Restaurants we list without phone numbers do not need reservations.

All larger restaurants accept credit cards. Be sure to ask first at smaller establishments.

Alive Price Scale – Restaurants
(dinner, per person, not including beverage)

Inexpensive . . . . less than US $6
Moderate. . . . . US $6-$13
Expensive . . . . over US $13

We reviewed here the best Cancún has to offer, in all price ranges, for fine dining in some fantastic settings. *¡Buen apetito!*

Favorite Italian Restaurants

Hotel Zone

CASA ROLANDI
Plaza Caracol Shopping Mall, lagoon side
☎ 9/883-2557
Moderate/Expensive

This is Cancún's best Italian/seafood restaurant. Just ask any of the faithful patrons who return here year after year since 1985 (we're one of them). Rolandi's features the low ceiling ambiance of a Mediterranean bistro – whitewashed walls, natural wood windows and Italian tile – and a menu to match. They offer an extensive wine list, with champagne available by the glass, and a cozy bar near the mall entrance.

Menu selections: homemade lasagna, salmon capriccio, lamb chops cooked with thyme fresh Caribbean lobster.

Mirco Bignotti has managed the restaurant since its opening and personally oversees the staff, so service is impeccable. Look for the jovial host when you dine and say hello for us. One of their signature dishes is Ravioli Neri Ripieni D'Aragosta (black ravioli stuffed with lobster). Another option is to pick a live Caribbean lobster from their tank and seafood counter in the middle of the dining room.

Cancún

Casa Rolandi is open daily from 1 pm to 11:30 pm, and reservations are highly suggested. If you are visiting Isla Mujeres, make sure to stop in the

Villa Rolandi Hotel for lunch or dinner – same fine dining with a beachfront view. Or, if you're just in the mood for brick-oven pizza, there is a Pizza Rolandi in downtown Cancún and one on Isla Mujeres.

LA DOLCE VITA
Av. Kukulkán, Km 14.6
☎ 9/884-1384
Expensive

Dolce Vita menu selections: antipasto di mare, green tagliolini, chocolate truffle cake.

After years of luring customers downtown to its pretty garden setting, La Dolce now perches on the lagoon's edge in the hotel zone. It has the same attentive staff and superb regional cuisine still comes at reasonable prices. The new décor, with twinkling lights and terraced seating under a skylight, is dazzling.

The house specialty is beautifully presented lobster medallions and shrimp simmered in white wine and herbs over green tagliolini (about US $15). Jorge Kaufer and George Savio are the owners, and one of them usually supervises and greets customers. With soft lighting, romantic live music played by a Cuban horn player and luxurious settings, La Dolce reeks of casual elegance. We always make a point of eating here when visiting Cancún. Open noon to midnight, reservations strongly suggested.

SAVIO'S
Plaza Caracol, Km 9
☎ 9/883-2085
Moderate/Expensive

Savio's menu selections: salmon carpaccio, osso buco Milanese, ricotta & spinach pasta, tiramisu.

George Savio, an expatriate Swiss businessman, features Northern Italian cuisine in his restaurant and gets rave reviews. The glass-enclosed interior with contemporary furnishings mixes the sunny feel of a greenhouse with the low-key buzz of a city café. The pastas are homemade, service is excellent, the presentation is stylish and the taste is superb. Try the fettuccine Neptune, a black fettuccine with shrimp and scallops in an oyster sauce. Very subtle. Open 10 am to midnight.

Downtown

ROLANDI'S RESTAURANT & BAR
Av. Coba & Tulum
Inexpensive/Moderate
Reservations not necessary.

Cool and private, this sister to the Pizza Rolandi on Isla Mujeres is less crowded but still features excellent brick-oven pizzas and basic Italian food in a cool romantic setting. Tasty and filling. Near the hectic atmosphere of Av. Tulum but far enough up Av. Cobá that it's away from all the hassle. Open 1 pm-midnight.

Favorite Mexican Restaurants

Cancún

Hotel Zone

HACIENDA EL MORTERO
Kukulkán, Km 9.5, across from Dady Rock
☎ 9/883-1133
Moderate/Expensive

The ambiance of El Mortero is one of the most intriguing in Cancún. Built in the style of its 18th-century namesake, the hacienda displays curved arches, hanging plants, soft lighting, adobe walls,

Spanish tile and beveled glass windows. The traditional menu features steak, prime rib and authentic Mexican dishes with such touches as homemade tortillas and homemade sauces. The bar offers 15 types of tequila and there's a cocktail on the house for diners.

El Mortero menu selections: prime rib (42 oz), chiles relleno, fajitas Mundo Maya, & chicken pibil.

Mariachis play nightly at 7:30, 9 and 10 pm and a romantic guitar trio serenades on Saturday. A non-smoking section is available. A dining experience. Open from 6:30 to 11:30 pm.

EL MEXICANO
La Mansion, Costa Blanca Shopping Center
☎ 9/883-2220
Moderate/Expensive

El Mexicano is reminiscent of a 19th-century hacienda with waiters in period costume, wrought iron railings and romantic lighting adding to the ambiance. In the evening there is a dinner theater with folk dancing and regional Mexican music. The fine menu includes charcoal-grilled steaks. For lunch they offer an all-you-can-eat buffet of traditional Mexican dishes. Open for lunch and dinner only.

IGUANA WANA
Plaza Caracol
☎ 9/883-0829
Moderate/Expensive

Iguana Wana menu selections: coconut shrimp in mango chile sauce, enchiladas de carnitas, jicama, nopal & spinach salad.

A décor that includes checked tablecloths, vertical striped walls, cane-backed chairs and odd little trees in large pots among the dining tables helps reinforce Iguana's contemporary Mexican reputation. The cuisine is eclectic, combining Mexican with Caribbean and North American in an irreverent but generally satisfying hodge-podge that offers something for everyone. The bar stocks 50 types of tequila and 25 different beers. A breakfast buffet is offered. Open daily 7 am-1:30 am.

Downtown

LA HABICHUELA
Av. Margarita No. 25
☎ 9/884-3158
Moderate/Expensive

La Habichuela menu selections: cocobichuela, shrimp and steak, coq au vin, chocolate pyramid of Chechén Itzá.

Capturing a quiet corner of old Yucatán with its lush green garden and Maya artifacts, the Habichuela (meaning stringbean) is a legend among locals and select tourists. Since 1977, the Pezzotti family has run this almost secret seafood restaurant with a Mexican-Caribbean flavor. Their specialty (about US $25) is *cocobichuela*, a dish of lobster and shrimp in a mild curry sauce and served in a coconut shell garnished with fresh fruit. They also serve fine cuts of steak, grilled to order. The romantic atmosphere includes beautiful table settings of linen and crystal, soft lighting and lush outdoor dining to the gentle sound of a fountain. Not very easy to find, but it's absolutely worth the effort. Take a taxi; they all know where it is. Near Palapa Park. Open for lunch and dinner.

LOS ALMENDROS
Av. Bonampak (opposite the bullring)
☎ 9/887-1332
Moderate

From humble beginnings in the town of Ticul, Los Almendros' reputation has grown and its food is now considered the epitome of Yucatecan cooking.

Cancún

A photographic menu displays pictures of the meals. If you've not eaten Yucatecan food before, try the combination plate of four typical dishes. One of them is *poc-chuc* – thinly sliced pork marinated and grilled with onions – which the restaurant first introduced in the late 1960s.

Poc-Chuc

Mayan for charcoal grilled steak

Ingredients:

3 kg. (6½ lbs) thin-cut pork steaks, marinated with salt and sour orange juice
1 kg. (2¼ lb) sliced onions
Chopped fresh coriander (cilantro)
1 kg. (2¼ lb) tomatoes
Juice of 10 sour oranges (available in bottled form; use enough to cover the meat)
Salt

Grill the pork steaks. Fry onions, add salt, coriander and bitter orange juice. Grill the whole tomatoes, smash and peel them, add to the onions. Serve the poc-chuc atop the onions and tomatoes. Serves 10. Recipe courtesy of Los Almendros.

This dish has become a traditional Yucatecan offering and can now be found in almost every eatery around the peninsula. If you're not heading out into the countryside, a stop at the Los Almendros' Cancún location is a must. Open 10:30 am-11 pm daily. Other locations are in Ticul and Mérida.

LOS AMIGOS RESTAURANT, among others
Av. Tulum
No telephone
Inexpensive/Moderate

Sit down and rest your bones on colorful painted ladder-back chairs at sidewalk tables with umbrellas. Los Amigos is one of several such indoor/outdoor eateries that serve generous meals with a distinctive taste of Mexico. These restaurants offer a free drink with your meal and Los Amigos is no exception. Sound too good to be true? It isn't. For dinner they display plates of steaks and fresh seafood that they guarantee will be just as appetizing and generous when served to you. We paid under US $8 for a large grilled filet mignon, baked potato, green salad and a margarita. Roving mariachis serenade you while you people-watch. Eating on a sidewalk downtown is a multi-sensory experience – and tons of fun!

The Mariachi

Mariachi music is an enduring tradition in Mexico. It's a standard feature of many Mexican restaurants in the hotel zone, while mariachis wander from restaurant to restaurant downtown. Part of their appeal is the interaction they enjoy with their audience and requests are welcome (with a tip for the ones downtown). Here are some of the most popular tunes in their repertoire:

Cielito Lindo (Pretty Sky). You'll recognize this one immediately, as it's the all-time favorite of most Mexicans.

Cancún

El Son de la Negra (He Who is of the Black Woman). This rousing piece is often the first loud song played by the band to let everybody know they've arrived.

Las Golondrinas (The Swallows). If you're crying in your beer, this song is a good choice. It's a moving, sad ballad about impending departure.

Other popular pieces include: *Volver, Volver* (Return, Return); *En El Rincón De Una Cantina* (In the Corner of a Tavern); *El Rey* (The King); *No Me Amenaces* (Don't Threaten Me); *¿De Qué Manera Te Olvido?* (How Can I Forget You?); *Cucurrucucu Paloma* (Coo-Coo Pigeon); *La Muerte de un Gallero* (The Death of a Gallant Man); *La Que Se Fue* (The One That Left); and of course, *El Mariachi Loco* (The Crazy Mariachi) and the risqué *Rancho Grande*.

PERICOS RESTAURANT
71 Av. Yaxchilán
☎ 9/884-3152
Moderate

Perico's continues to attract its customers with an extensive menu of Mexican food, steaks and seafood. The colorful bar and cantina, with huge murals of Mexican heroes and American movie stars, features saddles as bar stools. There's always a fiesta atmosphere at this venerable landmark. Open from 1 pm to 2 am, with lots of music and an infectious conga line. It's one of the downtown's most festive places and happy hour here is just that. Mariachis and Marimba music from 7:30 till closing. Well worth a visit just to see – and the food is pretty good too! One full block off Av. Tulum.

Favorite Seafood Restaurants

Hotel Zone

CAPTAIN'S COVE
Kukulkán, Km 16 (Royal Yacht Club Marina)
☎ 9/885-0016
Moderate/Expensive

Voted Cancún's best restaurant several years in a row, the Captain's Cove offers fine seafood, international favorites, and USDA-certified Angus beef steak. Obviously, they aim to please all.

Captain's Cove menu selections: coconut shrimp, soft-shell crabs, slow-smoked ribs, & flaming Maya coffee.

The wooden deck with a separate bar stretches out over the water where the sunsets on the Nichupté Lagoon are colorful, to say the least. Lots of greenery, thatched roofs and soft background music. The chef's speciality is lobster and shrimp Leonelo. Good food, good setting and fair prices. Open for breakfast through dinner, 7 am-11 pm.

LA FISHERIA
Plaza Caracol
☎ 9/883-1395
Moderate/Expensive

Owned by the same owners as La Dolce Vita and Savio's. The food here is cooked to perfection – and to order. The special attention to service and presentation has made this upstairs restaurant

La Fisheria menu selections: ceviche Cancún, seafood paella & seafood tacos.

Cancún

in an upscale shopping mall very popular. Floor-to-ceiling windows, bright colors, white linens and modern chairs give the dining room a light and open feel. The seafood paella is excellent, and as Chef Amilcar Vezquez assures us, is made from the freshest ingredients. Open 11 am-11:30 pm.

THE COVE
Playa Langosta, Km 5
☎ 9/883-06-09
Moderate/Expensive

The Cove menu selections: stuffed red snapper, lobster tail, seafood platter, flambé café sexy!

The playfully casual Cove, located in an octagonal-shaped building of palm and wood next to a fine public beach, is perennially popular. They claim that vacationing diners return an average of four times – quite a statistic considering the amount of quality competition. It opens at 7 am for an extensive breakfast buffet (everything from tamales to waffles) and remains open through dinner. The specialty is seafood. Mariachis appear – and play loudly – every night from 8-11 pm. Romantic tables are available directly on the beach.

RIO NIZUC
Km 25, south end of the hotel zone
No telephone
Inexpensive/Moderate

There's a small sign among the mangroves, easily missed, that announces the location of the Rio Nizúc restaurant. Fortunately, hardly any tourists find it despite hundreds of them passing by on personal watercraft as they enter the Laguna Nichupté on the Jungle Tour. You can sit in the cool shade and watch them watch you with envy as you enjoy this very special seafood-only restaurant. To get here, take a cab or jump on the bus that goes to Wet 'n Wild and tell the driver Río Nizuc restaurant. If you're driving, turn left just over the bridge at the far end of the hotel zone and park in the cement parking lot. Follow the path among the mangroves to this rustic, water's-edge eatery. One of the dishes they're famous for is Tikin-xic, fresh fish cooked in Maya anchiote spice and limes. Absolutely delicious. Bring your swimsuit and snorkel, have a beer or two and spend the day. Open for lunch all afternoon to dusk. Shhh... don't tell anyone. It's our secret.

FARO'S
Plaza Lagunas, Km 8.5
☎ 9/823-2080
Moderate/Expensive

The word "faro" means lighthouse in Spanish, so you know this is a seafood restaurant. The nautical décor of hanging fish nets and mounted fish in the dining room should assure you too. White linen tablecloths, bamboo blinds, brass fittings and blond vertical-slatted wood room dividers make you feel as though you're dining in a yacht. The extensive seafood menu is a draw for locals as well as vacationers. The *Dos Gringos* reviewers, a regular column in the local paper, named it as one of Cancún's Top 10 restaurants. Open noon to 11 pm.

Faro's menu selections: seafood grill, three-sauce fish filet, lobster and filet mignon combo, seafood fettuccine.

Cancún

LORENZILLO'S
Kukulkán, Km 10.5
☎ 9/883-1254
Expensive

Live lobsters and soft-shell crabs are the most popular dishes at this well-known seafood restaurant set on a pier over the lagoon. Somehow, they claim that they've been in business since 1683. The fish – some from their own farm – are super-fresh, but it's the lobster that is tops. Great views from a palapa-roofed restaurant balanced on pier pilings over tranquil waters. One of Cancún's "in" places to dine.

Downtown

EL PESCADOR
Tulipanes
☎ 9/884-2673
Moderate

Since its opening in 1980, the Pescador has built an excellent reputation for fine fish and other seafood. With competition from endless hotel zone restaurants, El Pescador, with upstairs dining and a palapa roof, has still kept its prices reasonable for delicious fresh seafood.

CARRILLO'S LOBSTER HOUSE
Claveles
☎ 9/884-1227
Moderate

Carrillo's is the older of the two top seafood restaurants downtown. For years this venerable landmark has been the place for lobster and seafood in Cancún. Its open-air patio dining, on a quiet side street, is particularly popular with travelers who appreciate fine seafood and good service. Needless to say, their specialty is lobster. Located in front of Carrillo's Hotel.

Favorite International Restaurants

Hotel Zone

BOGART'S
Kukulkán, Km 9.5, next to El Mortero
☎ 9/883-1133, ext. 108
Expensive

With a bronze statue in front showing the farewell scene between Humphrey Bogart and Ingrid Bergman from the movie Casablanca, you know this restaurant specializes in Mediterranean fare. The interior is lush and extravagant, with potted palms in brass planters, velvet foot cushions and Persian carpets. There's a grand piano in the main salon (not an upright, so there's no hiding space for those letters of transit). A free cocktail awaits at the Istanbul Bar. Middle Eastern and vegetarian dishes. Take a table tucked into an alcove for romantic privacy. Try the Ali Baba crème brûlée dessert. Open 5 to 11 pm for dinner only.

Bogart's menu selections: ravioli, taboule salad, rack of lamb in mint-tarragon sauce, crab and lobster, chicken supreme Casablanca.

MIKADO
Marriott Casa Magna Hotel, Km 16.5
☎ 9/881-2000, ext. 6325
Expensive

Thai and Japanese food are prepared with typical Marriott finesse in an ultramodern setting within the huge resort hotel. Sushi, lobster and steak are the featured menu items. Groups can get their own Teppan-Yaki tables for up to 18 with a personal chef who cuts and grills and creates to order. The menu selections come from all around the Pacific Rim. Order your Thai hot (as we like it)

Cancún

Mikado menu selections: spring rolls, tempura, tom yum gong, mussaman curry.

or gently spiced. Dinner reservations recommended. Open 5 pm to 11 pm.

MANGO TANGO
Kukulkán, Km 14.2
☎ 9/885-0303
Moderate/Expensive

Mango Tango's menu selections: lime-coconut shrimp, seafood & rice with black bean sauce, Caribbean lobster tail, seafood stir-fry.

Caribbean is the style and the flavor of Mango Tango, a huge, stand-alone restaurant facing the Nichupé Lagoon. The menu's strongest dishes are fresh Caribbean seafood, but they also serve steaks and beef shish kababs. The calypso atmosphere pulsates when the Caribbean Festival show begins at 7 pm and again at 9:30. Although Cancún has little culture in common with Caribbean islands such as Jamaica, the folklore show is both fun and festive. The food is good enough to keep diners coming back. If you like sweet, try the mango chutney shrimp. No cover. Open noon to 2 am.

Downtown

NAVAJO'S
Calle Alcatraces (south end of Parque de las Palapas – one half block west of Av. Tulum)
☎ 9/887-0657
Inexpensive/Moderate

Bigger mixed juice drinks (US $1 for fresh-squeezed) and a good selection of health foods distinguish Navajo's from the more famous "100% Natural" restaurant chain, which Navajo owner, Rodolfo Baca, helped found. With long salt-and-pepper hair and a quick smile, the distinctively handsome Señor Baca, part Navajo Indian (pro-nounced na-VA-ho in Spanish), oversees the service. Vegetarian specials, whole wheat tortillas and delicious natural chicken and beef dishes are served with fresh vegetables. It's under a grand cool palapa on the corner of Palapa Park. Generous servings and well-prepared meals.

PAELLA CLUB
Tulipanes
☎ 9/887-1724
Expensive

The Paella Club, a relatively new restaurant downtown, features a very Spanish (as in Spain) atmosphere, including subtle touches such as Spanish newspapers, magazines and music. The manager and chefs are from Valencia, Spain. The restaurant has live mariachis and flamenco music and dancers. The respected kitchen's specialties are: paella, seafood, lobster, tapas (varied appetizers served with drinks) and sangria. There's a separate bar and terrace. Reservations recommended for dinner. Open 11 am-11:30 pm.

YAMAMOTO JAPANESE RESTAURANT
Av. Uxmal #31 – opposite Howard Johnson's
☎ 9/887-3366
Moderate/Expensive

For those who crave raw fish and rice, Yamamoto's is the place to go. Long a favorite of Japanese food aficionados, this cozy eatery, tucked in a former private home at the corner of Uxmal and Rubia, features sushi, noodles and an extensive à la carte menu. It has a faithful following. Dress is casual. They're open 1:30 pm to 11:30 pm daily, except Sunday, when they close at 8 pm.

Favorite Casual Fun Restaurants

Hotel Zone

CARLOS & CHARLIE'S
Kukulkán, Km 5.5
☎ 9/883-1304
Moderate

This party-time restaurant bar is one of the most popular of a group of eateries in Cancún, Playa del Carmen and Cozumel all owned by the same people. Carlos & Charlie's combines international and Mexican food with live music and dancing. Featuring a beachside terrace, it is a favorite of the young, especially during Spring Break. Another favorite location on Cozumel. Open from noon-3 am.

SENOR FROGS
Plaza Caracol & Plaza Kukulkán
☎ 9/883-2198 or 883-1092
Moderate

Live reggae bands, separate bar, terrace dining and a party atmosphere. Dining here is similar to eating in the Carlos restaurants (Señor Frogs is owned/operated by the same group). Barbecue ribs are the food specialty, but party-hardy ambiance means drinks, and Señor Frogs serves up huge margaritas, tequilas and beer. The place is packed with revelers by late evening. The atmosphere is all fun and the restaurant and bar's motto is "It's Party Time!" Dancing and wet T-shirt competitions rule. Karaoke, too. Another location at the dock at Playa del Carmen. Open from noon to 2:30 am.

RAINFOREST CAFE

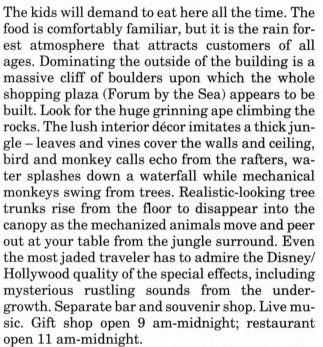

Forum by the Sea
☎ 9/881-8130
Moderate

The kids will demand to eat here all the time. The food is comfortably familiar, but it is the rain forest atmosphere that attracts customers of all ages. Dominating the outside of the building is a massive cliff of boulders upon which the whole shopping plaza (Forum by the Sea) appears to be built. Look for the huge grinning ape climbing the rocks. The lush interior décor imitates a thick jungle – leaves and vines cover the walls and ceiling, bird and monkey calls echo from the rafters, water splashes down a waterfall while mechanical monkeys swing from trees. Realistic-looking tree trunks rise from the floor to disappear into the canopy as the mechanized animals move and peer out at your table from the jungle surround. Even the most jaded traveler has to admire the Disney/Hollywood quality of the special effects, including mysterious rustling sounds from the undergrowth. Separate bar and souvenir shop. Live music. Gift shop open 9 am-midnight; restaurant open 11 am-midnight.

OTHER FUN PLACES: Fat Tuesdays (Km 6. 5), **Hard Rock Café** (Forum Mall), **Dady Rock** (near Convention Center), **Official All-Star Café** (next to the Forum), **Pat O'Brien's** and **Planet Hollywood** (both in Plaza Flamingo). Also see our list of nightspots for other fun dining opportunities.

Cancún

Downtown

CARLOS O'BRIAN'S
107 Av. Tulum
☎ 9/884-1659
Moderate

The word "cantina," meaning bar, was coined after a liquor store owner punched a hole in the wall to serve drinks to men in a side room. The Spanish term for this architectural passage is "cantina."

This fun-food cantina is a restaurant-bar that overlooks the crowded sidewalk of Av. Tulum, downtown. If it sounds and seems similar to Carlos & Charlie's, that's because it is owned by the same people.

There are two bars, terrace dining and live bands nightly. Popular with crowds heading on to the late-night disco nearby or those just people-watching. The specialty is barbecued ribs, a delicious plateful for about US $7. Open daily from 11 am until you leave at night.

Favorite Budget Restaurants

Hotel Zone

SANBORNS CAFE
Maya Fair & Flamingo Plazas
Reservations not necessary
Inexpensive/Moderate

Sanborns is a chain of restaurants similar to Denny's, with a touch of Pancake House thrown in. In fact, they serve breakfast 24 hours a day on linen table cloths with free coffee refills (good coffee too!). For lunch and dinner Mexican cooking is featured at reasonable prices.

The waitresses dress in colorful long cotton skirts and give prompt attentive service. The restaurant also offers a welcome non-smoking area. There's a dining area on a homey front porch and inside there's a diner look, complete with lunch counter. Another location is downtown on Av. Uxmal and Tulum, across the street from the bus terminal. Open daily 24 hours.

TY-COZ
Kukulkán, angled across the street from El Presidente Hotel
Reservations not necessary
Inexpensive

With only three patio tables beneath umbrellas, this little store-front place may not last in the "bigger-is-better" Cancún hotel zone. That would be a shame because it serves deliciously strong cappuccino, fresh coffee and great sandwiches on crusty French bread. Daily specials.

CHECANDOLE
Flamingo Plaza
☎ 9/885-1302
Inexpensive

A fast food off-shoot of a popular Mexican restaurant in Cancún City. The food here is tasty and well prepared, with hot spices served on the side. Specials offer two-for-one beers.

The Flamingo Plaza's cheap fast food eateries are the hotel zone's best kept secret. There is also a large mall-style food court in Kukulkán Mall, Km 13.

Cancún

Downtown

MESON DE VECINDARIO "LA BAQUETTE"
Av. Uxmal, near Av. Nader
Reservations not necessary
Inexpensive/Moderate

Open from 7 am to midnight, this trendy café began as a coffee shop/bakery, then grew into what has become one of the romantic gems of downtown restaurants. Set back from the road under a palm tree wrapped in romantic twinkling white lights. Its outdoor tables are under a green canvas awning. Inside, the softly lit walls are decorated with art, wine racks and magazines. Soft music playing in the background makes El Meson ambiance very alluring. Wood tables are hand-painted and the menu has developed from delicious sandwiches and coffee to gourmet offerings such as osso bucco and Chilean Cabernet. You can still try their delicious sandwiches on crusty French bread available for lunch or dinner. We love it. *C'est magnifique!*

EL CAFE
Av. Nader No. 5
☎ 9/884-1584
Inexpensive/Moderate

Only one block from crowded Av. Tulum, the local business people escape here to this clean and cool outdoor café that serves up coffee or tea and fresh-baked *pan dulce* both mornings and afternoons. Pleasant surroundings under drooping flamboyant trees. An excellent selection of varied Mexican food appears on El Café's breakfast-through-dinner menu, with both light snacks and full

meals. Unusually fast service, good food and reasonable prices are why those in the know come
here. We do!

SANTA CLARA ICE CREAM & CAFE
29 Av. Tulum at the corner of Av. Uxmal
☎ 9/884-9548
Inexpensive

Back in 1924, a horse-drawn cart began home de-
livery of dairy products in Pachuca, Hidalgo, Mexico. The uncompromising use of only the finest
and freshest ingredients resulted in the small local dairy expanding into a national franchise of
ice cream, bakery and coffee shops. Today, it is
still family-owned and offers only the highest
quality. This spotlessly clean Santa Clara shop,
with air conditioning, is a great place to relax and
snack. Their most popular products are the delicious natural yogurts, which are kosher and come
with nutritional charts. Very hygienic and very
tasty. We'll see you there!

Shop Till You Drop

Diamonds are a girl's best friend.
From *Gentlemen Prefer Blondes*, 1949

A strong dollar combined with high-quality
goods, fascinating folk art, handicrafts and
fun souvenirs make Mexico a shopper's paradise.
The problem is not so much what to buy among
Cancún's shops, malls and flea markets, but
where to begin. There are shopping plazas and
North American-style malls conveniently located

in the hotel zone. In addition, the downtown offers several flea market groupings, along with some fine shops and grocery/department stores. With limited time and a multitude of choices, even a veteran shopper could use help. Follow these hints for a fulfilling excursion into the mecca of Cancún bargains.

Helpful Hints

WHAT? As much as you can, decide what you're looking for in advance. Anything from T-shirts to designer clothes and accessories is available. Silver and gold jewelry are cheaper in Mexico and the craftsmanship is often exquisite. Large hand-woven string hammocks are the traditional bed, couch and crib here. Made of nylon, cotton, silk, or sisal, they are extremely comfortable once you get used to sleeping in them.

Traditional crafts from Campeche, on the peninsula's west coast, are carved wooden ships and replicas of the fortifications built to repel pirates in the 17th century.

Pottery and pewter are always good bets. Also check out hand-painted lacquerware, blankets and woven baskets. Once you have an idea of what you want, be flexible. The range of gifts is large.

🌀 TIP

Remember, you've got to get everything you buy back on the plane. Extra luggage is available for purchase in the markets and mall stores.

WHEN? Check out the malls first. You're probably familiar with their offerings and comfortable with their atmosphere. Additionally, there is less pressure to buy something right then and there. Boutiques and specialty shops often have bargains in designer labels as much as 30% off stateside prices. Jot down what you liked, the price and where you were. Shop now, buy later. Most established stores have fixed prices, but it can't hurt to ask for a break.

WHERE? Once you have an idea of what you fancy and what prices are like, check out the flea markets and smaller stores, especially downtown. We use the words "flea market" rather loosely to signify a market where there are numerous small stalls or clustered shops offering typical merchandise. If you show interest in an item in a market, the shopkeeper will begin the haggling process. There are some supermarkets/department stores in downtown Cancún that have items (such as liquor and clothes) at a distinct savings. Lastly, remember to check out the bargains over on Isla Mujeres.

Store Hours

Shops are usually open from 10 am to 1 pm and again from 4 or 5 pm to 9 or 10 at night. However, the traditional siesta break is not common in the hotel zone where the almighty dollar rules.

Cancún

Clothing Size Conversions

Although most clothes are made and sized for the North American market, Mexican made clothes may be differently sized. Use this chart to help you determine the right size.

	MEXICAN	AMERICAN
Women's Clothes		
	30	6
	32	8
	34	10
	36	12
	38	14
	40	16
Women's Shoes		
	3½	6
	4	6½
	4½	7
	5	7½
	5½	8
Men's Shirts		
	38	SM
	40	M
	42	L
	44	XL
Men's Shoes		
	6½	8
	7	8½
	8	9½
	9	10½
	10	11½
	10½	12

In the Hotel Zone

Malls

Plaza Caracol
Km 8.5

Plaza Caracol is centrally located in the busy convention center area that is often mistakenly referred to as "downtown." The large white mall rests on an island where Paseo Kukulcán divides and turns south. It is the second largest mall in Cancún, with 200 shops. These include designer specialty stores (Dominique France, Ultra Femme, Cartier, Fendi, Gucci, Piaget) and some of the best restaurants in the hotel zone (La Fisheria, Casa Rolandi, El Mexicano's, Iguana Wana, Savio's).

In the evening, sidewalk spray-paint artists attract big crowds in several of the outdoor mall areas. Their works are quite clever and very cheap.

Plaza Maya Fair
Km 8.5

This pleasing plaza was called Mayfair until a remodeling in 1998 put a Maya-inspired façade on the building, including a huge archway at one end. Now, it's known as Maya Fair. It's billed as an ecological mall (an oxymoron?) presumably because of its greenery, waterfalls and exotic gardens. Across from a good public beach, the Maya houses a playground, food court, lots of restaurants and shops. Other plazas (Terramar, Lagunas) connect to it. Featured restaurants are Faro's, Sanborns, American Classic, Danielli's, 100% Natural and Tu Tango.

Cancún

Coral Negro Mercado De Artesanías
Km 9

Across from the Official All Star Café is a Mexican artesians market, *mercado*, with a fancier outdoor handicraft gift section that imitates a village square (*El Zocalo*). The 65-shop market covers both sides of Kukulcán with more vendors next to Italianni's Restaurant. This is a popular stop for Americans who want a taste of real *mercado* shopping without leaving the hotel zone. Prices are reasonable here.

Plaza La Fiesta
Km 9.5

La Fiesta advertises itself as having the best prices in the hotel zone for myriad gifts and souvenirs. It's a large pinkish building next to TGI Friday's on the southern bend of Kukulcán. Rows and rows of handicrafts, clothes and typical gift merchandise at reasonable prices. It's a Mexican market that's inside and air conditioned. Well worth a look.

Forum By The Sea
Km 9.5

This shopping mall complex in Cancún is the hardest to miss, although you may not realize it's a mall at all. The huge guitar of the Hard Rock Café is cemented into the sidewalk out front and one half of the building looks as though it's made of huge boulders, where jungle animals, such as

King Kong, scamper. The cliff wall is part of the Rainforest Café, located on the second floor.

The Forum features a huge open atrium around which the 65 shops and attractions wrap. It is home to such exclusive designer boutiques as Tommy Hilfiger, Aca Joe's, Diamond International, Diesel, Bulgari, Berger Jewelry and Chronos de Peyrelongue, among others.

Eating and entertainment can be found at the Hard Rock Café, Zandunga, Santa Fe Brewery, Mama Roma, Coco Bongo, and the Rainforest Café. Situated across the street from the convention center, at the corner where Paseo Kukulcán turns to form the other leg of the number "7."

The monuments you see lining Paseo Kukulcán are fiberglass replicas of pre-Columbian structures found in many of Mexico's archeological sites.

Plaza Flamingo
Km 11

The Flamingo is a pleasant, air-conditioned mall with a good variety of shops, including Wayan, an exotic world gift shop; Roxana Pharmacy; La Casa de Habano, an excellent and reliable place to get Cuban cigars, and Deportes Martí, a large sports store. The small fast food court has a wide selection, and is very clean and open.

The wonderful paved walk that follows the Paseo runs behind this mall along the lagoon – very scenic. For food and fun it contains a Sanborns, New Orleans-based eatery Pat O'Brien's, Outback Steakhouse, and the Planet Hollywood.

Cancún

Plaza Kukulkán

Km 13

Plaza Kukulkán is a huge, American-style shopping mall where a series of restaurants such as Ruth's Chris Steakhouse and Splash compete for notice along the ground floor facing the Boulevard. It is Cancun's largest, in terms of interior size, at 60,000 square meters on three floors. Among the over 200 air-conditioned upscale shops are Señor Frog's Official Store, Harley Davidson Clothes, Corrado Luggage, Gaitán Leather, Cleopatra Beauty Salon, Mezza Luna, Sybeles and many more.

A Sierra Madre store, part of its namesake organization, sells nature-oriented items, with profits contributed to various ecological efforts such as the Sea Turtle Program. These altruistic-inspired crafts and gifts are on the second floor.

An upstairs food court offers 16 fast food choices and there are some good restaurants downstairs. The mall is also home to Tele-Cines, an English-language cinema that plays first-run Hollywood movies, as well as a video and laser-game center and a bowling alley.

La Isla Shopping Village

Km 12.5

Cancún's newest and most ambitious shopping area is located along the lagoon in the hotel zone. Opened in mid-2000, *La Isla* features a city street-like "downtown," full of upscale shops and restaurants that line its traffic-free walkways. Huge canvas roofs attached to massive metal poles protect pedestrians in inclement weather. A moat crossed by pedestrian bridges meanders through the retail area. *La Isla* is also home to the popular Ma'ax'o discotheque, an aquarium, a multiplex cinema, and Pasaje del Terror, a scary multi-media theatrical experience that is drawing crowds worldwide. The artwork and crafts of the Huichol Indians, indigenous Mexican Indians well known for their artistic skills, are sold as the Huichol Collection. Profits benefit their efforts to preserve their traditional lifestyle.

Isla Mujeres

Consider taking one of the party boats/hotel zone cruisers over to Isla Mujeres for shopping. Prices are great and it makes for a fun day-trip, and *La Isla* is virtually crime-free, despite what you may hear. If food is included in your cruise price, you'll miss some inexpensive and delicious dining opportunities in town. Adventuresome travelers should consider taking the people ferry across from Puerto Juárez, just north of Cancún downtown (around US $3).

Downtown

Downtown, everything's waiting for you.
Petula Clark

Downtown Cancún has several shopping choices. There are three flea market-type shopping areas along Av. Tulum, as well as traditional and upscale stores. The Av. Tulum's stores include Ultra Femme, which features fine jewelry and expen-

Cancún

sive perfumes at duty-free prices (as does a smaller competitor on the next block). The exclusive shop Sybele opened there in 1980 (there are also branches in plazas Caracol and Kukulkán). Sybele is a department store on two floors that features elegant timepieces, gifts, shoes, designer clothing and fashions, dresses, jewelry, and accessories, for men, women and children. The Varsity Club clothing store sells designer clothing from big names like Ralph Lauren and Tommy Hilfiger for men and women. There are also several stores with quality merchandise in sportswear, bathing suits, sporting goods, souvenirs, gifts and art – most of which boast lower prices than can be found in the hotel zone.

Malls, Markets & Plazas

The flea markets for shoppers along Av. Tulum are typically Mexican. They feature several outside stalls with sidewalk hawkers to attract you to their merchandise. Inside the buildings you'll find a warren of little walkways between what seems like hundreds of stalls offering jewelry, cloths, gifts, souvenirs, food, and more. It can be a little claustrophobic, and having every stall owner invite you in because their stuff is cheaper than Kmart can be annoying, especially if you're used to begging for sales help when you shop back home. However, once you get used to it you can become very comfortable saving lots of money. These markets are safe (in any crowded area anywhere, watch your purse, wallet, and camera) because shop owners do look out for their customers. And the bargains inside are genuine.

Plaza Garibaldi

This market on Av. Tulum, at the corner of Av. Uxmal, contains stalls of serapes, tablecloths and traditional clothing, gifts and crafts. The north end of the avenue.

Plaza Mexico

A flea market at Av. Tulum No. 200 squeezed into a cluster of 50 handicraft shops.

Ki-Huic

The oldest and biggest flea market downtown is located in the center of Av. Tulum between two banks. Open daily from 9 am-10 pm (some take a siesta), this streetfront and indoor labyrinth of stalls has 100 vendors of gifts and crafts.

Good bargains can be struck at these flea markets, but be prepared to haggle if you like what you see. You'll be "eagerly invited" to enter every shop.

Plaza Bonita

Av. Xel-Há

Near the post office downtown, Plaza Bonita is an attractive outdoor mall that looks like a little village street, right next to a typical Mexican municipal market. This is a favorite shopping and eating area of local residents and expatriates. Upscale goods without the high prices.

Mercado

SM 23

The middle of the large triangular block behind the bus station at Av. Uxmal and Av. Tulum houses a municipal market that local workers fre-

Cancún

quent. Gringos are scarce here, but bargains are not. Gifts and clothing.

Supermarkets/Department Stores

Prices on beer, liquor, tequila and Ixtabentún are better in the supermarkets than in regular liquor stores.

Supermarkets that sell souvenirs, gifts and liquor in downtown Cancún are **San Francisco de Asis**, in the middle of Av. Tulum; the **Comercial Mexicana**, at the circle of Av. Tulum and Uxmal; and the **Chedraui**, a great department store at the corner of Av. Tulum and Cobá. They're good places to stock up on water, food and miscellaneous necessities as well as gifts.

Bakeries

Chedraui has a good bakery called **La Hogaza.** To choose what you want in a bakery, take an aluminum pizza tray and some tongs and pick from the open racks. The sales clerk will add it up and bag it at the register. Baked goods are very inexpensive.

Chain Stores

There's a large **Ace Hardware** on Av. Tulum, south of the city center (☎ 9/887-6800), plus a huge Chedraui shopping center across the street. A **Sam's Club** (the USA-based membership club) is tucked behind Av. Yaxchilán and Av. Labna, near the Telemex microwave towers. If your annual membership is expiring soon, think about renewing here – it's cheaper. They offer a list of stores and restaurants that discount with a Sam's card. At the same location is a **Wal-Mart**, open 24 hours. Around the block is another membership club, **Costco**.

Dawn to Dusk

There was a young lady named Bright,
Whose speed was far faster than light;
She set out one day in a relative way,
And returned home the previous night.
Professor Arthur Buller, 1874-1944

There is something for everyone, every hour of the day in Cancún, including swimming, sunning, fishing, watersports, exploring, shopping – and everything in between. Cancún rocks 24 hours a day. You could spend three months down here and still not do it all.

When your sightseeing itinerary involves day-trips or quick overnight jaunts, there's no shortage of ways to reach your destination. Choices include a travel-agent-arranged tour, renting a car, or taking public transportation.

Sightseeing

A must-see is **Tulum**, a Post-Classic ruined walled city, set high upon a bluff, with spectacular views of the turquoise Caribbean below. Tulum is now the most visited archeological site in all of Mexico. **Chichén Itzá** is an even more

Cancún

impressive sight, not because of its location, but because of its massive size and architecture. The giant pyramid El Castillo, where human sacrifices once occurred, dominates the fascinating abandoned city. On the way, a stop or an overnight in the historic Colonial city of Valladolid gives a sense of the Yucatán not found in the modern streets of Cancún.

Wear sunscreen and a hat when touring outside, even on cloudy days.

Visit the **Xke'ken Cenote** (sinkhole) near Dzitnup and Valladolid, or the **Balankanché Caves** near Chichén. The ancient lost city of **Cobá** is also within reach, as is the **Gran Cenote**, both near Tulum. And if you're down there, don't miss a tour of the Aktun Chen caves and underground cenote. Exciting educational trips into the **Sian Ka'an Biosphere**, a 1.3 million-acre nature reserve, are arranged by Amigos de Sian Ka'an, headquartered in the Plaza America at ☎ 9/884-9583. If you're tempted to explore more of the countryside, check out our *Adventure Guide to the Yucatán*, also from Hunter Publishing, for full details. Otherwise, see the *Field Trips* chapter at the end of this book for information on quick trips to Tulum and Chichén Itzá or other archeological or natural spots on the peninsula. Below are some of the local Cancún activities that are bound to please.

Jungle Tour

The tour of the "jungle" that you'll be offered everywhere is actually a guided foray – on either small speedboats or a one- or two-person personal watercraft, such as a Jet Ski – into the mangrove lagoon. This is less a tour of the jungle than a chance to zoom around the ocean and lagoon and get wet. Some tour operators offer snorkel stops. There are several major suppliers of the extremely popular tour, which leaves from various marinas in the lagoon. Either contract directly at one of the marinas or via your hotel's travel agent. Look for discount coupons.

Croco Cun & Botanical Garden

About 45 minutes south of Cancún near Puerto Morelos is this crocodile research station, breeding farm and fun zoo that offers a fascinating glimpse of the ugly prehistoric beasts up close. It's a good kid spot with excellent photo ops. Open daily 8:30 am-6 pm. Admission: $6 (kids under age six enter free). No phone.

Very close by is Dr. Alfredo Barrera Marín's Jardín Botánico (Botanical Garden), 150 acres of land with nearly two miles of walking trails through the natural plants and trees of the peninsula. Open daily from 9-5, a guide is available. Get to both places by taxi, organized tour, or via car. No phone.

Use insect repellent when you're going back to nature.

Cancún

Sports & Activities

Go-Karts

Go-kart racing is very popular with the young and restless. Cartwheel over to **Karting International Cancún**, open daily from 10 am to 11 pm, south of downtown. Some special cars can reach the scary speed of 80 mph (130 kmph) on a competition standard track. Others putter along at much lower speeds. When we passed, they were advertising free taxi rides one-way.

Golf

Pok-Ta-Pok golf course is named after the ancient Maya ball game in which the losing team's captain is thought to have been beheaded!

Floggers can enjoy the **Pok-Ta-Pok Golf Club**, open 6 am-6 pm, along the lagoon at Km 7.5. Designed by Robert Trent Jones, Jr., the 18-hole course incorporates ancient Maya ruins with real sand traps. Restaurant, bar, pro shop, equipment rental, swimming pool, tennis courts and driving range. ☎ 9/883-1230.

The **Meliá Cancún** boasts an executive course and pro shop. ☎ 9/885-1114. The **Hilton Beach & Golf Resort** has its own championship 18-hole, par 72 course, designed around the Ruinas del Rey archeological site on the Nichupté Lagoon. ☎ 9/881-8000. The **Oasis Hotel** at Km 17 has an executive course. ☎ 9/885-0867, ext. 6655. There's a **Mini Golf Palace** for the sacrilegious at the Cancún Palace, Km 14.5, featuring 36 holes of mini-golf around pyramids, waterfalls, a river, and a lagoon. ☎ 9/885-0533, ext. 6655.

Bowling & Battles

There's a bowling alley, Bol Kukulcán, in **Kukulkán Plaza**, open from 10 am to 1:30 am (☎ 9/885-3425). The mall is also home to one of those **laser combat centers** as well as a **video game** room.

Bullfights & Special Events

Bullfights take place at the **Bullring** (☎ 9/884-8372), downtown on Av. Bonampak at Av. Sayil, every Wednesday at 3:30 pm. Los Almendros restaurant is across the street. Professional matadors fight bulls (some to the death) and cowboys, *charros*, put on an entertaining show of horsemanship and rodeo skill. Get your tickets (US $35) through travel agents or downtown in front of the San Francisco Asis supermarket on Av. Tulum. Look for the big plaster bull.

For music lovers, Cancún hosts a respected **Jazz Festival** over the Memorial Day Weekend (☎ 9/884-5895). July features a **Country/Western Fest** and a **Rockfest** plays in October.

Expo Cancún, a crafts and exhibits fair/festival, is held the end of October, also downtown.

Horseback Riding

Horsing around is a popular pastime for visitors. The largest ranch, **Rancho Loma Bonita** (☎ 9/887-5465), has 987 acres on Highway 307 south of Cancún. Book directly or through a travel agent. **Rancho Grande**, Km 41.5, Hwy 307 near Puerto Morelos, features beach rides (☎ 9/887-5465).

Isla Mujeres

La Isla should be more than a quick shopping trip. Its quaint personality survives on the slip of an island only a few miles off the coast of Cancún.

Cancún

For beginner snorkelers the island has an underwater park, **El Garrfón**, and the rocky northeastern coast is dramatically beautiful.

There is also a great snorkel and nature trip from either Isla Mujeres or Cancún to **Isla Contoy**, a bird sanctuary. Adventuresome souls may consider taking the people ferry over to the Island of Women from Puerto Juárez, just north of downtown. (See the *Isla Mujeres* section, page 137, for more information.)

Fun in the Water

Swimming offers year-round fun, whether it's in the warm waters of the Caribbean or the languid hotel pools. Some beachfront hotels offer **parasailing**, an activity in which you are pulled by a motorboat above the sea or the lagoon attached to a parachute. If your hotel doesn't offer this, inquire at Lorenzillo's Restaurant (☎ 9/883-3073).

⚡ WARNING

Be aware that parasailing is a dangerous sport and injuries are not unheard of.

Sailboarding, or windsurfing, also has its fans here. At Playa Tortugas, Km 7 (distances are marked along the 16-mile-long Paseo Kukulcán beginning in the downtown), there's the **International Windsurfer Sailing School** (☎ 9/884-2023) that features rental equipment and lessons.

You can **sail** your way out to sea from any number of lagoon marinas. A Sunfish is ideal for the calm lagoon. Or rent a personal watercraft to zoom around on.

Deep-sea fishing lures many Cancún residents from April through September when the best varieties of fish come to local waters, but the catch is good year-round.

Cancún hosts a **Billfish Tournament** from late April through June. Several marinas in Cancún and over on Isla Mujeres will arrange charters of four, six or eight hours. Charters include captain, first mate, gear, bait and beverages. And a boat.

Wet 'n Wild

A kid favorite is the exciting 17-acre, $20 million Wet 'n Wild amusement park with splashy water rides. Tall towers and long twisting slides are the big attractions in this beachside park located south of the hotel zone, past Rio Nizuc (Km 25). The 2001 admission prices were US $28 adults, US $18 for children. It's easy to reach. Just look for hotel zone buses displaying a Wet 'n Wild logo; they'll drop you in the parking lot. ☎ 9/885-1855.

Cancún

Marinas

Almost all marinas listed offer the works: fishing charters, jungle tours, snorkeling trips, sailing and motorized watersports.

Marina Aqua Rey – Km 10.5 Paseo Kukulkán, at Lorenzillo's Restaurant. They offer jungle tours and their own floating sports center as well as the *Subsea Explorer,* for underwater viewing (☎ 9/883-3007).

Marina Barracuda – Km 14, next to Mango Tango. Open 8 to 8, they are a full-service marina offering jungle tours, waterskiing, WaveRunners, fishing and a banana ride (☎ 9/885-2444).

Marina Aqua Tours – Km 6.25 by Fat Tuesdays. Fishing, waterskiing, snorkeling, jungle tours and lobster dinner cruises (☎ 9/883-0400).

Royal Yacht Club – Km 16.5 by Captain's Cove Restaurant and the Royal Mayan Hotel. Watersports equipment rentals, showers and lockers (☎ 9/885-0391).

Aqua Fun – Km 16.5 by the Omni and Royal Mayan Hotels. Canoes, sailing, snorkeling, diving, etc. (☎ 9/885-3260).

Pelican Pier – Km 5.5. Offers an air-taxi and sportfishing (☎ 9/883-0315).

Mundo Marina – Km 5.5. Snorkeling and diving trips, fishing and a cruise (☎ 9/883-0554).

Marina Playa Langosta – Playa Langosta (☎ 9/883-2802). Trips and rentals.

Aqua World – Km 15.2 in front of the Meliá Cancún Hotel. *Sub See Explorer* underwater viewing ship, jungle tours and "Paradise Island," a private watersports island in the lagoon (☎ 9/885-2288).

More than just a quick shuttle, the ***Dolphin Express*** (☎ 9/883-1488) wanders over to Isla Mujeres from the Playa Langosta dock at 10 am, and returns at 4:30 pm. The daytime cruise costs about US $30, which includes continental breakfast, shopping and exploration time on the island, swimming, buffet lunch, open bar and a chance to watch dolphins close up. Snorkel gear rental extra.

You can have a hands-on dolphin swim experience on Isla Mujeres with ***Dolphin Discovery***, which also departs from the dock at Playa Langosta in Cancún's hotel zone. Each session lasts one hour with a half-hour of swim time and photo ops. Safe for anyone who can swim. Minimum age of eight. Reservations are suggested, ☎ 9/883-0779.

On the ***Asterix*** party fishing cruise (☎ 9/886-4847) you catch your own food and the crew cooks it for you. If you're not lucky enough to land the big one, they provide dinner while you drown your sorrows at their open bar. Departure from Nautico Club in Caracol Beach.

Atlantis Submarine is an Isla Mujeres-based, Coast Guard-approved, passenger submarine offering underwater excursions. Tours include cruising the reefs and an interactive high-tech marine show. Hourly departures from the Embarcadero at the Playa Linda pier (☎ 9/883-1442). ***Nautibus*** (☎ 9/883-3552) is a floating submarine available to reveal the mysterious world of Neptune to us mere mortals.

The ***Sub See Explorer***, like the *Nautibus*, is a glass-bottom boat that has a very deep draft with

Cancún

portholes under the water line. A jaunt in AquaWorld's *Sub See* is usually combined with a trip to **Paradise Island**, a tiny artificial island built over a reef. Paradise Island provides a platform where you can swim, snorkel or just sun. Hourly departures. Cost is about US $35 for either trip (lunch, beer and refreshments included). In combination, the two excursions run US $45 per person.

After Dark

Come on baby, light my fire
Try to set the night on fire.
The Doors, 1967

Cancún's reasonable prices, proximity to the United States and lax drinking laws contribute to the city's reputation as a year-round "party town." Fortunately, not all night-time entertainment revolves around getting plastered. Cancún features something of everything – from evening dinner cruises, oldies concerts and Mexican folklore shows to wet T-shirt contests and chest-throbbing rock and roll discos. And we have peppered your choices with places downtown, as well as those in the hotel zone. Here is how to make the most of your evenings.

Dancing & Drinking

Beaches, beer, and bikinis... sand, surf, and sex.
Dave Mazur, Canisius College freshman, 1986.

There is so much demand for late-night entertainment that there are a half-dozen clubs within walking distance of each other at the center of the hotel zone near the convention center. Most have a cover charge, but there are often special nights with no cover or a Ladies Night, when women enter free. The real action doesn't start till after 11 pm and it heats up around 1 am.

For pulsating palpitations, try **CoCo Bongo**, the hottest hotel zone nightclub, attached to the Forum by the Sea shopping plaza. It packs them in every night from after 10 pm until the wee hours. Two of its bars open earlier: the Tequila Bar at noon and the Terraza Bar at 6 pm.

Dady'O, across the street at Km 9.5, is another "in" disco in town. Expect long lines, especially on the weekends. This place throbs with nightlife, featuring cavern-like décor with a projection screen TV. A sister bar and grill is **Dady Rock**, where they party just as hard.

The latest entry in Cancún's night life is the **Ma'ax'o**, conveniently located in the front of La Isla Shopping Mall. It's huge, it's big, it's popular, it's full of *jovenes*.

The **Hard Rock Café** serves its drinks, food, and music in the center of the Forum Mall, at the turn of the Paseo, opposite Dady'O's. A large **Planet**

Cancún

Hollywood, the California-style restaurant club, is a part of the Plaza Flamingo. Video bars **La Boom**, with a live rock band, and **Tequila Boom**, next to it, boom their high-tech music out at Km 3.5. Singles welcome. **Up & Down**, in the Oasis Hotel, Km 17, combines a cozy restaurant (Up) with an ultra-modern disco that can host 2,000 gyrating bodies (Down).

Rock Lobster Garage at Plaza Terramar is a restaurant with a party atmosphere and a karaoke bar with a DJ. **Pat O'Brien's** is a New Orleans-style eatery in the Plaza Flamingo. **Señor Frog's** (Plaza Caracol and Plaza Kukulkán) and **Mango Tango** (Km 14.2 opposite the Ritz Carlton) are restaurants with rocking bar areas and live music.

The **Rainforest Café** is entertaining for sight and sound. **Carlos & Charlie's** features a house band after 7 pm.

Late night downtown brings restaurants and bars open along the street. Options include **Carlos O'Brian's** on Av. Tulum; and **Karumba Disco**, open at 11 pm and a favorite for alternative lifestyles, located over the Casa Italiana restaurant on Av. Tulum.

The perennially popular hotspot downtown is **Péricos**, Av. Yaxchilán, No. 61, one of the most happening places in town. Péricos is an eatery and bar with live Mexican music from 7:30 pm to midnight. The constant party atmosphere makes a festive night out. Their unique bar stools are crafted from saddles.

If you are looking for a lively Latin atmosphere and dancing in the hotel zone, consider **Azucar** ("Sugar") an elegant bar and nightclub next to the Hyatt and Camino Real hotels. Bands are flown in from Cuba and Puerto Rico to play hot salsa and Caribbean dance music. It's the kind of atmosphere that makes it impossible to sit and not tap the tabletop, shuffle your feet, or sway your shoulders to the beat. We went in for a drink one night (it opens at 9:30 pm) and closed the place at 4 am. What fun!

The dress code at Azucar is slacks for men and skirts, slacks, or dresses for women. No shorts or T-shirts.

Christine's, attached to the nearby Krystal Hotel, attracts well-heeled locals and visitors with its enormous dance floor. Very elegant décor.

Batachá is another salsa hotspot, located in the Miramar Misión hotel. It features live tropical bands with a full range of Caribbean music – merengue, rumba, salsa, danzon, cumbia, lambada and reggae. Cool jazz plays out at the **Blue Bayou** dinner club in the Cancún Caribe Hyatt.

Mr Gee! (across from the Marriott at Km 16.5) attracts couples and lovers to its terrace restaurant and bar overlooking the lagoon. From 8:30 on, you can dance to merengue, salsa and rock and roll. Reservations recommended at ☎ 9/885-1615.

Ballet Folklórico Nacional de Mexico features traditional Mexican music and folk dancing at the convention center at the turn opposite Punta Cancún. Dinner and show or show-only tickets available (☎ 9/883-0199, ext. 193/194).

Several upscale hotels also offer a dinner show with similar Ballet Folklórico performances.

Cancún

Cruises & Dinner Shows

 Almost all marinas offer a selection of activities and excursions, so drop by the one closest to your hotel and see what's going on. You can also make reservations with your hotel's travel agent. If your hotel doesn't operate a travel desk, just go into another hotel and ask there. Additional agencies can be found in all the shopping plazas.

The *Cancún Queen*, a Mississippi-style paddleboat, plies Laguna Nichupté on romantic dinner cruises every evening at 6 pm. It departs from the AquaWorld Marina. Dinner, open bar, dancing and live entertainment. Reservations can be made via your travel agent or directly (☎ 9/885-2288). Menu choices are lobster or steak at a fixed price (US $60 p/p) or fish or chicken (US $40).

You can also enjoy a lobster or steak meal aboard the **Columbus Lobster Dinner Cruise**, which takes place on a replica Spanish galleon (capacity 80 people). This ship unfurls its sails in a lagoon cruise from the Royal Mayan Marina, Km 16.5, in front of the Omni Hotel. Departures every evening at 5 pm and 8 pm (☎ 9/883-1488). Price of US $55 includes an open bar, dinner with salad and dessert. Dress is casual.

Yo-ho-ho and a bottle of tequila. **Pirate's Night** is a dinner cruise on a faux pirate ship featuring a three-course buffet and live entertainment (US $50; kids under 12 half-price). The excursion emphasizes fun with "avast ye maties" pirate dress-up costumes provided. Casual dress (no heels).

Reservations required (☎ 9/883-1488). Departure is at 6:30 pm from Playa Langosta dock next to the Casa Maya Hotel. Return at 11:30. Closed Sundays.

Gambling

Luckily, there are no gambling casinos in Cancún. Sports betting is allowed in the **L.F. Caliente** restaurant-bar, open 11 am to midnight in the Fiesta Americana Hotel in the hotel zone and in Plaza Caribe Hotel, downtown. Also in Cozumel.

Entertainment

There is an American movie theater in Plaza Kukulkán called **New Telecines** that features Hollywood movies in English. Comfortable and air conditioned, the theater's sound is in Dolby stereo. Wednesdays are half-price. A larger multiplex movie house for first run movies is located nearby in La Isla Mall at Km 12.5 on the Paseo.

Play night-time miniature golf at the **Mini Golf Palace** at the Cancún Palace Hotel, Km 14.5. The lighted course features 36 holes in and around pyramids, waterfalls, a river and a lagoon.

Release your aggressions at the **laser combat center**, located in Plaza Kukulkán.

At least one nude bar/show has crept into the hotel zone. Enough said.

Cancún

❓ Cancún A-Z

All men by nature desire knowledge.
Metaphysics, Aristotle

American Consular Help

A US Consular Agency is located in Plaza Caracol, 3rd floor, in the hotel zone. ☎ 9/883-0272. Open 9 am-1 pm.

In the event of an emergency, call the Mérida office at ☎ 019/925-6366 or 925-5011. The Embassy itself is located in Mexico City, ☎ 015/211-0042.

American Express

The Amex office (☎ 9/884-1999) is open weekdays from 9 to 6, Saturdays from 9 to 1 pm. It's on Av. Tulum, near the Hotel America.

Babysitting

Most of the major hotels offer babysitting services (often provided by a chambermaid), so ask in advance. This service is additional, even if you've paid for "Kids Club" activities, which entertain children during the day.

Banks In The Hotel Zone

Banks are generally open for money exchange from about 9 am to 1 pm.

Banamex – Plaza Terramar; **Banco Santander Mexicano** – Plaza Lagunas, 2nd floor; **Bital** – Plaza Caracol. Most of these and the other banks scattered in the shopping malls have ATM machines, a great way to get money at the official rate.

Banks Downtown

Banamex, Tulum No. 19; **Banca Serfin**, Coba Ave at Tulum; **Banco del Atlantico**, Tulum No. 15; **Bancomer**, Tulum No. 20; **Banpaís**, Tulum and Azucenas; **Inverlat**, Tulum No. 26.

British Consular Help

The Queen's subjects can find consular help from their representative in the Royal Resorts Hotel, 8 am-5 pm. ☎ 9/881-0100.

Canadian Consular Help

Plaza Caracol II hosts consular service for citizens of the Great White North. The third-floor office is open between 9 and 5. ☎ 9/883-3360; for emergencies outside office hours, ☎ 91/5/724-7900 (Mexico City office).

Electricity

Electric is the same as the States, 110 volts.

Friends of Friends

There's a **Narcotics Anonymous** meeting in English every Monday. It's held at 7:30 pm at Plaza Centro (3rd floor) on Av. Nader, downtown. English-language meetings of the **Friends of Bill W**, another support group, also assemble at Plaza Centro, 3rd floor, on Av. Nader. Meetings run daily from 6:15-7:15 pm. ☎ 9/884-3375; emergency group, ☎ 9/874-3082.

German Consular Help

Achtung. The consular office of Germany is downtown at 36 Punta Conoco, SM 24. Monday-Friday, 10 to 2, Saturdays, 8 to 1, ☎ 9/884-1261.

Health Clubs

Most hotels in the zone contain their own health clubs for exclusive use by their guests. However, there are two public gyms: **Gold's Gym**, ☎ 9/883-2933, is open Monday through Friday, 7 am-9 pm, and Sunday from 9 am-9 pm. It's at the Plaza Flamingo in the hotel zone. **Michaels' Gym** (☎ 9/884-2394) is on Av. Sayil No. 66, SM 4 (near the bullring).

Italian Consular Help

Open Monday through Friday (9 am-2 pm), the Italian consul is located downtown at 39 Alcatraces Street, SM 22. ☎ 9/884-1261.

Immigration Office

To renew your tourist card or to replace a lost one, go to the Servicíos Migratorios at the corner of Av. Uxmal and Nader and take a number. Opens at 9 am and closes for the day at noon.

Laundry

A laundromat that does a good job is **Lavanderia Tulum**, between the Comercial Mexicana and the big McDonalds on Av. Tulum. It's open Monday through Saturday, 7 am-8 pm, and on Sunday from 9 am-6 pm. Full-service laundry runs about 80¢ per kilo. Another one that is larger and closer to the hotel zone is **Alborada** located on Av. Nader, #5, just a dozen meters from Av. Uxmal.

Medical

The Red Cross is open for first aid (24 hours a day) on Av. Labna No. 2 (☎ 9/884-1616). Hospital Americano (15 Calle Viento, ☎ 9/884-6133) and Total Assist (Claveles, ☎ 9/884-1058) have English-speaking staff. Both are located just off Av. Tulum.

In the hotel zone there is an American Medical Center (☎ 9/883-0113) and Ameri-Med, next to La Boom's (☎ 9/883-0985).

Pharmacies

There are several pharmacies in the hotel zone malls and plazas, two in Plaza Caracol and several downtown. The **Farmacia Canto** (☎ 9/884-4083), a drugstore on Av. Yaxchilán and **Sunyaxchen**, is open 24 hours.

Police

The police can be reached at ☎ 9/884-1913 or 884-2342.

Post Office

The post office is on the corner of Av. Sunyaxchen and Av. Xel-Há and is open Monday through Friday, 8 am to 7 pm, and Saturday, 9 am to 1 pm.

Tourist Information

Tourist info can be found downtown in a kiosk building near the Municipal Palace in the middle

Cancún

of Av. Tulum (☎ 9/884-8073). The Quintana Roo State Tourism office is in the FONATOUR building on Av. Cobá at Av. Nader (☎ 9/884-3238).

Isla Mujeres

Not all those that wander are lost.
J.R.R. Tolkien, *Fellowship of the Ring*

If your fantasy is a vacation on a small peaceful island where time passes at its own slow pace, then we have the place for you. Nearly seven miles (11 km) off the Cancún shoreline rests a wisp of an island with a name right out of a 1950's grade-B movie – the "Island of Women," Isla Mujeres. It's close enough to Cancún to provide easy access, but far enough away to offer a taste of real Mexico. The sandy slip of land – only one mile at its widest and five miles end to end – is a lower-priced, low-key alternative to the shopping-mall atmosphere of Cancún itself. Many Cancún-based tourists take advantage of bargain shopping prices by commuting from the mainland on party boats, but by the late afternoon they've upped anchor and the "real" island comes alive.

No bikini-clad Amazons here. The Spanish coined the name "Isla Mujeres" after they found some stone idols of bare-breasted women, believed to be Ixchel, Maya goddess of fertility. If the conquistadors returned today, they would find topless sunbathers on the North Beach. The Maya temple-lighthouse on the rocky southeastern tip provided an important link in a chain of pre-Columbian lookout signals around the peninsula. Sadly, after a thousand years of guard duty, Hurricane Gilbert reduced it to rubble in 1988. Just in time for the Millennium celebration it was partially restored and two concrete paths and a bench were added for visitors to enjoy the sensational view. Early risers can watch the sun come up over the Caribbean from *La Isla's* dramatic eastern rock cliff headlands. You'll be standing on one of Mexico's easternmost points, the place where the first warm morning rays of sunlight strike the land – a very sacred place to the Maya.

The lone town is a simple fishing village where the island's shops and low-rise hotels are set in a basket weave of narrow streets of cobblestone and sand. Despite the inevitable conversion from fishing to tourism as its main income, *La Isla* has managed to retain much of its native charm. A bright-white and red painted lighthouse rises above the palms to welcome home fishermen while the island's clapboard and stucco houses – painted in whites and blues and pinks – lean helter-skelter in an easy-going tropical jumble. It's a fantastic place to enjoy the sea – around which life on this ancient fishing island still revolves.

Finding Your Way

Isla Mujeres is separated from the mainland by the Bahia de Mujeres (Bay of Women). The island serves as a buffer for Cancún against the Caribbean Sea.

The best way to get to *La Isla* is by boat. Shuttle, water taxi or ferry service is available from three locations: the hotel zone, Punta Sam and Puerto Juárez, a small port city just north of downtown Cancún. Several boats depart from the hotel zone from a variety of piers, playas and docks along Paseo Kukulcán, including Playa Linda, Playa Tortuga, Playa Caracol and the dock at Playa Langosta. These cost from US $13 (round-trip) for a shuttle, to US $30 for a party boat that includes lunch and activities.

There's no sense in taking a car to the island unless you live there.

The less-touristy (and much less expensive) ferry terminal is in Puerto Juárez. The Puerto Juárez ferry requires a double bus ride or a taxi. Our favorite way across is on the "people" ferry (about US $2), a rickety-looking, brightly painted wooden boat named *Beatriz Blanca*. It looks something like Humphrey Bogart's *African Queen*. The *Beatriz* takes 45 minutes to cross the bay, an introduction to Mexico's slower lifestyle.

Isla Mujeres was a popular stopover for pirates, including the famous Jean Lafitte.

Even we see the advantages of Puerto Juárez's high-speed boats that zip across the blue-green waters in 15 minutes for about US $4. They run every half-hour or so. Unless you're patient or (we think) just lucky, chances are you'll get one of the high-speed boats, which depart frequently from the same dock.

Isla Mujeres

There is also a larger car ferry that leaves and returns to Punta Sam, only a few miles north of Puerto Juárez.

To get to either ferry from downtown Cancún, take a cab or catch a bus marked "Puerto Juárez" from in front of the Comercial Mexicana supermarket (look for its Pelican logo) on Av. Tulum, north of the *glorieta* (circle) with Av. Uxmal. This is less than one block north of the busy Tulum shopping area.

When you arrive on Isla Mujeres you'll be docking at a wooden pier in a quaint harbor – home to fishermen, yachtsmen and pirates for generations. People mill about the pier as each boat arrives, some selling handicrafts or offering rides, and others just hanging out people-watching. Pink Colonial-style arches straddle the ends of the narrow streets facing the waterfront. This is the northwest end of town, where all the shops, the best beaches and most of the hotels are situated. There's a taxi stand to the right of the pier, although most of the hotels are within walking distance. If you don't take a taxi, men with three-wheeled bicycles that have open storage areas can load your luggage in the front – and sometimes you too – and take them to your hotel. These cleverly designed *triciclos* are ubiquitous throughout the Yucatán. Tips are US $1-$2.

The most common mode of island transportation is by foot; you can easily walk the entire downtown. But to see the entire island with the wind in your hair and the sun on your back, rent a motor bike or a slower golf cart.

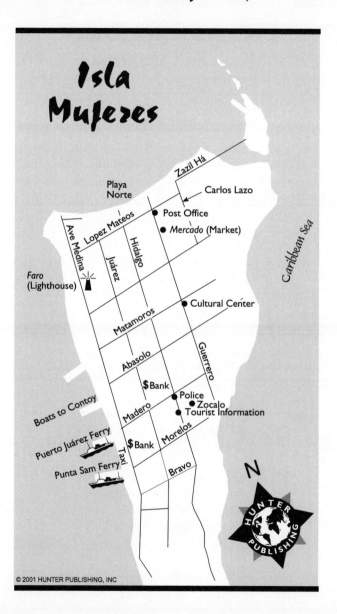

Isla Mujeres

Playa Norte

Zazil Há

Carlos Lazo

Ave Medina

Lopez Mateos

Juárez

Hidalgo

Post Office

Mercado (Market)

Faro (Lighthouse)

Caribbean Sea

Cultural Center

Matamoros

Abasolo

Guerrero

$ Bank

Police

Zocalo

Tourist Information

Boats to Contoy

Madero

Puerto Juárez Ferry

$ Bank

Morelos

Punta Sam Ferry

Taxi

Bravo

N

© 2001 HUNTER PUBLISHING, INC

HUNTER PUBLISHING

Isla Mujeres

> ### 🗕 WARNING
>
> Wear a helmet and drive care-
> fully. Watch out for *topes*, speed
> bumps in the road. Talk about
> going bump in the night!

Wave to the policeman directing non-existent
traffic and head south for *El Garrafón* ("The Jug")
National Park, an underwater coral reef. The island's southern end is less populated and its roll-
ing hills are covered by scrub brush and an
occasional house. At the eastern/southern tip is a
working lighthouse. A little farther toward the
cliffs are the remains of the Maya lighthouse de-
stroyed after a thousand years in a 1988 hurricane. Bring your camera.

The road loops back along the eastern shore, the
windward side of the island, where large waves
crash against the rocky coastline. This fun drive
presents many opportunities to stop and beach-
comb for shells and coral.

 **Best Places to Stay**

Whoe'er has travelled Life's dull round,
Wher'er his stages may have been,
May sigh to think he still has found
The warmest welcome, at an inn.
At an Inn at Henley, William Shenstone, 1714-1763

*L*a Isla's hotels run the gamut from budget to
moderate and plain to fancy. Because of the

laid-back lifestyle and proximity to the beach, staying anywhere on the island is a delight. We have always gloated in our ability to find good values here. The jewels of the island for most travelers are the moderately priced hotels on or near the beach. Some have impressive accommodations and/or locations even by Cancún resort standards – yet they cost significantly less than they would in the hotel zone.

Reservations at the hotel of your choice are absolutely necessary at Christmas and Easter, and are strongly advised for Spring Break, too. Lately the island's hotels have been completely filled for Christmas so book in advance to avoid disappointment.

Most of the island's accommodations can be reached or investigated on the internet at **islamujeres.com.mx.** If you're into budget digs, *La Isla* has a fair number of clean small hotels. Check out our ***Adventure Guide to the Yucatán*** for a more in-depth look at other properties.

Alive Price Scale - Accommodations
(per night/two people per room)
Prices do not include a 12% tax.

Inexpensive. . . . . under US $40
Moderate. . . . . US $40-$100
Expensive . . . . US $101-$200
Deluxe. . . . . US $201-$300
Super. . . . . US $301-$400
Ultra . . . . over US $400

Isla Mujeres

Favorite Island Hotels

VILLA ROLANDI
Laguna Mar, Sac Bajo
☎ 9/877-0700, fax 9/877-0100
www.rolandi.com
All inclusive/Expensive

From humble beginnings at Pizza Rolandi – and years of experience with the Hotel Belmar and Casa Rolandi restaurant in Cancún – the Italian/ Swiss owner opened this small hotel, restaurant, and beach club. It is, by far, the best hotel and the best restaurant on the island. Colonial styled and Mediterranean-influenced, the hotel features a deep blue infinity pool that overlooks the Cancún skyline, and all its 20 suites face the Bahía Mujeres. Each room features a huge bathroom and an individual balcony with a hot tub. Guests arrive to the hotel by Rolandi's private yacht from Cancún. Continental breakfast is subtly served through an access in the wall, for intimacy. Your choice of lunch or dinner at Casa Rolandi, the Northern Italian cuisine restaurant on the large veranda, is included. The price may be Cancún-like, but the luxury and personal attention far exceed what those large hotels across the bay offer.

PLAYA LUNA MEDIA
on the beach behind the Centro de Convenciones
☎ 800/223-5695; in Mexico 9/877-0759
E-mail: mar@cancun.rce.com.mx
Moderate/Expensive

Opened just in time for the turn of the millennium, the Playa Luna is owned by the same hard-working family as the Maria del Mar. Rooms in the four-story, two-wing hotel are offset from each other, and feature verandas or patios with hammocks; each has a view of the Caribbean. Two full beds are in the smaller size rooms with a refrigerator and a large bathroom. Its half moon beach – the hotel's name – offers a protected cove to go wading in a surf that is too rough in other spots. Besides the pool with wet bar, safe swimming is just a shortcut away on the north beach of the Na Balam.

NA BALAM
At the end of the north beach
☎ 9/877-0279, fax 9/877-0446
www.nabalam.com
Moderate/Expensive
31 rooms with air conditioning, pool, dive shop, master suite with hot tub, restaurant and bar, optional meal plans.

All the appealing rooms here are semi-luxurious – with terraces or balconies, large beds and bath. They are decorated in Maya motif with attractive paintings or artifacts on the walls. The baths are all tile.

Peeking out from along the paths through carefully tended gardens at Na Balam is some of the most artistic pottery we've seen. Pieces have been strategically placed by owner Judith Fernandez.

The deluxe Na Balam has expanded in recent years to include cabañas, a small pool and palapas which are used for yoga meetings, attracting a gentle crowd of cosmic-conscious travelers. Second-floor beachside rooms are vine-covered and look over palm trees to the fine sand playa, where topless sunbathing is common. The happy hours' two-for-one drinks special pack the beach bar with friendly folks who chat while the sun sets. The adjacent indoor-outdoor Zazil-Ha restaurant is one of the island's finest.

Isla Mujeres

CASA ISLENO II APARTMENTS
Guerrero
☎ /fax 9/877-0265
Moderate

*Next door to Casa Isleño is a medical emergency clinic and across the street is **Chen Huaye**, a good little Maya-Mexican restaurant.*

Owned by long-time *Isla* resident Hen-rietta Mor-ris de Avila. In her home, one street off the Carib-bean, she has made three small apartments with fans and complete kitchens that rent by the week or month. Very small and quiet, the rooms have a "built-above-the-garage-at-a-beach-house" feel to them. We found them homey and appealing.

FRANCIS ARLENE
Guerrero
☎ /fax 9/887-0310
Moderate
22 rooms with air conditioning or fans.

This soft peach-colored family-run establishment has guests who return annually for its quality and peaceful atmosphere. It's no wonder: the beds are comfortable and the showers hot. All the rooms have small terraces or balconies, with limited views of the Caribbean, which is just a block away. Three rooms have kitchenettes and a suite on the top floor has a king-size bed. A good value with high standards. The Magaña family has added two large rooms over the top between the two connected buildings. Perennially popular.

ROCA MAR
Bravo
☎ /fax 9/877-0101
www.mjmnet.net/HotelRocaMar/home.htm
Moderate
22 rooms with fans plus a suite, pool and patio.

Perched on the edge of the Caribbean where it meets the town center, the Roca Mar hotel is one of the island's oldest – but doesn't look it. The medium-size rooms, with two twin beds and windows with thick wooden shutters, have been recently remodeled and each has a spectacular ocean view from its balcony. The lone suite has two bedrooms (a single and a double) and a kitchenette; it's a good value for families.

Roca Mar is a good choice for roar-of-the-surf sleepers and those who love the sea.

AQUALODGE HOUSEBOAT
moored in the lagoon at Villa Rolandi
☎ 9/884-5333
www.aqualodge.com
Expensive

The most unusual vacation hotel in the area is this attractive two-bedroom houseboat, capable of sleeping eight in tight quarters. Moored in the protected lagoon, the floating villa can cruise around or stay put while guests paddle around in the courtesy sea kayaks. Honeymoon packages available. Rent daily, weekly or monthly. Rates in high season range from US $300 daily to US $6,000 monthly. Price includes maid service, continental breakfast, and two crew members during the day. A vacation to brag about.

CASA DE LOS SUENOS B&B
near Garrafón Park
☎ in US 800/551-2558, in Mexico 9/877-0651
www.lossuenos.com
Expensive

The "House of Dreams" is a dream house built high on a bluff above the bay, close to Garrafón. Behind a tall wall with large wooden doors, enter the Casa's hidden garden fronted by a fountain

Isla Mujeres

pond and lush green plants. The house is divided by an open-air, sunken living room protected by a second story causeway. Beyond the living room is a picture perfect infinity pool facing the bay and the hurried life of Cancún. La Casa delivers on its promised relaxation with an adults-only atmosphere. Master suite features a hot tub and one junior suite has a kitchen. The rocky beach has a wooden swim platform with a beachside shower. Morning juice and coffee brought to your room, and a full American breakfast is served in the dining area. La Casa has a no-smoking policy – our kind of place! Romantic and intimate.

PERLA DEL CARIBE
Madero
☎ 9/877-0306, fax 9/877-0011
Moderate
90 rooms, restaurant, pool, telephone, a/c.

In the middle of the *malecón*, the modern Perla is the most hotel-looking of the island's accommodations. Straddling Av. Madero, its twin three-story buildings form a horseshoe around a bit of pleasant green grass and a large pool. All the rooms, each with terrace or balcony, face the Caribbean. There is no-swimming beach on the windward side of the island, but the option for a dip is only a hop, skip and a jump away on glorious beaches.

CIELITO LINDO APARTMENTS
Av. Medina
Moderate
Fax 9/877-0585
joy@cancun.com.mx
Two studio apartments with a/c or fans.

Cielito Lindo means "beautiful sky," which is what you'll see at sunset from the apartments' terraces.

Minimum stay is three nights. The property is owned by a former New York advertising executive who dropped out of the rat race after falling in love with the lifestyle of Isla Mujeres. You'll wish you could too. The rooms have cable TV, good closets, pretty tiles, tiny bathrooms and rearrangeable furniture. The shared balconies face the beach and *La Isla's* famous sunset.

Pull the bell behind the iron grate to access Cielito Lindo's two second-floor studios.

CASA MAYA GUEST HOUSE & CABANAS
Punta Norte at Zazil-Ha
☎ /fax 9/877-0045
Moderate
12 rooms, including eight in a palapa building.

Jose Lima's guest house is nestled next to the North Beach inlet, behind a dive shop near the larger Na Balam Hotel. There are signs around the island advertising a low rate, but that's either low season or the daily rate for weekly stays. Still, the four rooms in the large beach house are attractive and well furnished. There is a communal kitchen and sitting room with a library, TV and videos. The eight rooms in the cabañas each have private baths and either two twin or one king-size bed.

MARIA DEL MAR
Lazo and Zazil Ha
☎ 9/877-0179 or 0213, fax 9/877-0213
Moderate
56 rooms with air conditioning or fans, pool, restaurant, bar.

Isla Mujeres

Maria del Mar does not allow its beach chairs to be taken out of a fenced-in area in front of the hotel. (It costs US $3 to rent one on the beach.)

Along with Na Balam, the Maria del Mar sits on the north beach of the island. There are 18 newer rooms over the restaurant/bar (which the hotel calls the "castle") and a main hotel building styled like a hacienda. Upstairs rooms with dressers, wardrobes and balconies are better than those on the ground floor. Near the ho-hum little pool there are 15 cabañas offering large rooms with low ceilings. They have big palapa-covered front terraces – great for shade when it's hot or on rainy days.

POSADA DEL MAR
Medina
☎ 9/877-0044, fax 9/877-0266
Moderate
28 rooms, 15 bungalows, pool, restaurant, bar.

Across the street from the beach and close to all the shops and the ferry, the Posada has been a favorite for a long time. It was one of the island's first hotels. Each room in the main building faces the shore and has either a balcony or porch and air conditioning. Upstairs rooms are much better than those downstairs. Penguinos is the hotel's palapa-covered restaurant and bar. It got its name many years ago when a slightly inebriated customer happily remarked that his beer was "as cold as a penguin." Order a penguin and you'll get an ice cold Superior.

CRISTALMAR
Laguna Macax, Sac Bajo
☎ 9/877-0390, fax 9/877-0007
www.cristalmar.com
Moderate - Expensive
38 suites with air conditioning, kitchenettes, very large pool, restaurant.

One of the few hotels on the slender slip of land between the lagoon and protected waters of the Bahia Mujeres – along a road populated with the private homes of wealthy North Americans – is the suite-only Cristalmar. Each large suite has a kitchenette, one or two bedrooms, dining room and sitting area. Inviting and pleasantly apportioned, the hotel is well worth considering because of its lovely beach – right next to a sea turtle research area – large pool and kitchenettes. Friendly staff. It's around US $2 for a taxi ride into town, or a little less to Garrafón. Offers full or partial meal plans. We enjoyed our stay.

MARIA'S KANKIN
Next to Garrafón Park
☎ 9/877-0015, fax 9/877-0395
Moderate
Eight rooms with air conditioning, including three suites.

You can walk to Garrafón from this tiny hotel, which was the "in" spot for the jet-set yachting crowd when Cancún was still a swamp. Now you can see the city's lights across the bay at night. The hotel rooms have high windows, which make them somewhat dark, and a decorative scheme heavy on bamboo for tropical ambiance. They are overdue for a remodeling. Maria's palapa-covered French restaurant, down the flowered walk to the beach, is the island's most exclusive place to eat. The excellent (but pricey) gourmet restaurant is open from 8 am to 9 pm and makes huge drinks. This is a sentimental favorite, so even if we're not staying here, we often buy a margarita or Mai Tai and swim all afternoon at their soft sand beach. The first time we stopped here it was quite in-

Isla Mujeres

triguing to wonder what strange romantic tragedy brought a French woman to this tiny island so far from her home. For years we tried to catch a glimpse of the mysterious Maria. We imagined her to be madly in love with a Latin lover. Perhaps he went to sea and never returned, or disappeared into the jungles of the Yucatán, searching for the lost civilization. She had a long and hearty laugh at our vivid imaginations when we finally met and told her of our theories. Say hello if she's around when you're there – she's a character. Stay for dinner or stay the night, you'll enjoy it. Ask about a Yoga package.

Favorite Budget Hotels

For lodging, the budget category here emphasizes inexpensive *pensiones* and "mom and pop" hostels. These Isla Mujeres hotels have been the traditional abode of students and frugal travelers looking for a more Mexican experience, often willing to sacrifice amenities. The accommodations we surveyed are clean and well-run, but lack ambiance. They are simple, basic hotel rooms with beds and bathrooms. Unless it's super-high season, chances are you'll find a room in one of these without a reservation – and they're all within walking distance of each other, which makes for easy comparison shopping.

The cheapest in town is the **Poc Na Youth Hostel** at the end of Matamoros. These other low-price simple hotels – **Caribe Maya** on Madero, and **Hotel Isleño** at the corner of Guerrero and Madero are all basic and serviceable. The **Xul-Ha** is on Hidalgo, **El Caracol** is on Matamoros, and the **Hotel Gomar** is hard to miss on Medina, near the dock.

VILLAS PUNTA SUR
Km 6 near Garrafón
☎ 9/877-0572, fax 9/877-0371
Coralscubadivecenter.com
Moderate
12 rooms in six villas, pool.

These lovely one- and two-bedroom apartment villas are set on a wooded hill overlooking the bay, but not on the beach side of the road. Colonial-styled but modern. Large and airy, with fully equipped little kitchenettes, they attract many repeat customers, especially families or two couples sharing. Quiet little pool. The owners run the Coral Dive shop downtown.

VISTALMAR
Medina
☎ 9/877-0209, fax 9/877-0096
Inexpensive/Moderate
43 rooms with air conditioning or fans.

The best rooms at this perennially popular but basic place – the three back apartments around a friendly little terrace – are next to impossible to get as they are rented long-term during the winter. The front rooms' balconies and the hotel roof are favorite hangouts for regular guests who watch the beach-goers across the street or the crowd that comes off the ferry. Ideally located both downtown and near the waterfront, the rooms here are simple and clean. A favorite of college students.

Isla Mujeres

HOTEL GOMAR
Medina
☎ /fax 9/877-0541
Inexpensive
16 rooms with air conditioning or fans.

Up a hallway behind a gift store is the surprisingly pleasant lobby of this modern hotel across the street from the ferry dock. There's a large wall mirror and plants and the overstuffed furniture is tastefully color-coordinated. However, the bedrooms have rough cement walls that are impossible to keep clean of furniture marks. The bathrooms are newer, large and well lit and the housekeeping seemed satisfactory.

 Best Places to Eat

People, like wines, have their moods and no restaurant is suited to every mood and every occasion.... There are days when one does not feel like making love. There are days when I don't like to shave and I have a favorite restaurant for these non-shaving days, which are not necessarily non love-making days.

David Schoebruen, *Esquire*, February 1961

The tiny island has nowhere near the huge variety of restaurants that feed Cancún's appetite. But because there are fewer choices, that doesn't mean the dining here is of an inferior quality – just lower priced. Naturally, fresh seafood is the specialty of most restaurants in the village, whose residents have always been seafarers. Some island women joke that their sons could sail before they could walk.

We found meals on *La Isla* very reasonable and the standard of cleanliness and service quite good. Prices, for the most part, are lower than those found across the bay in Cancún. Whichever cost range you select, that same fine food, service and ambiance in a metropolitan area of the United States would cost significantly more. Restaurants listed without phone numbers do not need reservations. We reviewed here the best Isla Mujeres has to offer, in all price ranges, from fine dining to bar food. *¡Salud y Buen Provecho!*

Alive Price Scale – Restaurants

(Dinner per person, not including beverage)

Inexpensive . . . . less than US $6
Moderate. . . . . US $6-$13
Expensive . . . . over US $13

Favorite Island Restaurants

VILLA ROLANDI
Laguna Mar, Sac Bajo
☎ 9/877-0700
Expensive

With a Northern Italian cuisine and a superb setting on the beach, the Villa Rolandi is the choice of other restaurant owners – including many over in Cancún – when they dine out. The dining room is relatively informal, set on a large covered veranda overlooking the beach and bay at the Villa

Isla Mujeres

Rolandi hotel. Owner Sandro Muller Rolandi was raised in a family of hotel and restaurant owners along the Swiss-Italian border, so the standards here are very high. Whether lunch or dinner, the seafood and Northern Italian specialties are mouth watering and the wine list impressive. If you're looking for a special meal, a romantic evening, or just great dining, you'll find it at Rolandi's.

Reservations for dinner strongly suggested.

MIRAMAR
Next to the ferry dock
Reservations not necessary
Inexpensive

This small and personal restaurant sits beneath a palapa roof, unchanged and undiscovered by the crowds of tourists that disembark from the nearby ferry and charter boats from Cancún. Open for breakfast through dinner with a complete menu that includes beef, chicken and pork as well as fresh fish.

The Miramar is an idyllic spot to while away the hours over a beer or a delicious meal. You can watch the local fishing launches bring in their catch. Close your eyes and listen to the melodic sound of the fishermen talking or the hypnotic rhythm of boat owners who scrape barnacles from their beached boats with handfuls of sand. Sit and watch the daily pelican show as the fishermen throw scraps from their cleaned catch. If you're in a hotel with a kitchenette, consider buying fresh fish as the boats come in and cooking for yourselves.

CAFE CITO
Matamoros
Inexpensive/Moderate

The influx of residents who have chucked the rat race for the slow pace of the island has spawned many restaurants that combine an artistic ambiance with creative cuisine. One of these surviving the test of time is Café Cito. A black and white cat purrs lazily on one of the open-shuttered streetside windows, beckoning you into this neat breakfast and dinner café. The blue and white dining area is split in two by a custom-made stained glass wave. There are beach scenes under each small glass-topped table. The ice cream sundaes here are outrageous. This is one of Mexico's rare no-smoking eateries.

Café Cito owner, Sabrina, is into New Age soul searching; if you'd like, you can arrange to have a reading.

LA CASITA BAKERY AND RESTAURANT
Madero
Inexpensive/Moderate

The continental breakfast here features a toasted loaf of homemade bread (US $1.50) instead of sliced "Bimbo," the brand name of Mexican commercial white bread. La Casita is open for all three meals and they have excellent coffee with free refills. Like other places that have discovered the pleasures of soft lighting (you'd be surprised at the number of restaurants in Mexico that light their dining rooms with harsh fluorescent) it has a romantic atmosphere at night.

BISTRO FRANÇAIS
Matamoros
Inexpensive/Moderate

Open from 8 am till noon, then again from 6 to 10 pm for dinner, the Bistro is one of the island's

Isla Mujeres

larger charming storefront restaurants. It does a good business because of its reasonable prices, colorful ambiance (the menu is painted on the walls) and excellent presentation. Its rare-in-Mexico bottomless cup of coffee is delicious and refilled often. The French toast is "oo-la-la" and includes a fresh fruit plate. There's a friendly and relaxed atmosphere.

CAFE EL NOPALITO
Corner of Matamoros and Guerrero
Inexpensive/ Moderate

This health food restaurant (open for breakfast and dinner, 6 to 9 pm) is combined with a folk-art gift shop called El Nopal. Homemade breads, granola and good service make this a popular spot to sit and chat. The gift store carries ¡Qué Bárbara! clothes – produced and designed by an American expatriate who lives on the island – and many local women's co-op crafts.

PINGUINO'S
Posada del Mar Hotel, Av. Medina
Moderate

Pinguino's is near the north lighthouse. Its dance floor heats up late into the night.

The best seats in the palapa-roofed Pinguino's restaurant are on the balcony that overhangs the sidewalk facing the beach along the main drag downtown. The large menu features Mexican dishes and fresh seafood. Order a "penguin" and get an ice cold bottle of Superior beer.

PIZZA ROLANDI
Hidalgo
Inexpensive/Moderate

Across the street from Meson del Bucanero, another good restaurant, Rolandi's is the island's most popular eatery. Its open dining porch extends out into the shopping avenue in front. The good-time atmosphere can be warm and inviting. Excellent brick-oven pizza. See also their sister restaurant in Cancún, page 85.

CAZUELA M&J
Bravo
Inexpensive/Moderate

The Cazuela is a little treasure of a restaurant tucked into a corner next to the Roca Mar hotel with a great view of the pounding surf. Owners Marco and Julie named it after the popular egg dish they developed, cooked in a ceramic chafing dish called a *cazuela*. Their *cazuela* dish comes with a variety of fillings and is a cross between an omelet and a soufflé. The hand-colored menus reflect the care and consideration that makes Cazuela popular with both expatriates and visitors. They also serve deli sandwiches.

FREDY'S
Hidalgo
Inexpensive/Moderate

Fredy bought the old Mano de Dios restaurant – a local bar and one of our favorite cheap eateries on Isla Mujeres – and brightened it up both inside and out. It is a bargain restaurant that offers good homemade Mexican cooking and tasty fresh fish. It's next door to the Red Eye Café.

Fredy's is no stranger to the yacht crowd who often come here for a good meal.

CHILES LOCOS
Hildago

Jorge learned his cooking in Campeche, where food is an art form. Here on *La Isla*, he and his partner, Marianne, operate a storefront restau-

Isla Mujeres

rant that features sidewalk dining under a red clay tile roof. One evening we ordered *Chiles en Nogada*, a regional dish from Puebla that contains the tri-colors of the Mexican flag – green, white and red. A green poblano pepper, stuffed with a meat and fruit filling, is covered by a white cream sauce made with ground cashews and sprinkled with red pomegranate seeds. What a delightfully delicious experience! Excellent Chiapas coffee in glass mugs at breakfast; we'll be back. Open for breakfast and dinner only.

TONYNO'S
Hidalgo
Inexpensive/Moderate

Exposed brick walls covered by clay suns and moons and masks lend atmosphere to this narrow storefront restaurant down the street from the fancier and pricier Rolandi's. Tonyno's offers delicious Italian food – such as meat lasagne with a béchamel sauce or wood-oven-baked pizza. Very reasonable prices. If you stay for the nightly live music you may be handed a bongo or tambourine and invited to join in. Free tequilas are delivered with your bill. We'd go back. Dinner only; during the day it's a gift shop.

RED EYE CAFE
Hidalgo
Inexpensive/Moderate

Inge and Gus Kasulke own this little corner breakfast/lunch café on a quiet side street near the north beach. It's the first place open in the morning (6 am), and is often crowded with early birds. Lunch is traditional German food, such as bratwurst, with daily specials like fish, hamburgers, or roast turkey. Their home-baked breads and potato salad are excellent and the word is out among visitors. Closed Tuesdays. Look for the large red awning.

LONCHERIA EL POC CHUC
Juárez
Inexpensive/Moderate

Six tables rest against two long walls painted with primitive art murals in this narrow little restaurant. The Mexican menu offers some of the best prices in town from breakfast to dinner. Sandwiches come on toasted kaiser rolls. Try the *torta loca*, or crazy sandwich, for about US $2. It's filled with chicken, ham, eggs, sausage, refried beans, salad – just about anything but the kitchen sink!

MARIA'S KANKIN
Near Garrafón Park
☎ 9/877-0015 in Cancún; 9/882-0015
Expensive

We never come to the island without having at least a drink at this excellent beachfront French/ seafood restaurant (see its entry under *Hotels*, page 149). *Bon appetit!*

CHEZ MAGALY
☎ 9/877-0259

Hidden behind the Nautibeach Condos on the north shore.

Another fine French restaurant. Magaly Marmy's place may be expensive but she has a gourmet's high standards. Great sunsets and beachside dining.

Isla Mujeres

ZAZIL-HA
Na-Balam Hotel
☎ 9/877-0446
Moderate/Expensive

When islanders and tourists are up for a night out
with friends, an intimate dinner, or just a great
meal, they often choose the Zazil-Ha. There are
three separate restaurant/bars here. The outdoor/
indoor restaurant (with air conditioning) has a
superb atmosphere and gourmet cooking at relatively moderate prices. The Palapa restaurant
and bar is open from 10 am until 4 pm and serves
light meals and snacks. The beachfront bar,
packed with people to its palm-topped rafters
around sunset, serves bar food and drinks all day.

 **Shop Till You Drop**

If you want to spend money where it'll show,
spend it on a woman.
Kin Hubbard, 1868-1930

Life on Isla Mujeres (population 13,000) is laid-
back and unpretentious. Pink Colonial arches
frame sandy side streets lined with shops that offer fine coral jewelry, gifts, handicrafts and the
latest sportswear. Boatloads of sunburned shoppers descend on *La Isla* daily for better bargains
than can be had in the hotel zone or simply to
wander the town's quaint boulevards.

Thatched-roof restaurants and funky hotels dot
the fishing village that's been a favorite spot for
visitors since pirates discovered its natural pro-

tected harbors in the 17th and 18th centuries. Tourists began hiding out there in the 1950s, enamored with its unforgettable charm. Quality shopping got its start here in response to the wealthy jet-set yacht crowd that discovered *La Isla's* appeal. Today there are many interesting shops and vendors to choose from; many close for afternoon siesta.

Where to Go

Van Cleef & Arpels

At the corner of Av. Morelos and Juárez, this is one the most upscale jewelry shops on the island. The knowledgeable staff speaks English.

Casa Isleñoli

Henrietta Morris de Avila, instrumental in the production of *Islander* magazine, owns this shop. It sells custom-painted T-shirts and shells. You'll find it on Guerrero, across from Chen Huaye, a famous family-owned eatery that specializes in home-made Yucatecan cooking. Well worth locating for breakfast, lunch or dinner. Henrietta also offers some of her artwork for sale (☎ 9/877-0265).

¡Qué Barbara!

The name translated means, "How Very Barbara!" and she is a designer and manufacturer of comfortable custom tropical clothing. Barbara combines practicality with flair and sex appeal. She began her business in Guatemala and Mexico and settled here for the less hectic lifestyle. For a chance to buy designer clothes and meet the designer, stop in her little shop at Matamoros No. 18 (☎ 9/877-0705).

Paulita's

This corner store on Av. Morelos in front of the police station will lure you inside with its large collection of arts and crafts. There is a wide variety of incredible collector's masks. We think this is a fun place.

Valentina Artesanías

Valentina's is located across the street from the main square and park. This shop is owned and operated by a native islander, Blanca Rosa Schmied de Ramos. She features quality hand-selected gifts and crafts.

Artesanías Arco Iris

Alejandro Trejo, the owner of Arco Iris, comes from a skilled weaving area of central Mexico. In addition to regular crafts, he features unique hand-woven wall-hangings. Located on Av. Júarez.

Artesanías El Nopal

Sharing space with a delightful café, El Nopal features Mexican folk art and Women's Co-op crafts; You'll find it at the corner of Guerrero and Matamoros.

Body Map

Body Map, Av. Júarez and Morelos, features con-temporary fashion and beach wear. A second Body Map location is on 5th Ave. in Playa del Carmen. Great name for a store and sexy fashions to go with it.

Mention the Body Map's ad in the phone book for a 10% discount.

Boutique Elenita

This family-owned gift shop – in a typical Carib-bean wood slat building on Av. Hidalgo No. 13 – has interesting gifts and crafts. However, their ad in the *Islander* magazine loses something in the translation: "Wallets and Bags of Skin."

A Few More...

Other shops worth mentioning for their wares and prices are: **La Sirena, Tlaxcalteca**, **Casa del Arte Mexica** – all on Av. Hidalgo; **Azteca** and **El Grillo** on Juárez; **Crazy Cactus** on Me-dina; **Pancho Villa** on Abasolo; **El Coral Negro** on Matamoros; **Mambo** at Garrafón de Castilla; and the **Handicraft Co-op** on the road to Garrafón, Km 6.

Mercado

La Isla's tiny *mercado*, where locals buy and sell fresh vegetables and meats, is located next to the post office on Av. Guerrero. There are several loncherias, lunch stands, serving inexpensive Mexican food. The last vestige of the island's orig-inal Maya/Yucatecan culture.

Isla Mujeres

Dawn to Dusk

*I like to collect experiences the way other people
like to collect coins and stamps.*

Michael McGuire, adventurer

Life in this former fishing village is more tranquil and relaxed than in the megalopolis of
Cancún, whose highrise hotels are visible across
the bay. It has been some time since fishing was
the main source of income for islanders. However,
their lives – as well as those of the visitors – still
revolve around the sea. Isla Mujeres took the
brunt of Hurricane Gilbert in 1988, which did tremendous damage to the island, including destroying the pre-Columbian Maya lighthouse on the
island's majestic eastern cliff. We may have one of
the last photos of it standing.

But with change comes change and *La Isla's* water supply, streets and public facilities have all
improved as a result. Hotels took advantage of the
damage to upgrade and improve and the hurricane's aftermath began a building boom that continues today.

Even after all that you'll still find Isla Mujeres
quiet and a welcome relief from the unfocused energy of Cancún. *La Isla's* laid-back attitude does
not mean there isn't plenty to do, it just means
you *can* do nothing at all. If you're here for the day
or here to stay, read on.

Beaches

While clashing Caribbean currents make swimming dangerous on the spectacular and rocky eastern shore, calm water and gentle surf mark the idyllic western and northern beaches. Several splendid beaches with soft white sand and tranquil water grace the leeward shores. Local families favor the beach just west of the ferry dock.

All the major beaches have beach chair and/or umbrella rental concessions (about US $5 per day). The best beach for very young children is the inlet around the **Na Balam Hotel**, where the blue water is warm and very shallow and there are no people except for those who wander across the wooden bridge to the sand island of the now-defunct and deserted Presidente Hotel (rumor has it that it might reopen under new owners).

Playa Cocos/Playa del Norte (North Beach) is a pristine white sandy beach with bathtub-warm shallow surf. This long beach, in front of several hotels and condos, has its share of topless sunbathers, probably honoring Ixchel (goddess of fertility), and is a great place to watch the sun go down.

Playa Paraiso, Playa Lancheros and **Playa Indios** have more secluded locations near each other, close to Mundaca's Hacienda. Thatched hut restaurants dot the shore, along with gift shops, wandering jewelry vendors and hair braiders. Excellent swimming and a warm atmosphere. These

Isla Mujeres

beaches are favorites of the local families that live in the island's interior – and ours too!

El Garrafón National Undersea Park has a close-shore reef that teems with colorful fish and is excellent for beginner snorkelers. Time your visits for the early morning or late afternoons to avoid the crowds. Well worth a visit. The popular park features a tranquil swimming beach near the southern tip of the island on the western shore. Changing rooms, showers, restaurant and picnic area, equipment rental and a gift shop. Take a taxi here. The nearby cliffs at the lighthouse are fabulous for watching the sunrise. The dawn's rays first strike Mexican soil here at the country's easternmost point.

Isla Contoy

Isla Contoy has no fresh water supply, so birds' natural predators (such as rats) cannot survive. The island is a natural bird sanctuary.

We took Captain Ricardo Gaitán's six-hour cruise to the uninhabited coral island of Isla Contoy (US $50) for a day of nature hiking, bird watching, snorkeling and beachcombing. His boat, the **Estrella del Norte**, a 36-foot motor sailboat, was the last one to be built on the island in 1968. The island is a bird sanctuary for 70 species, including some large nesting colonies. During the summer, sea turtles lay their eggs along its sandy bays. After snorkeling on a colorful coral reef on the way over, we spent our time beachcombing among the rock pools while the others sunbathed and swam.

There's a small museum and a lookout tower to climb for a panoramic view. Gear and lunch are included – grilled fish, deliciously spiced *à la*

Yucateca, caught by the first mate on the way over. (Just in case you don't catch a fish, they bring one along.) Buy your tickets at the Fisherman's Cooperative (*Cooperativa*), west of the ferry, or phone the captain at ☎ 9/877-0434. You can take a much faster launch, at the same price, from the cooperative, but it doesn't match the romance of a journey under a red sail in a wooden hull.

To go fishing or snorkeling over other reefs is easy. Just visit the *Cooperativa* and ask to be set up with a qualified fisherman. Captain Francisco Sosa and first mate Pedro Rodriquez run two of the smartest boats for fishing charters, dive charters and snorkel runs. A two-hour snorkel trip costs about US $40 for two, or US $50 for four. They offer a three-hour fishing trip and one all-day run, with guaranteed fish, for US $400. It's a great deal for groups.

Diving & Snorkeling

About 50 years ago Carlos Garcia, a young island lobster diver, discovered a deep sea-cave where sharks went in, but didn't come out the other side. Curious, he entered the cave to find sharks asleep with their eyes wide open. It's now known as the **Cave of the Sleeping Sharks** and dive shops such as the one at El Garrafón (☎ 9/877-0572), Bahia Dive Shop (☎ 9/877-0340) and Buzos de Mexico (☎ 9/877-0274) near the dock will take certified divers on this popular professional 65-foot scuba dive. The slumbering sharks were made world-famous

Isla Mujeres

when Jacques Cousteau and his crew filmed them for one of his television specials.

Other snorkel and dive spots are the **Cuevones Reef** at 35 feet deep (10.5 meters) and the **Manchones and Banderas Reefs**, wide coral stretches .6 miles long at a depth of about 35 feet. A bronze cross weighing approximately one ton, 39 feet in height and 9¾ feet wide, was planted into the Manchones Reef between Isla Mujeres and the coastline in 1994. The **Cruz de la Bahia** is the island's tribute to the men and women of the sea. Divers celebrate the founding of Isla Mujeres in 1854 with a mass dive on August 17.

Events

The waters surrounding La Isla offer year-round fishing for bonito, grouper, kingfish, mackeral, and amberjack year-round.

Boating and sailing regattas are organized by the Club de Yates the last week of April/first week of May. For specific information call them at ☎ 9/877-0173. The 12-day **Isla Mujeres International Music Festival** begins the second week in October. There are **fishing tournaments** February through May. For more information, check out the Isla Mujeres website, islamujeres.com.mx.

For Landlubbers

The western shore north of Playa Paraiso is home to Centro de Investigaciones, **a turtle research station** funded by the government and private donations. This is a fascinating and popular educational stop for some of the party boats from

Cancún, whose passengers walk along the beach to reach it.

Isla Mujeres was an ancestral hatching ground for giant sea turtles who lumbered ashore from May through September to lay their eggs in the silky sand. Many turtles were captured by local fishermen and killed for their meat and shell. Their eggs were dug up for food. Finally, a concerned fisherman convinced his brethren to spare the precious eggs. His efforts led to the founding of the research station where turtles are now bred for release into the wild. Local school children participate in the annual releases. Take the guided tour. A suggested donation is about US $1.

From the Garrafón underwater park it's a short walk up to the ruins of the **Ixchel temple** and the rocky headlands of the island.

A large modern **lighthouse** is here and the keeper lets people climb to the top (for a tip). At the other end of the island, crowds gather for the sunset on the northern beach. The deserted Caribbean eastern shore makes a great walk for beachcombers who explore rocky pools and washed up coral and shells.

Check out the spectacular dawn from one of the rocky outcrops on the headlands.

Mundaca's Hacienda (see *Pirate's Treasure*, below) has some cement paths that weave through the former gardens of this partially restored hacienda. Even in the hot air you can feel a cold chill while thinking of the old fool's tragic efforts to woo a local island girl after a life of debauchery and slave trading.

Isla Mujeres

Pirate's Treasure

As you are, I was. As I am, you will be.
Words carved on Mundaca's grave marker.

Fermin Mundaca de Marechaja lived life as a pirate and slave trader, getting rich at the expense of others who paid with their lives for his greed. For many years he plied the seas from Africa to Cuba with human cargo destined to labor as slaves and die in the sugar fields. By 1860 the British Navy's campaign against slavery cramped his style, so he furled his sails and retired to the sheltered harbor of Isla Mujeres. Once there, he fell in love with an 18-year-old girl, famous on the island for her beauty, called *La Trigueña*, "the Brunette." But the young girl rejected the former pirate and slaver. Determined to win her love, he built a whimsical hacienda surrounded by gardens filled with exotic plants and entered by arches carved with her name. But instead of changing her mind, *La Trigueña* married a young island fisherman whom she loved. She bore her husband child after child while Mundaca slowly went insane. He died in Mérida but the grave marker he had carved for himself is located in the island's sandy cemetery (in the front to the right of the gate). His ruined hacienda and gardens – a tragic example of "love's labor lost" – makes an interesting short visit.

One of our favorite visits is the **cemetery** along the North Beach on Av. Lopez Mateos. Mexicans build shrines to their dead and leave objects on them as a celebration of their life. We wept over a little girl's tiny pink slippers left on her grave.

After Dark

*The game of love is never called off
on account of darkness.*
Tom Masson, 1866-1934

Isla Mujeres' nightlife pales in comparison to Cancún's, except when the whole island has a celebration – then it can be like Carnival (which is tons of fun here on the island). Most of the nightlife is bar action with dancing. **Las Palapas** on the north end beach kicks up some sand. You could try **Buho's** at Cabañas Maria del Mar or the nearby **Zazil-Ha** bar at the Na Balam Hotel. **Sunset Bar** and **Pinguino's** on Medina also have some action.

Isla Mujeres A-Z

Knowledge is power.
Francis Bacon, 1626

Banks

Banks with money exchanges (open 9 am to 2:30 pm, Monday-Friday) are **Banco Serfin**,

Bancomer, **American Express** and **Banco Atlantico**. They are all near the docks downtown. There are also change booths downtown, but most shops have no problem taking dollars.

Health Clubs

Everyone should have good health on an island like this. If you need pumping up, discover **Isleños' Gym**, Av. Guerrero. After a hard workout (without air conditioning), head for the showers – or in this case the beach, as the street-front gym has no running water. Basketball and volleyball enthusiasts will find pick-up games at the park in the main plaza.

Laundry

Two laundromats compete in town, but there's no question, **Wash Express** is hands-down cheaper than the more established **Tim Phós**. The two rivals are set just one block apart on Av. Abasolo. Both do a good job washing and folding, but Tim charges double to separate whites and colors.

Library

The **Cultural Center** on Av. Guerrero hosts frequent activities for children and also has a paperback library where you can trade English-language titles from the open shelves.

Medical

There is a decompression chamber at the **Hospital de la Armada** on Medina (☎ 9/877-0001). Several doctors on the island speak English: **Dr.**

Antonio Torres Garcia (☎ 9/877-0050) makes house calls and is available 24 hours for emergencies. He's located on Matamoros at the corner of Guerrero. **Dr. Antonio Salas** offers general medicine and emergency treatment on Calle Hidalgo No. 8 (☎ 9/877-0477), next to the pharmacy, Farmacia Lilly.

Police

The police station is near the main square on Av. Madero (☎ 9/877-0082).

Post Office

The post office is on Av. Guerrero at Lopez Mateos.

Tourist Information

The office is located on Av. Medina, not far from the ferry dock next to the bank (☎ 9/877-0316).

Cozumel

*We were very tired, we were very merry, we had
gone back and forth all night on the ferry.*
Edna St. Vincent Millay, *Recuerdo*, 1892-1950

The kaleidoscope of colors found in waters
around Cozumel is amazing. Sergeant major
fish are striped in bright yellow and black. Parrot
fish shine as if under a dayglow lamp. French
grunts with blue-green shimmering stripes dart
among white angelfish as two schools mingle to
avoid the human swimmers ogling them.

The garlands of reefs around Cozumel were discovered by Navy divers stationed on the island
during World War II. Word spread quickly among
divers and snorkelers, who flocked here for the in-
describable beauty of life undersea and visibility
reaching 250 feet. Jacques Cousteau filmed an
underwater documentary that opened a floodgate
of diver tourists to the area (it's now considered
one of the top five dive spots in the world). Later,
cruise ships began an annual migration, like huge
pregnant white ducks, to the docks of Cozumel.
Now both the reefs and the seafront downtown become crowded with divers and cruise passengers
making the most of their time here.

With an atmosphere somewhere between the resort life of Cancún and the *laissez-faire* attitude of
Isla Mujeres, Cozumel casts a magical spell over
anyone who sets foot on shore. The island somehow manages to absorb a daily dose of tourists

and still maintain a charm all its own. The area is only about 5% developed, and beyond the tourist meccas are spectacular natural wonders and a relaxed lifestyle.

For centuries, Cozumel has been a destination and refuge for people leaving their troubles behind on the mainland. The island was originally a religious ceremonial center for the ancient Maya, who built a temple to Ixchel, the goddess of fertility. By 1600 the native population was wiped out due to disease brought by the Spanish Conquest. For a hundred years the island was virtually deserted and used only as a fishing base. By the mid-1800s it was repopulated by 700 refugees fleeing the Caste War, and then became a boom/bust port for the chicle trade. During World War II, the American Air Force built the airstrip from which they launched anti-submarine patrols and Navy divers found the beautiful underwater world along the shore.

Cozumel became a port of call for Caribbean cruise lines after Jacques Cousteau filmed its amazing reefs for a 1961 documentary – now an average of 600 cruise ships visit the island annually. It's also a favorite hop-over for tourists from Cancún. You can "do" Cozumel – which means "Place of the Swallows" in Mayan – in a day, or spend a month and still not "do" everything. The reasons for the island's popularity are obvious: sparkling emerald waters that hold a coral coat of many colors and a population of warm and friendly *Cozumeleños*.

Cozumel

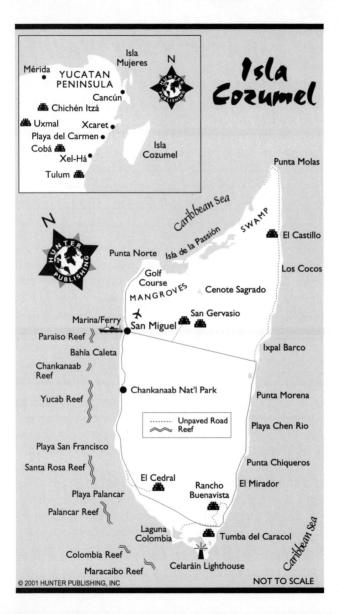

Isla
Cozumel

© 2001 HUNTER PUBLISHING, INC

NOT TO SCALE

Finding Your Way

San Miguel (population 60,000) is the only city on Mexico's largest island – 28 miles (47 km) long and 11 miles (15 km) wide. It rests in the Caribbean 12 miles (19 km) off the coast of Quintana Roo, some 42 miles (68 km) south of Cancún. A scrub brush jungle covers the northern half of the island, which is virtually uninhabited (along with the southern portions, the interior and the windward east coast). A road loops the entire southern part along the sea, then cuts back into town, dividing the island in half. The **windward eastern beaches**, best suited to beachcombing and shell collecting, are rocky, dramatic, impressive, gorgeous and too rough and dangerous for swimming (Playa Chen Rio is the exception). The **leeward western beaches** feature picture-perfect white sand, gentle lapping waves, warm turquoise blue water and a series of vibrant living reefs. They offer good swimming, snorkeling and diving.

Two **ferry services** – a car ferry from Puerto Morelos and a people ferry from Playa del Carmen – serve Cozumel from the Yucatán mainland. Reach "Playa" using one of the frequent public buses from Cancún's downtown terminal; a cab will take you for about US $30 (negotiated). The ferry service from Playa to Cozumel (45 minutes, US $5) changes schedule as often as we change underwear so check at one of the ticket booths.

San Miguel also has an **international airport** with some direct flights from the United States and numerous 15-minute connecting flights from

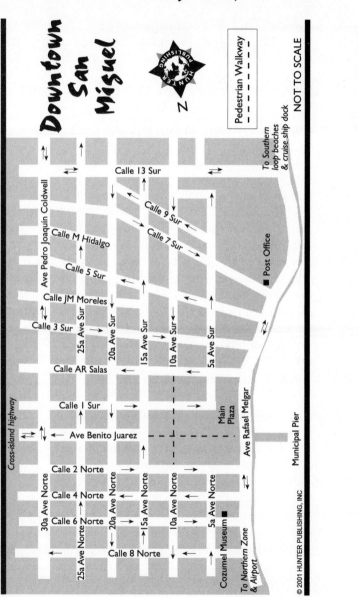

Downtown San Miguel

N

HUNTER PUBLISHING

Pedestrian Walkway

NOT TO SCALE

Cozumel

Cross-island highway

Ave Pedro Joaquín Coldwell

Calle 13 Sur

Calle 9 Sur

Calle M Hidalgo

Calle 7 Sur

Calle 5 Sur

Calle JM Moreles

Calle 3 Sur

25a Ave Sur

20a Ave Sur

15a Ave Sur

10a Ave Sur

5a Ave Sur

Calle AR Salas

Calle I Sur

Main Plaza

Ave Benito Juarez

Ave Rafael Melgar

Calle 2 Norte

30a Ave Norte

Calle 4 Norte

25a Ave Norte

20a Ave Norte

15a Ave Norte

10a Ave Norte

5a Ave Norte

Calle 6 Norte

Calle 8 Norte

Cozumel Museum ■

Post Office ■

Municipal Pier

To Southern loop beaches & cruise ship dock

To Northern Zone & Airport

© 2001 HUNTER PUBLISHING, INC

Cancún (call **Aerocozumel** at ☎ 9/884-2000). If you're on a cruise, you'll find taxis lined up at the pier to take you downtown or on an island tour. Even if you are just there for the day, we'll point out the best places to eat and shop, as well as what to do.

Cozumel streets are laid out well and it's easy to know where you are once you get used to them. **Av. Rafael Melgar** is the main road running along the western waterfront. It becomes the North Road and South Road out of the downtown. Streets running north and south, parallel to the water, are *avenidas* and those running perpendicular to the sea, east and west, are *calles*. The sole exception to this is **Av. Benito Juárez**, which cuts San Miguel and the island into northern and southern halves. The streets north of Juárez are marked *norte* and have even numbers (2, 4, 6, etc.). All the *calles* south of Juárez are *sur* and are given odd numbers (3, 5, 7, etc.). Vehicles traveling north and south are *supposed* to have the right of way, while those traveling east and west are required to stop on every corner.

N WARNING

Drive carefully and look before you cross the street.

Besides taxis (a good choice when going direct from one place to another), three types of personal transportation are available: motorbikes, bicycles and rented cars or Jeeps. Many major hotels rent motorbikes or cars and every street corner downtown near the dock has men hawking rentals. The

Cozumel

prices are pretty much the same between individual renters, especially near the dock, but you could try going to some of the shops in town or waiting until the crowd disburses before negotiating.

⚡ WARNING

It's illegal to ride without a helmet and motorbikes may not come with insurance, so check first. Drive more carefully than you might at home.

Parking can sometimes be scarce in town so be careful of No Parking zones (including red curbs). Your car could be towed or the license plate removed so that you pay a fine at the rental agency. If you are in a group, or want to really see every detail of Cozumel's wilderness, try getting a good deal on a Jeep.

⦿ TIP

Cozumel's official tourism website is www.islacozumel.com.mx.

Last but not least, pick up a free *Blue Guide* to Cozumel, available all over the island and at the ferry. It has some valuable discount coupons and fun-to-read tidbits.

Best Places to Stay

Night, with her train of stars
And her great gift of sleep.
W.E. Henley, 1849-1903

As in resort areas around the world that cater to North American visitors, new Cozumel properties are increasingly opening as all-inclusive resorts. They offer complete vacations that include food and drink, watersports and activities, enough that you never need to leave the hotel. We note which hotels are all-inclusive, so be sure to compare the two.

The areas north and south of the town of San Miguel host the more expensive but generally gorgeous beachfront hotels and resorts. If you're on a budget don't despair – the island is small enough that the downtown hotels are also close to the beach.

The Mexico Tourism Office has developed their own star hotel-rating system (which we repeat here by use of stars like this one ☆). It's based not just on perceived class or elegance, but also on location and amenities. So far, Cozumel does not have any Gran Turismo hotels (the highest ranking, indicated here by a 🌿), but its five stars are also fabulous. Amenities include: beachfront location (Caribbean or Bay); cable/satellite TV; air conditioning; laundry and dry cleaning service; mini-bars; combination baths (tub and shower); banquet and convention facilities; travel agency; car rental; gift shop; watersports facilities.

Cozumel

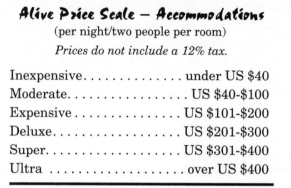

Alive Price Scale — Accommodations
(per night/two people per room)

Prices do not include a 12% tax.

Inexpensive.	under US $40
Moderate.	US $40-$100
Expensive	US $101-$200
Deluxe.	US $201-$300
Super.	US $301-$400
Ultra	over US $400

Cozumel has a 12% room tax.

If you are shopping for weekly stays in villas or condos, try **Cozumel Vacation Villas,** ☎ 800/224-5551, or **Los Arrecifes'** two-bedroom bungalows, ☎ 9/882-5930.

Beachfront Hotels

North End (North to South)

PARADISUS ☆☆☆☆☆
Northern Coastal Rd., Km 5.8
☎ 800/336-3542; in Mexico, 9/872-0411
Fax 9/872-15-99
www.solmelia.com
Super/Ultra – All-Inclusive
300 rooms, TV, telephone, air conditioning, game room, motorscooter rental.

The northernmost hotel on Cozumel is owned by Meliá (meli-A), a quality Spanish chain of international hotels. The all-inclusive Paradisus, "Paradise" in Spanish, boasts a perfect beach, as well as excellent food and fine accommodations. Rooms are housed in three buildings, a 200-room, 12-story highrise and two smaller wings. The resort was completely remodeled in 1994 with terrazzo floors, king-size or double beds, muted floral fabrics, balconies or terraces and tiled baths in each room. A huge palapa-topped buffet restaurant, with terrace dining, separates one of the hotel's two large swimming pools from the white beach. One pool is the "activity" pool for children and watersports, the other is for more adult swimmers and "floaters." A second, more intimate restaurant, surrounded by tropical flowers, serves items à la carte, while a third grills to order. There's nightly family-style entertainment in a separate theater, kids' club, health club, watersports facility and tennis courts. Also offers dive packages, ☎ 888/341-5993.

EL COZUMELEÑO ☆☆☆☆☆
Northern Coastal Rd., Km 4.5
US, ☎ 800/742-4276; Mexico, 9/872-0050
Fax 9/872-0381
www.elcozumeleno.com
Deluxe/Super – All-Inclusive
100 rooms, TV, pool, restaurants, bars, hot tub, disco.

A modern six-story hotel, El Cozumeleño features ocean-view patios or balconies accessed by sliding glass doors from the large and airy rooms. It has a fine sand beach with a small rocky portion and two restaurants – one beachside and the other, a more formal affair, off the Mediterranean-style tropical lobby and lounge. Rooms feature bright colors and tile baths. There is a tennis court, inviting free-form pool and health club.

SOL CABANAS DEL CARIBE ☆☆☆☆
Northern Coastal Rd., Km 5.1
☎ 888/341-5993; in Mexico, 9/872-0017
Fax 9/872-2008
Expensive
48 rooms plus nine beachfront cabañas, pool, bar, restaurant.

This attractive, quiet hotel is one of two good Sol Meliá properties on Cozumel. A bit of a forgotten sister to her bigger brother the Paradisus, Sol Cabañas is an older, low-rise hotel on a fabulous beach. The rooms (32 of which face the sea) all have terrazzo floors, beamed ceilings, warm wood trim and a small anteroom for sitting (some with fridge). A huge woven wall hanging depicting a sea scene decorates the open stairway to the second floor. Caribbean pink beach bungalows sit next to the hotel's small pool and bar. Outside, they have compact front sitting patios while inside the one-bedroom studio layout features tile floors with throw rugs, Colonial furniture and tiled showers. Divers' packages offered (☎ 888/341-5993).

PLAYA AZUL HOTEL ☆☆☆☆
Northern Coastal Rd., Km 4
☎ 9/872-0199, fax 9/872-0110
www.playa-azul.com
Expensive
53 rooms & suites, air conditioning, TV/VCR, Mexican restaurant, two bars, telephones.

The name, "Blue Beach" refers to the turquoise water in front of this bright-white hotel toward the north end. Despite spacious rooms, the hotel maintains an intimate, relaxed feeling and the staff is especially attentive. Playa Azul, family-

Owners of the Playa Azul, an academic couple, traded both their teaching careers in Mexico City for the soft sand of Cozumel. You might be tempted to do the same!

run with high standards of service, is one of our island favorites. A remodeling in 2001 added a large pool flanked by a three-story expansion where rooms with balconies face the beach. The beach is small, but there's a natural cove entrance ideal for children. A four-bedroom garden house in front of the hotel is available to rent. Despite its recent growth, it's still an idyllic setting for a romantic getaway.

HOTEL FONTAN ☆☆☆☆
Northern Coastal Rd., Km 2.7
☎ 800/462-6868; in Mexico, 9/872-0300
Moderate
49 rooms, restaurant, TV, small round pool, dive shop, bar.

After seeing some of the fancy hotels on the north coast road, we were prepared to be disappointed by the plain-looking, white-painted Fontan. But we found something appealing in its unpretentious Mexican atmosphere and surprisingly low price. With no beach to speak of, the Fontan has a small, sheltered lagoon-like natural swimming area formed by the coral reef. Forty clean, basic rooms with ocean views and balconies face the beach in the three-story hotel (no elevator). Boat trips leave from their small dock for dive and snorkeling trips.

CORAL PRINCESS ☆☆☆☆☆
Northern Coastal Rd., Km 2.5
US, ☎ 800/253-2702; Mexico, 9/872-3200
www.coralprincess.com
Expensive/Super
139 suites, restaurants, bars, kids' play area, TV, telephones, pools.

This attractive hotel rises high above the reef along Cozumel's north shore. Built in two phases, the taller tower features electronic keys and electricity-saving lights in rooms that have a bright teal and white modern décor, balconies and combination tile baths. There are well-equipped kitchenettes in the "Princess," a two-bedroom deluxe suite with two baths and a living room, and in the "Coral," the hotel's large one-bedroom suite. The third style of accommodations is a studio, the equivalent of a medium-size hotel room with either one king-size bed or two double beds.

Although the hotel is hard against the Caribbean, rock coral lines the shore, so the hotel utilizes a seawall platform to create a soft sand beach for sunbathing. The hotel's large blue, double pool makes for fine swimming anyway.

South End (North to South)

A new highway built early in 2001 bypasses the old winding beachfront road beginning just after the southern most ferry dock, before the Presidente. We have kept the order and addresses of hotels along the old road the same, as the two roads had yet to be well marked. By press time, signs should make the difference clear.

HOTEL BARRACUDA ☆☆☆
Av. Melgar
☎ 9/872-0002, fax 9/872-1243
Moderate
51 rooms with private terraces, dive shop, in-room fridge.

This is an old favorite of scuba divers who flock to the island for the incredible underwater delights it offers. Despite an energetic clientele, the rooms themselves are somewhat tired.

VILLABLANCA ☆☆☆
Southern Coastal Rd., Km 2
☎ 9/872-0730
Moderate
25 rooms and 25 suites, two villas, TV, telephones, pool, tennis.

Just a few miles south of downtown is this easy-to-miss low-rise hotel set back from the road in a tropical garden setting. The office is located in the small white kiosk next to the Colonial archway in the parking lot. Across the street is their private pier and beach club. Although the hotel caters to divers (ask about their packages) it's a pleasing find for simple tourists like us. Low-key and quiet, it features a tennis court and a swimming pool centered in a large lawn and garden area with stone walkways among the colorful plants. Rooms are comfortable and clean with wood-trim Mexican décor. Not pretentious, a good value.

PARK ROYALE
Southern Coastal Rd., Km 3.5
☎ 9/872-0700; fax 9/872-1301
Super – All-Inclusive
322 rooms, tennis courts, restaurants, lobby bar, pool, beach club.

The Park Royal, originally known as Crown Princess, then Sol Caribe, is one of Cozumel's first all-inclusive deluxe hotels. The open lobby is under an impressive octagon-shaped thatched roof supported by huge wooden beams. The front entrance is up a small hill across the street from the beach (an underground tunnel provides easy, safe access). Follow the sounds of a waterfall down the steps to the lagoon-like pool and courtyard restaurant. In a jungle setting, an artificial waterfall splashes down a gigantic Chac Mool idol into a stone basin. The tropical feeling is replicated in the rooms, where the furniture is dark wicker, the fabrics light and the bathrooms marble tile.

EL CID – LA CEIBA COZUMEL ☆☆☆☆☆
Southern Coastal Rd., Km 3.5 near the old cruise ship dock
US, ☎ 800/437-9609; Mexico, 9/872-0844
Fax 9/872-0065
Expensive
112 rooms, big pool, hot tub, tennis, gym, sauna, restaurant and bar.

Recently purchased by El Cid Resorts, the resort is undergoing a $2.5 million renovation, but will still cater to the dive, family and group markets.

The restaurant offers a great homemade coconut pie. There's a small beach – with optional topless sunbathing – within sight of the giant cruise ships that anchor offshore. Just beyond the wooden pier in back of the hotel, a large Convair 40-passenger plane was sunk in the crystal-clear water for a disaster movie by a Mexican film company. Now it's a frequent dive and snorkel spot that you can swim to even if you're not staying here. Del Mar aquatic shop on the beach runs frequent trips to the wreck and the reefs. Dive packages are offered by the hotel. Very pleasing rooms and buffet breakfast included.

PRESIDENTE INTER-CONTINENTAL ☆☆☆☆☆
Southern Coastal Rd., Km 6.5
US, ☎ 800/327-0200; Mexico, 9/872-0322
Fax 9/872-1360
www.interconti.com
Deluxe/Super
253 rooms and suites.

If you can afford to spend an extra $50 or so for the "Superior" room at the Presidente, do it!

We can't think of a hotel in the Yucatán we enjoyed more than the fabulous El Presidente on 100 acres of beautiful Cozumel. Its location on a crescent-shaped beach is absolutely perfect for swimming and snorkeling. Schools of colorful fish provide great photo ops.

We loved our room, a superior, #2125, whose terrace – surrounded by a flowering hibiscus hedge – faced the little beach and the sunset. The main building's rooms are equally attractive. Suites are also available. Features a large pool with hot tub, two tennis courts, motor scooter, scuba and snorkel rental, two great restaurants and a bar.

CLUB DEL SOL ☆☆☆
Southern Coastal Rd., Km 6.8
☎ 9/872-3777
Moderate
41 rooms, air conditioning, restaurant / bar, small pool.

The very efficient, friendly staff at Club Del Sol has an assistant manager who calls himself Peter Pan.

Painted a deep sunflower gold, Club Del Sol sits across the street from a tiny beach and marina that runs snorkel/scuba trips. This establishment is not nearly as pretentious as its name.

Each room in the two-story building that runs back from the road has a table with two chairs and faces a pretty garden. Some rooms have kitchenettes that include fridge, stove, pots and plates. A super value so close to the beach.

FIESTA AMERICANA COZUMEL REEF ☆☆☆☆☆
Southern Coastal Rd., Km 7.5
☎ 800/343-7821; in Mexico, 9/872-2622
Fax 9/872-2666
www.fiestamexico.com
Expensive/Deluxe (breakfast rate available)
162 rooms and suites, TV, three restaurants, pools, beach club.

Located only a short distance from the Chankanaab Park, a beautiful natural park for snorkeling, the Cozumel Reef complex straddles both sides of the road. On the ocean side is a sea-walled beach club and restaurant connected to the hotel gardens by a pedestrian overpass. The five-story orange tile-roofed hotel is set back from the road behind a free-form pool with swim-up palapa bar.

The hotel rooms feature balconies, terrazzo tile floors, light fabrics and painted tropical furniture. In 1997, in the jungle behind the hotel, the Fiesta Americana built 14 charming Maya-style casitas, "cottages." These house four junior suites in each. Our romantic nature liked them very much, especially those super-private suites that feature a view of the jungle. The intimate lodgings boast a sunken sitting area, king-size beds, attractive wood furniture and a terrace or balcony, complete with a Yucatecan hammock.

Downtown

Alive Price Scale — Accommodations
(per night/two people per room)

Prices do not include a 12% tax.

Inexpensive. . . . . under US $40

Moderate. . . . . US $40-$100

Expensive . . . . US $101-$200

Deluxe. . . . . US $201-$300

Super. . . . . US $301-$400

Ultra . . . . over US $400

B & B CARIBO ☆☆☆☆
Av. Juárez
Mexico, ☎ 9/872-3195
www.visit-caribo.com
Moderate
12 rooms with air conditioning, including 4 kitchenette suites.

Rates by the week and month are a real bargain at Caribo.

The American owner of this welcoming, gringo-friendly hotel is Cindy Cooper. She delivers what pleases *norteamericanos* – pleasant, spotlessly clean rooms and bathrooms, and congenial communal living and dining rooms. Some bedrooms are plainer than others mostly because a bitter marital custody battle for the hotel delayed promised upgrades. But things were looking up when we stopped back. Homey rooftop suites are available for weekly rental, and a big meatless breakfast is served every morning. The B&B is inland along busy Av. Juárez, the road that leads from the ferry dock to the windward side of the island.

Cozumel

VILLA DEL REY HOTEL
Av. 11 Sur, No. 460
☎ 800/325-2525, in Mexico 9/872-1600
Fax 9/872-1692
Moderate
45 rooms, pool, air conditioning, cable TV.

Located in a quiet comfortable and affordable area of downtown San Miguel, it is a good choice for dependable lodgings in the budget/moderate category. The Mexican-style building, within easy strolling distance of local shops and restaurants, features a lush tropical garden surrounding its pool. Double beds, electric coffee makers (we're addicted) and free local calls. Some rooms have kitchenettes. Restaurant open for three meals.

CARIBE HOTEL
Calle 2, between 15th & 20th
☎ 9/872-0225, fax 9/872-1913
Inexpensive/Moderate
14 rooms with fans.

This pink motel, in a peaceful section of town, has a small L-shaped pool in the center of a pretty garden. The medium-size, single-story accommodations are bright Caribbean blue inside, which makes them slightly dark with the door closed, but they're nice and clean. Comfortable and quiet.

TAMARINDO B&B
Calle 4, between 20th & 25th
☎ /fax 9/872-3614
Moderate

Native Frenchwoman and former language teacher Elaine Godement met her husband, Mexican architect Jorge Ruiz Esparza, in San Francisco before settling in Cozumel and opening this

magnificent but hard-to-find B & B. There are five
rooms total. Two bright and airy upstairs rooms
are in the white stucco main building. With
French doors, narrow balconies, a circular staircase to a little patio, skylights in the bathrooms
and Elaine's continental decorating touch, they're
very inviting. Two new attractive rooms with air
conditioning and kitchenettes are located in a de-
tached stucco building at the back of the fruit-tree
garden. The garden also houses one very attractive palapa Maya hut with a private bath. The two
main rooms and the bungalow share a kitchen off
the upstairs patio. There is a generous European-
style breakfast included in the price, adding one
more reason to search out the Tamarindo. Child
care and French lessons are also available, so in-
dulge yourself. They have a second dramatically
styled rental home nearby, so if they're full at the
B&B, they'll offer you rooms there. It's more private but equally distinctive.

HACIENDA SAN MIGUEL
Calle 10 Norte #500
☎/fax 9/872-1986
E-mail: vogakin@cozumel.com.mx
Moderate

Hacienda San Miguel is a luxury all-suite and
"spa" hotel located a few minute's walk from the
central downtown restaurant and shopping area.
In hacienda style, the hotel's suites, townhouses,
and studio apartment enclose a tropical courtyard
garden. Their spa service offers skin and body
therapies, and they have an agreement with
Playa Azul Hotel & Beach Club, on the north end,
for guest use of all amenities including the pool,
beach, and restaurant. All of Hacienda San

Miguel's 10 rooms are air conditioned with kitchenettes and cable TV. Cute breakfast nooks.

VILLAS LAS ANCLAS
Av. 5 Sur
☎ 9/872-6103, fax 9/872-5476
Moderate

Although this small hotel of seven staggered attached upstairs/downstairs villas was built in 1988, it looks new. What has matured nicely is the tiny green garden facing the villas' doorways. Downstairs quarters contain a well-equipped kitchen and sunken living room with comfortable furniture, day bed, attractive artwork, and a large picture window. The upstairs sleeping loft, accessed by a wrought iron spiral staircase, features a queen-size bed, bathroom and huge closet. Very much like staying in someone's apartment, someone with good taste. New American/Mexican owners in 2001 have spruced up the place even more.

Best Places to Eat

You can get anything you want at Alice's Restaurant.
Arlo Guthrie, 1966

For a resort destination, Cozumel's dining prices are quite reasonable, inexpensive even. The same fine food, service and ambiance in a metropolitan area of the States would cost significantly more. There are plenty of places on Cozumel where you can get a good meal for a bargain price.

> ### ◎ *TIP*
>
> If you're low on funds, the abso-
> lute cheapest places to eat are
> the small, limited-menu fast
> food *loncherias* near the *mer-
> cado* and the central plaza.

In the afternoon, the lunch crowd – which includes cruise passengers – spreads down the
south coast, where a series of Mexican restaurants dot idyllic white sand beaches. They serve
up cold beers, fresh seafood and tasty Mexican
dishes, while you swim or sun or stroll the beach.
In some, you can eat under individual palapa umbrellas right on the beach.

If you're looking for good food at a good price,
we've selected a number of sit-down restaurants
that are well worth visiting. Many of the nightlife
places in Cozumel are a restaurant with a bar on
the side – or vice versa – so check in the nightlife
section for additional eateries of note.

Reservations are virtually unheard of on
Cozumel. If they are needed, we note it in our
description. *¡Buen apetito!*

Alive Price Scale - Restaurants
(per person, not including beverage)

Inexpensive . . . . less than US $6
Moderate. . . . . US $6-$13
Expensive . . . . over US $13

Favorite Mexican Restaurants

EL MORO
75 Bis Norte #124, between Calle 2 & 4
☎ 9/872-3029
Inexpensive

El Moro is impossible for most tourists to find. Get a cab or go west past the circle on Av. Juárez until you get to the large Pemex station on the left. Make a left just before, then make the first right and the first left. You'll find El Moro, or "The Moor," on a bumpy dirt street in a residential area. It's a very popular place with diners in the know, offering an extensive menu (in both English and Spanish) of Mexican regional dishes and fresh seafood. Once you try any of the varied menu choices, you'll wonder why you bothered to eat anywhere else on the island. Giant drinks, excellent food – it's an unbeatable value. Closed Thursday.

LA CHOZA
Calle Rosado Salas at Av. 10 Sur
☎ 9/872-0958
Inexpensive/Moderate

La Choza has a big palapa roof over its corner dining area with large windows. It has the reputation for the best *comida tipica* (typical Mexican food) on the island. Our pork stew and beefsteak in pepper sauce was well prepared and very tasty. La Choza is owned and operated by the extended Peralta family who are from Guanajuato, a beautiful colonial "silver" city in central Mexico.

CASA DENIS
Calle 1 Sur
☎ 9/872-0067
Inexpensive/Moderate

The yellow wooden house on the right as you walk up Calle Uno is Casa Denis. A few tables are set out front in the pedestrian-only street, but there are two small dining parlors inside and some more tables in the shady back garden patio. It offers tasty light or full Mexican and Yucatecan home-style meals – as well as fresh seafood. Been there, doing that, since 1945.

LAS PALMERAS
At the ferry pier
☎ 9/872-1386
Moderate

The best seats at Las Palmeras are those that allow diners an unrestricted view of the crowds coming and going on the malecón.

When it comes to location, location, location, Las Palmeras has got it, got it, got it. Certainly not the cheapest nor even the best restaurant on Cozumel, this cool and breezy palm-planted open-air corner spot is nevertheless very tempting. Its décor is appealing, it's right at the ferry dock and the food smells good. We find it awfully hard to get off the ferry hungry and pass by without at least a look at their menu. Sea breezes and over-sized awnings keep it cool inside.

MORGAN'S
Av. Juárez on the north side of the plaza
☎ 9/872-0884
Moderate

Morgan's offers a 10% discount voucher in the Blue Guide: *(find it in hotels and all over the island).*

There is enough polished wood in this Caribbean-styled restaurant to make another ship for the pirate Henry Morgan, who once used Cozumel's protected waters to hide from the English and

Spanish navies. The distinguished building, with a large wrap-around porch for dining, is the harbor town's former Customs house. The international and seafood menu, impeccable service and nautical ambiance make Morgan's the place for a refined night out or a celebratory lunch after striking good shopping bargains in the mercado nearby. Live music in the evening. Open 11 to 11.

PANCHO'S BACKYARD
Av. Melgar and Calle 8
☎ 9/872-2057
Moderate/Expensive

Pancho's Backyard is in the rear of Los Cinch Soles, Cozumel's most famous shopping store. This lovely courtyard restaurant is set under Colonial arches with loads of greenery. In the early 1900s the building was a warehouse that stored bales of dried resin from the zapota tree.

Beautiful hand-painted dinnerware and blown glassware (certified lead free) are sold in Pancho's store.

★ DID YOU KNOW?

Zapota resin is the basic ingredient of chewing gum and Quintana Roo's main export.

In 1960 the building was opened as a hotel. In 1990, after four years of extensive renovation, it became a large store, art gallery and restaurant. The charming atmosphere is matched by delicious food – generous servings of Mexican dishes and seafood, cappuccino and espresso coffees and awesome Margaritas. Try the bananas Susana dessert with a café Maya espresso. Yum!

Favorite Seafood Restaurants

LA CABANA DEL PESCADOR
"THE LOBSTER HOUSE"
Northern Coastal Rd., Km 4
☎ 9/872-0795
Expensive

Follow the coast road north, past the airport and marina, until you find an incongruous red British telephone booth. Cross a wooden footbridge and discover the best lobster dinner on the island. The Lobster House, a Cozumel fixture since 1983, is located in a Maya-style hut beneath a traditional thatched roof. Hidden back from the road among banana trees and jungle vegetation, the lobster-tail-only restaurant is a small, dark, intimate eatery with a nautical décor and screened windows overlooking the thick jungle. They've served dinner the same way since their inception: You choose a locally caught, fresh lobster – usually a Caribbean spiney – from a tray. The tail is then grilled to order. Meals come with all-you-can-eat rice and steamed vegetables. Prices change daily, depending on the market and weight, but the average dinner price is around US $20. No credit cards. Open from 6 pm to 10:30 pm.

Next door and across a small wooden bridge and raised walkway over the mangroves and jungle floor is El Guacamayo, the "King Crab House." The restaurant's candlelit interior features a nautical décor of fish nets, lobster pots, and floats. Soft music plays in the background. A photo menu shows king crab, seafood or steaks. No credit cards, same hours as La Cabaña.

EL CAPI NAVEGANTE
Av. 10 Sur
☎ 9/872-1730
Moderate/Expensive

A block or two from the main plaza and all those other crowded restaurants resides Cozumel's most famous seafood restaurant, El Capi Navegante. With the obligatory nautical décor, Capi Navegante serves what many claim is the freshest fish on the island. And the fact that they run out of certain dishes attests to that. Open from 11 am-11 pm, this is one of the island's early pioneers in fine dining and a local favorite. Say hello to José Santos, *el capitán.*

LA VERANDA
Calle 4, 1½ blocks in from the seafront
☎ 9/872-4132
Moderate/Expensive

La Veranda is a Caribbean-style eatery with a relaxed atmosphere, classy ambiance and fine fusion cooking. Tucked on a side street in a typical Caribbean house behind a small front garden and long porch, its wooden beams and trim dominate the air-conditioned interior dining and bar area. The menu is creative and appetizing, a pleasant change. Seafood dishes are the specialty. Their signature dinner is a mixed platter of fish, shrimp, octopus, lobster and squid (US $36 for two). More to our tastes was the jerked chicken, a spicy hot chicken with rice. For the most romantic setting, try the back porch – la veranda – where tables are set up to overlook a softly lighted tropical garden patio. A few wrought iron tables are also available in the garden, which boasts a fountain and antique lamppost. Opens at 6 pm.

Favorite International Restaurants

PRIMA
Av. Adolfo Rosado Salas No. 109
☎ 9/872-4242
Moderate/Expensive

Breezy terrace dining upstairs is primo at Prima, an Italian restaurant specializing in Northern Italian seafood dishes, brick-oven pizzas, calzones and handmade pastas. Though you can argue the better Italian restaurants are actually across the strait in Playa del Carmen, the festive roof-top dining room at Prima attracts Americans by the dozens for dinner. They take credit cards and sell Cuban cigars. Open for dinner only.

TONY ROME'S
Calle Adolfo Rosado Salas near Av. 5 Sur
☎ 9/872-0131
www.tonyrome.com
Moderate

If you're walking along the street and hear the music of Frank Sinatra, Tony Bennett and modern standards, you're near Tony Rome's. Tony was a nightclub headliner in Vegas and Atlantic City before settling down with a dinner show restaurant in Cozumel. Tony has a wonderful voice and entertains diners nightly with songs. As to food, we can sing his praises – he features Kansas City steaks and a good barbecued ribs, as well as tasty Mexican dishes. Tony personally visits your table to ask how everything is – everything was fine with us when we ate there. If you're from Jersey, be sure to say a special "howya doin'."

JEANIE'S WAFFLE HOUSE
Oceanfront in Hotel Vista del Mar
☎ 9/872-0545
Inexpensive

We could only love an eatery with a name like "Waffle House." It's the kind of place where we can relax our "going native" façade and chow down on what we haven't had for a while – feelgood food such as hot cakes and ice cream. Besides waffles and crêpes to crow about, owners Raul and Jeannie DeLille feature excellent steak and regional dishes. Even more to our plebeian tastes is digging into a big home-style breakfast for dinner. Open 6 am-10 pm.

DIAMOND BAKERY CAFE
Corner of Calle 1 Sur and Av. 15
Inexpensive

We must qualify our review of the Diamond by first saying: we like bakeries. And we absolutely love this precious gem of a bakery/café across from a hilly miniature golf course. Inside, the aroma of baking and fresh brewed coffee excites the senses.

The café features a cheerful and bright, air-conditioned seating area, usually crowded, and glass counters displaying delicious looking sweets and savories. Not to mention homemade ice cream. We practically lived there. Well-used bulletin board for rentals and for sales. Open 7-11 weekdays and Saturdays, Sundays, 8-11.

More Munchies

Other restaurants that deserve a mention include **Sonora Grill** (Av. 15 Norte between Júarez and Calle 2 Norte). They open at 7 am for breakfast (try *huevos rancheros*) and don't close again until midnight. Our favorite dish is their Mexican *fajitas*. Owners Victor and Rosa give it their personal attention.

Another very good Mexican restaurant is **El Abuelo Gerardo** (Av. 10 Norte #21). Grandfather Gerardo's is another local favorite eatery that specializes in seafood and home-cooked Mexican meals. There's a bright open dining room with colorful tablecloths and an *al fresco* dining area under umbrellas in the back. No cruise shippers come here, so the food is authentic and the prices are excellent. Check out the old photos of Cozumel.

The **Coffee Bean** is an appealing coffee shop and café on Calle 3 Sur. Mmmm, cappuccino. The string of beachside restaurants along the south shore are all excellent for kick-off-your-shoes dining on fresh seafood and Margaritas. And if you're wandering on the east coast of the island, try **Coconuts**, a little place on a bluff overlooking the sea at Km 22. It is open 10 am until sunset. Texas gringo owned.

Shop Till You Drop

How sweet it is.
Jackie Gleason

With thousands of daily cruise ship visitors, guests in the island's hotels, plus day-trippers from Cancún, Cozumel is a natural place to set up shop and sell. And sell they do. Downtown is alive with good places to shop for jewelry, clothes, handicrafts, gifts and souvenirs of your Mexican vacation. Store hours are not set but vendors will likely open if tourists are in town.

Where to Go

The island has three main commercial shopping areas. **Downtown**, along the waterfront on Av. Melgar and its side streets, has more than 150 stores selling a variety of quality merchandise. Behind the main plaza is the **Crafts Market**, a flea market kind of set-up where stalls and store-fronts feature Mexican crafts, jewelry and clothes. Another **flea market** exists across the street from the cruise ship terminal south of town. These stalls sell a variety of Mexican crafts, blankets, T-shirts and jewelry in a shaded hollow off the road. There are too many little places down-town – and even more in the flea markets – to mention them all, but below are some of the most notable places to spend your pesos.

Los Cinch Soles

The most appealing downtown gift shopping is found at this large store housed in a remodeled former hotel on Av. Melgar, a few blocks north of the Playa del Carmen ferry dock. In this clean, well-organized store you can shop for metal works from Jalisco, enamel painted animals, table-cloths, onyx and silver jewelry, embroidered clothing, papier mâché fruit, high-quality repro-ductions of Maya artifacts and gift items from all over Mexico.

You can buy big chairs, mirrors, tables and pots at Pancho's and they will ship your goods to anywhere in the world.

When you're loaded up with bargains, just walk through the Colonial arch to Pancho's Backyard, a charming casual Mexican restaurant located in a terrace garden area to the rear of the store. (See our review of Pancho's Backyard in the *Best Places to Eat* section.) Los Cinch Soles, which means "The Five Suns," also has a very interesting art gallery in its courtyard. It features paint-ings, sculpture and woodwork from local as well as national craftsman.

The store is kind enough to supply public rest-rooms, thank you!

Van Cleef & Arpels

Av. Melgar No. 54

The famous jeweler shines here in Cozumel com-fort along the *malecón* (waterfront road) and spe-cializes in the finest jewelry, gems and diamonds. Van Cleef makes their own jewelry so it is the place to buy one-of-a-kind pieces and be assured of getting what you pay for.

La Casita

Av. Melgar

This corner shop features high-quality gifts, arts and crafts and fashionable resort wear. They sell the authentic limited-edition Bustamante figures – those distinctive and unusual hand-painted animals and birds from the mind of Mexico's famous artist. A Cotton Country section boasts tropical clothes. Also find an assortment of silver jewelry.

Plaza Del Sol

Three locations: PDS Palancar, downtown on Av. Melgar, No. 15; PDS Cozumel in the Plaza del Sol Building on the main square; and PDS Taxco in the airport terminal. Since 1978 the Plaza del Sol has offered several choices in gold coin jewelry (14k and 18k), as well as silver and semi-precious and precious stones. They also feature Cozumel's famous black coral as well as handcrafted jewelry and gifts from other parts of Mexico.

Other Shopping Treasures

Two other interesting shops are **Na Balam** (Av. 5a on the main square), which sells batik clothing, high-quality Maya art reproductions and jewelry, and **La Concha** (Calle 5, No. 141), which features a large selection of good Mexican and Guatemalan folk art, belts, jewelry and clothing. To be honest, we could go on and on in this section, but the most fun in shopping is to discover your own favorite places. And don't forget the crafts at flea market-style places for some good bargains and an authentic Mexican market experience.

Dawn to Dusk

I'm picking up good vibrations.
The Beach Boys

Somewhere between the hustle-bustle of Cancún and the laid-back attitude of Isla Mujeres lies Cozumel, the paradise best known for its colorful reefs that braid the ocean floor. It's a no-brainer that activities on Cozumel center around the water. If you're an experienced diver with PADI certification, there is no end to the number of dive trip operators who will gladly run you out to the 11 big dive spots offshore, including a sunken airplane near La Ceiba Hotel. You can even learn to dive in certified courses. Snorkelers can find their paradise at Chank-anaab National Park. Landlubbers will find things to do and see around the Maya ruins, driving or walking the spectacular eastern coastline, or exploring and shopping in town.

Beaches on the Loop

The beaches north of the pier on the leeward (western) side are sublime, especially around Playa Azul, but access to them is limited because of the numerous hotels and private residences. The strange unfinished lighthouse-looking structure, near the marina, is part of an abandoned mansion, supposedly connected with the main house by a tunnel under the road.

Rumor has it (spread to us by a wildly imaginative security guard) that a previous owner of the lighthouse killed his family and himself here.

Cozumel

With the north beach filled with buildings, it's the long southern coast that beckons most tourists to its shore. Here's how to get your feet wet:

Even if you're in Cozumel for only a day you should at least take a ride around the island's long southern loop road. Beautiful beaches dot the western shore until the road swings east to the dramatic scenery of the rugged windward coast. Rent a motorbike, car, or take a taxi tour. Follow the leeward loop about 5½ miles (9 km) south of town to the **Chankanaab National Park** (admission around US $10), a natural lagoon with botanical gardens containing over 400 plant species, and a fantastic beach. The lagoon used to be connected to the sea through an underground passage (now collapsed), which created a living aquarium with over 60 different aquatic species. A research project precludes going into the lagoon now, but swimming and snorkeling on the seashore is still sensational. The fish in the Caribbean hang out waiting for food scraps. It's also a marvelous place to relax in the sun or read a book in the shady picnic areas. Swimming beaches, restaurants, museum, snorkel and dive areas with rental and lessons are available.

The park fills up with cruise ship passengers by the middle of the day.

The small beach near Chankanaab is **Playa Corona**, with a fresh fish and Mexican food restaurant and snorkel rental. **Playa San Francisco**, a beach south of Chankanaab, is very popular with cruise tourists who stop for lunch and a swim. It's one of the best beaches in Cozumel. As you head south, at **Playa Sol** there are interesting gift shacks, a little zoo and a wide swimming beach with recreations of Maya idols sunken in the sea for snorkelers. The large palapa restaurant is slightly more reasonable than the one at San Francisco. **Playa del Cedral** is opposite the turn for the El Cedral ruins (small). It's a public park where fisherman land their boats on the bright white sand beach. **Playa Palancar** is opposite the famous reef of the same name. Dive boats dot the waters offshore. The beach features a restaurant and good swimming.

After a long ride through the jungle bush along the bottom of the island you come to the **Paradise Café**, a reggae bar along the rough windward (eastern) side. Just north of the café is a blowhole in the rock – great for getting wet and a fun photo op. A right turn at the café takes you to the entrance to the 247-acre **Punta Sur Ecological Reserve** featuring a dedicated swimming and snorkeling beach recreation area and an observation tower. Visitors between May and September can observe the sea turtles that nest here on the beaches. The US $15 entrance fee covers your parking, unlimited bus rides in the reserve, a visit to the Maya ruins of El Caracol (see below) and a museum, as well as an ecology education center. Guests can experience the park at their own pace, the bus circles the route continuously or electric bicycles are available for rent. The **Museum of Navigation**, tracing seamanship from the pre-Columbus times to present day, is located at the site of the 19th century Punta Celerain Lighthouse. Great birdwatching too, but remember insect repellent. The Late Postclassic Maya ruins at the southernmost tip are **El Caracol**, one-of-a-kind in Maya architecture.

North on the road along the east coast is **El Mirador snack bar**, a tiny place with outdoor tables among the dunes. Sometimes there's a guy with a huge iguana who hopes to get a US $1 tip for photos of his pet. As you drive the road there are plenty of herons, pelicans and iguanas to be seen in the wild. Pretty **Playa Bonita** can be camped on and the **Chen Rio beach**, with its seafood restaurant, is shielded by rock formations that break up the waves and form a cove. It's excellent for swimming and snorkeling and a peaceful place to hang a hammock. The paved road north ends in the center of the east coast and you'll need a four-wheel-drive and stamina to continue on to Punta Molas. Turn left on the paved road to return to San Miguel, past the San Gervasio ruins.

Sightseeing

The end of the human race will be that it will eventually die of civilization.
Ralph Waldo Emerson, 1803-1882

San Gervasio

One of the most popular excursions on the island are the ruins at San Gervasio (100 BC to 1600), Cozumel's only excavated Maya ruins. To get there from town, follow Av. Benito Juaréz (which transverses the island) east until the town thins out. About halfway between town and the east coast a small sign announces the left turn for the ruins. You'll have to pay a small "road-use" fee at a toll booth and an entrance fee of about US $3.50 to enter. If you take a taxi out here, about US $25, have it wait for you in the parking lot.

The ruins are not impressive if you've seen others such as Tulum or Chichén Itzá, but they are archeologically significant. The temple was built to worship Ixchel, fertility goddess and the wife of Itzamná, king of the Maya deities. The ancient Maya canoed across from the mainland in hollowed logs to visit this important Cozumel ceremonial center. The first Catholic mass performed in Mexico occurred here in 1518. The trails between the individual sites follow ancient *sacbé*, sacred roads raised above the ground and made of white limestone. The shade of jungle trees gives it a natural ambiance and is perhaps more fun to walk around than the ruins themselves.

Cozumel Museum

The interesting Museum of Cozumel opened in 1987 in an airy building along the seafront, 2½ blocks north of the main plaza. It presents local archeological, geographic, ecological and Colonial history in four *salas,* exhibition halls, on two floors. A Maya *otoch*, "house," is on display in a side courtyard with a Maya woman cooking traditional handmade tortillas.

The well-arranged museum is open 10 am to 6 or 7 pm weekdays and 1 to 6 pm on Saturdays. No flash photography is permitted. Upstairs, under a canvas awning on a breezy terrace overlooking the harbor, is the **Museum Café** – a very popular eatery open breakfast through dinner. Good service, light Mexican fare.

Sports & Activities

Horseback Riding

A number of independently owned ranches offer horseback riding into the bush (there's one near El Presidente Hotel and another on the east coast road). Arrangements can be made with your hotel travel agent, or just take a chance and find one as you drive. We liked the horseback ride and hike offered in the tiny inland town of El Cedral, on the southern half of Cozumel. There is a tiny Maya ruin to the left of the church, and an unrestored mound to its left again. Park in the shade under the overhang in the square. Horses are tethered nearby. A tour to explore a small cave and cenote is available.

⊘ TIP

We advise that you use mosquito repellent for any non-beach outdoor activity on Cozumel.

Fishing

Cozumel was a fishing paradise long before it became one of the top five diving spots in the world. The island still attracts deep-sea fishing enthusiasts from around the world for wahoo, mackerel, barracuda, amberjack, bonito, snapper and shark.

The sports fish of blue marlin, white marlin, sail-fish, dorado and albacore are best from March through June. The marina, one mile north of town and the airport just before the big bend in the road, is where most of the fishing charters dock.

If you express an interest in fishing, chances are you'll be approached by a fishing broker known as a *comisionista*. These men are legitimate. They work off commissions and tips and should put you on a trip with a reliable captain. Boats range from a small "ballenera" boat (US $100 for a half-day) to a deluxe fishing yacht for six people (US $1,200 for the day). **Club Nautico**, located at the marina, arranges trips (☎ 9/872-0118), as does **Cozumel Adventures** (☎ 9/872-0489) on Av. Salas. Also try **Marina Aqua World** (☎ 9/872-1210) on the Southern Coastal Road at Paráiso Beach. Any travel agent can book your excursion too. Try **IMC Travel**, Calle 2 North, ☎ 9/872-1535. A sailfish and billfish fishing tournament is held every year in May. Contact any of the above companies for more information.

Diving & Snorkeling

Cozumel's favorite dive spots:
Chankanaab Reef
El Mirador
La Ceiba Reef
Los Atolones
Maracaibo Reef
Palancar Reef
Paraíso Reef
Punta Molas
Punta Morena
Santa Rosa Reef
Yucab Reef

If you're one of Cozumel's estimated 1,500 daily divers, most hotels – even many smaller ones that we did not mention in town – offer dive packages and you could save money by arranging one. If you're the independent sort or want to learn, the island is crawling with reliable dive shops and dive operators, but there are some things beyond price to consider before choosing one.

- Verify their certification for PADI or NAUI. FMAS is the acceptable Mexican equivalent.

- Verify the certification and experience of the dive master. Your safety could depend on his/her decisions.

- Make sure your operator's boat carries safety equipment, a radio and oxygen.

- Make sure you're comfortable with the operator and their operation. Choose someone who cares about your buoyancy and the protection of the reefs. Personal attention can make a difference, if not in your safety, at least in your enjoyment.

Emergency Recompression Chambers

There are two emergency recompression chambers on the island: **Cozumel Recompression Center**, Calle 5 South No. 21B, ☎ 9/872-2387, VHF channels 16 and 21; and **Dr. Pascal Piccolo Hyperbaric Center**, ☎ 9/872-3070, VHF channel 65. Both are physician-staffed 24 hours a day.

The CRC is supported by a diver surcharge of US $1 per day so they have excess medical insurance, assuring no out-of-pocket expenses should you have the misfortune of a pressure-related problem. They welcome tours of the facility during business hours.

To capture the beauty of the reefs you can rent underwater cameras – everything from point-and-shoots to advanced rigs and videos. Try **Cozumel Images** (Calle 2 between Av. Melgar and 5th, ☎ 9/872-2238) or **Island Photo Center** (at the La Ceiba Hotel, ☎ 9/872-5833). The center also offers a short course in underwater photography.

Snorkelers can find any number of shoreline locations to swim to and float around, including the Chankanaab Park, El Presidente Hotel, La Ceiba and more. Many of the same dive operators also run snorkel trips in their boats to ideal locations above the offshore reefs. Ask in your hotel, at a travel agency, or at any of the many dive shops.

> ★ **DID YOU KNOW?**
>
> Coral is a slow-growing living object that will die if you touch it. A careless kick can destroy 20-200 years of growth. Please be careful.

After Dark

*Come a little bit closer, you're my kind of man,
so big and so strong. Come a little bit closer,
I'm all alone and the night is so long.*
– Jay & The Americans, 1964

A large number of island visitors return to their cruise ships by the early evening. After the ships weigh anchor, light up their rigging and sail off, the nightlife in Cozumel begins. Although it is not quite as much a party town as Cancún – perhaps because alcohol and diving don't mix well – it still swings. The hottest eating, dancing and "ass-kicking" party place is **Carlos & Charlie's** rooftop dance and grill restaurant, near the ferry dock on Av. Melgar. It's up a steep set of stairs that guarantees a problem coming back down after a few drinks! Dine on the terrace overlooking the harbor and the main drag below. When Carlos closes at 1 am,, the sleepless from Seattle may wander over to find you at **Joe's**, a crowded bar and live-music super party place on Av. 10 between 1 & 3 South; or at **Raga**, the live reggae, salsa and rock music Caribbean restaurant and bar, on Av. Salas between 10 and 15 (opens at 10:30 pm). The oceanfront drive boasts a popular **Hard Rock Café** and a **Planet Hollywood**, both smaller and more intimate than their Cancún counterparts.

A piano bar type evening can be found at **Black and White**, a trendy bar/nightclub that draws a hip local crowd. It's near the central downtown. Head east on Juárez four blocks from the plaza and turn right at the Pemex on Av. Pedro Joaquin (30a) and go four blocks more to this happening spot. Cool, baby.

If you'd rather listen to a real singer go to **Tony Rome's** (Av. 5 South, No. 21), where Tony Rome himself croons relaxing music with two shows nightly at 7:30 and 9:30. Tony's offers good food and loaded drinks.

If you're traveling with children or just prefer to party early, the **Hotel El Cozumeleño** (☎ 9/872-0050) has great nightly beach parties with live music. Locals and visitors alike love to spend hours at night people-watching downtown. If that appeals to you, go to the **Aladin Video Bar** on the northeast corner of the main square. Actually, any of the plaza-side or street-side places on the island are great for absorbing the environs in the evening.

Discos

The disco dance floors can become very crowded in Cozumel. **Scaramouche** opens at 9:30 and closes at 3 am, two blocks south of the square on Av. Melgar. **Neptuno Disco**, five blocks south of the plaza is always filled with a good mix of locals and tourists who love to dance and mingle. They have huge TV screens and a sharp laser light show.

? Cozumel A-Z

Beauty Salons

Shampoo is a full-service beauty parlor open Monday through Saturday, 9 to 9, at the corner of Av. Melgar and Calle 3 South.

Vogue Salon will come to you, by appointment only, if you call Mirna Molina (☎ 9/872-4010; cellular, ☎ 9/879-1987). **Caribbean Massage** (☎ 9/872-5068) does beauty and hair on Av. 5 between Calles 3 and 5 South. Therapeutic massage and aromatherapy is available from **Massage With**

Sue by appointment only at La Ceiba Resort, ☎ 9/872-0812, or home ☎ 9/872-4612.

Bookstore

A bookstore with English-language titles is the **Agencia de Publicaciones Gracia** on the east side of the plaza. They should be carrying both our Hunter guides!

Friends Indeed

English-language **AA** group meetings are held Sun., Mon., Wed., Fri. and Sat. at 6 pm in the Hotel Colonial on the corner of Av. 5 and Calle 7 Sur (☎ 9/872-1007). English **NA** meetings are held in the same place, a half-block from the main plaza, Tues. and Thurs. nights at 6 pm. Subject to change.

Laundry

Lavanderia Margarita is on Av. 20, near Calle 3 Sur.

Medical

There are several **pharmacies** in town, including one on the plaza, another at the *zócalo* near the Hotel Lopez and a 24-hour one at the Medical Center on Av. 20 Norte No. 425 (☎ 9/872-2929).

There's a 24-hour **tourist medical service** on Av. 50 between Calles 11 and 13 Sur (☎ 9/872-0912). Call an **ambulance** at ☎ 9/872-0639. There are also several English-speaking doctors on the island. Try **Dr. Lewis** on Av. 50 (☎ 9/872-1616) or **Dr. Ricardo Segovia**, who can obtain bed-to-bed transfers to several stateside hospitals, at Av. 15 North No 320 (☎ 9/872-3370). **Unidad Medica del Sur** is a group practice on Av. Pedro Joaquin Coldwell, between 21 & 23 (☎ 9/872-5787, emergencies, 9/874-5720). A **diver's recompression chamber** is on Calle 5 Sur off Melgar at ☎ 9/872-2387 or 9/872-3070.

Movies

English-language movies are shown every night at 9 pm at **Cinema Cozumel**, Av. Melgar between Calles 2 & 4, and **Cine Cecilio Borge**, on Benito Juaréz between Av. 30 and 35.

Phone

Phone home from the **Calling Station** on Av. Melgar at Calle 3 Sur, open until 10 pm daily.

Police/Fire

The police can be reached at ☎ 9/872-0409 in the Palacio Municipal on Calle 11 Sur. For English service, ask for James Garcia. Call the fire department at ☎ 9/872-0800.

Post Office

Mexico has some great stamps.

Found on Av. Rafael Melgar at Calle 7 Sur.

Tourist Information

Brochures and advice can be obtained at the Plaza del Sol building facing the central square (☎ 9/872-0972) or at the Consejo de Promocion Turistica on Av. Rafael Melgar at Calle 11 Sur (☎ 9/872-4379), open weekdays only, 8-1 and 4-7.

Playa del Carmen

*Not bound to swear allegiance to any master,
wherever the wind takes me I travel as a visitor.*
Horace, 65-8 BC

The once-sleepy village of Playa del Carmen has twice doubled its population in the last few years. This is largely due to Europeans who discovered the alabaster-white beaches, gentle surf, coral reefs and slow lifestyle. Playa's dock is the pier for the people ferry to Cozumel, so it's only a short trip over to snorkel or dive on Cozumel's incredible coral reefs.

The strong Italian and German influences have created a unique vagabond traveler ambiance. Numerous outrageously delicious Italian restaurants provide sustenance and several German-owned hotels raise the standards of service to exacting levels. Combine that with a relaxed Mexican-Caribbean feeling and a sprinkling of American free spirit and you've got Playa. It's definitely not the place to "get away," but it is a place to enjoy marvelous beaches by day and a lively nightlife in the evening. The mix of backpackers, archeological buffs and new-age sunworshippers makes Playa very interesting and worth some time. It's also ideally located to reach the many nearby day-trips we recommend. See the *Field Trips* section for details.

Finding Your Way

To reach Playa, 42 miles (68 km) south of Cancún, take a bus from the station downtown (a trip of about one hour) or negotiate a fare (around US $30) with a Cancún taxi driver to scoot you down. The main road into town, Av. Juárez or Av. Principal (depending on whom you ask), leads you right to the ferry dock and the pedestrian-only "5th Avenue," running perpendicular to the beach. This street boasts many of the town's hotels, stores and restaurants. The bus station is right there at Av. 5 and Juárez and is a hub for further journeys down to Tulum and south to Belize. Most hotels are within easy walking distance from the bus station. Near the bus and ferry dock you'll find men with large yellow tricycles (*triciclos*) who will ride just your luggage – in a Mexican version of a rickshaw – to a hotel or to the Cozumel ferry.

The Xaman-Ha Aviary in Playacar, south of Playa del Carmen, is a haven for 30 species of birds indigenous to the Yucatán. Great photo ops.

Playa del Carmen

Restaurants and gift shops jostle each other for space along Playa's pedestrian walkway, part of 5th Avenue (as even many locals call Avenida Cinch). There are so many places here, beach-side or within a few blocks from the shore, that we selected only a sampling of the most comfortable hotels and best restaurants. Live well.

Best Places to Stay

Alive Price Scale – Accommodations
(per night/two people per room)
Prices do not include a 12% tax.

Inexpensive	under US $40
Moderate	US $40-$100
Expensive	US $101-$200
Deluxe	US $201-$300
Super	US $301-$400
Ultra	over US $400

TREE TOPS HOTEL
Calle 8
☎/fax 9/873-0351
www.treetops.com
Moderate

Imagine if someone built a wall around virgin jungle while a city grew around it, unaware of the life within. That's pretty much how Tree Tops began, a cabaña hotel in a piece of jungle sealed off before Playa grew from 3,000 to 130,000 people. There are still three rustic bungalows left under the tall trees and heavy tropical vegetation, but owners Bill and Sandy Dillon built additional hotel rooms in tall modern white stucco buildings to meet the demand. With a North American sensibility, the Dillons' quiet 12-room, three-suite hotel exudes privacy and cool comfort, without rip-off prices. A half-block from the beach. At the entrance is a pub restaurant that serves breakfast and lunch. Continental breakfast is included with your room rate.

LA ZIRANDA
Calle 4, between 15 and 20
☎ 9/876-2476
www.hotellaziranda.com
Moderate

The enticing Ziranda, which features a leafy ceiba tree as its symbol, boasts modern Mexican architecture to host guests on a quiet Playa side street. Opened in December 1999, all the double rooms here have small verandas or patios, some facing the backyard garden. The color scheme is soft gold and adobe red and bathrooms have exhaust fans (which many more expensive places lack). Owner, Nora Quiroz, who fled the chaos of Mexico City for the relative quiet life of Playa, built her outside hallways in such a way that some trees that grew on the property were not cut down but rise right through both floors, with openings to accommodate the trunks. A nice touch. A nice place.

HOTEL ALEJARI
Calle 6, beachfront
☎ 9/873-0372, fax 9/873-0005
www.xaac.com/playacar/alejari.htm
Moderate

The garden path weaves through a labyrinth of hibiscus bushes and flowers and leads to duplex rooms and studios, some with air and some with kitchenettes. Choose a good room and you'll never want to leave. Reasonable prices in the beachfront restaurant where you can eat in the dining room or under individual palapa shades.

ALBATROS ROYALE
Calle 8, beachfront
☎ 800/538-6802; in Mexico: 9/873-0001
www.mexicoholiday.com
Moderate/Expensive

These modern interpretations of Maya *naj* homes (traditional Mexican dwellings) are romantic, absolutely clean and pleasant. Rooms on the top have palapa roofs and balconies; downstairs all have porches and all come with hammocks for lounging or sleeping outside. A stone walkway leads from the white-tiled rooms and winds through lush flowering bushes out to the beach. This is a well-designed hotel. It's also one of several Turquoise Reef properties in Playa, some others being the Pelicano Inn, Chican Baal Kah apartments and Quinta Mija efficiencies. Tur-

Playa del Carmen

quoise is a booking/public relations firm that handles boutique properties. They also handle Apartmentos Jacques in nearby ritzy Playacar.

PELICANO INN
Calle 8, beachfront
☎ 800/538-6802; in Mexico, 9/873-0997
www.mexicoholiday.com
Moderate/Expensive

The rooms of this appealing Pueblo-styled hotel have red-tiled roofs and private balconies or patios that surround a private village-like courtyard. Completely rebuilt within the last five years, the hotel knows what guests like and offers it. The rooms are either beachfront, garden-view or ocean-view and the ambiance is more like that of a small apartment in the center of town, than of a hotel. Behind huge glass windows facing the beach, Ronny's Steakhouse specializes in fine cuts of beef.

SHANGRI-LA CARIBE
Av. 38, on the beach
☎ 800/538-6802; in Mexico: 9/873-0611
www.mexicoholiday.com
Expensive

The Shangri-La is famous among long time Playa del Carmen visitors. Once located well north of the downtown, the city has moved up to it, yet it retains its private club feeling and great beach location. The palapa-topped housing units are furnished with two queen-size beds and bathrooms with wonderful hand-painted porcelain basins and tile. Verandas with hammocks are ubiquitous, rooms do not have TVs. Breakfast and dinner included. Next to a great public beach.

MAYAN PARADISE HOTEL
Av. 10
☎ 9/873-0933
www.playadelcarmen.com/mayan
Expensive

Pricey for off the beach, this is nevertheless the best place to splurge in Playa del Carmen. The small hotel is probably the most attractive and luxurious of anything in town, with high palapa roofs and polished woods that give its cabaña rooms a Polynesian feel. The luxurious quarters all have kitchenettes and lovely shaded terraces. With an owner named "Palacio," how could you not expect palatial accommodations? One-bedroom suites have a hot tub and steam bath. The pleasing pool is figure-eight shaped. For those who prefer sand, the hotel offers its own beach club. You'll find this gem three blocks off the beach to the north of the ferry dock.

HOTEL KINBE
Calle 10, between 1 & 5
☎ 9/873-0441, fax 9/873-2215
www.kinbe.com
Moderate

Of the gazillion boutique hotels in Playa, the Kinbe stands out as a pleasant and pretty three-story hotel with a wonderful view from the top floor and very comfortable rooms. Five mini-suites have sea views from their balconies and feature king-size beds. The seven "executive rooms" also boast king beds; Seven standard rooms come with double beds. The exterior has flowering vines growing from balcony to balcony. Inside, white walls are accented by fabrics and artwork in bright primary colors. Air conditioned. Rates are reasonable.

HOTEL LUNATA
5th Ave., between 6 and 8
☎ 9/873-0884, fax 873-1240
www.lunata.com
Moderate-Expensive

Readers of our *Adventure Guide to the Yucatán* recommended we include Lunata in Playa and when we checked it out, we could see why. It's a luxury boutique 10-room hotel right on the main drag. Original furnishings from around Mexico make up the beautiful décor and each room features queen or king-size beds, tiled baths and safety deposit boxes. Terrace/balcony views of the ocean, garden or street. A colonial-styled building with intriguing common areas. Above the Boutique Mango on 5th Ave. Rates include continental breakfast.

Best Places to Eat

Alive Price Scale – Restaurants
(per person, not including beverage)

Inexpensive . . . . less than US $6
Moderate. . . . . US $6-$13
Expensive . . . . over US $13

Reservations generally not needed anywhere in Playa Del Carmen. At restaurants with no phone number listed, this is definitely the case.

DA GABI RESTAURANT
Calle 12 at Av. 5
☎ 9/873-0048, fax 9/873-0198
Moderate/Expensive

This is one of the best – if not the best – in the plethora of Italian restaurants in Playa. We had a delicious gourmet meal for only a few dollars more than we would have spent at a less-interesting sidewalk café on the pedestrian walkway. The evening ambiance is romantic in a giant palapa decorated in twinkly lights. It's an excellent value with great Italian and Mexican cooking.

EL CHINO
Calle 4, between 10 and 15
Inexpensive/Moderate

Despite its name it serves not Chinese food (try the one at Mom's Hotel), but specializes in Yucatecan cuisine. We found El Chino to be the best value in Playa. It's under a palapa roof, with wooden chairs and tables, big arched windows on either side, and an extensive Mexican menu, a block and a half off of 5th Ave. The *dueña*, Reyna Beltrán, supervises the staff personally so service is impeccable. Open from 7 am to 11 pm.

RESTAURANT & BAR JAGUAR
in Hotel Jungla Caribe, 5th Ave & Calle 8
Moderate

An upstairs bar/restaurant has views overlooking the busy street below or the quiet garden court-yard of the Jungla Caribe Hotel. Wood-burning pizza oven. In the courtyard beside the pool is the main dining room, surrounded by lush tropical foliage. The Italian and seafood menu offerings are well prepared and the atmosphere was pleasant

Playa del Carmen

and unhurried. A very nice hotel as well (with bidets!).

KAREN'S GRILL & PIZZAS
Av. 5, between Calles 2 and 4
Inexpensive/Moderate

More fun than gourmet, Karen's fills up and up and up with a boisterous crowd watching TV, music videos, or listening to live music. Italian and Mexican menu. Don't bother to ask for Karen – she ain't here.

LIMONES RESTAURANT
Av. 5 at Calle 6
Moderate/Expensive

This highly romantic restaurant set down in a hollow right on the pedestrian mall features international and French cuisine. Soft candlelight, numerous plants and a terraced dining area enhance the amorous atmosphere. There's live music in their "Red & Black" Bar. Daily specials help make this a great night out.

OTHER RECOMMENDED OPTIONS

There are some fine dining restaurants along the beach, usually associated with hotels, with excellent food – **Ronny's Steak House** is a tasteful example. Many little seafood restaurants and bars, however – such as **La Tarraya** between 2 and 4 – set up on the beach looking across the strait to Cozumel. Not much in the way of fancy ambiance – except for the Caribbean sea a few feet away – but they offer good food at good prices.

Additional eateries worth mentioning are, **Johnny Cairo's**, which serves excellent contemporary cuisine on 5th Ave between 12 and 14;

Yaxche, Yucatecan food at Calle 8 between 5 & 10; **Spaghetteria**, pasta on Calle 12 at 1; **Media Luna** and **Zaz**, vegetarian menus on 5th between 8 & 10 and 5th between 12 & 14, respectively; and the **Coffee Press**, a great place for breakfast and a shot of coffee all day long, Calle 2 between 5th and the beach. The **Hot Bakery** is on Calle 10 between 5 and 10.

Shop Till You Drop

*O*ne of Playa's most addicting attractions is its shopping. **Fifth Avenue** is chock full of a variety of stores that sell gifts, clothes, cigars, tequila, Mexican folk and fine art, and just about everything else you never thought you needed until you saw it here. We have no favorites among the many shops, it's always best to walk the Avenue to check prices before making a major purchase. Of course, some places have more unique offerings or higher quality or more appeal or better design. Most shops have fixed prices but it never hurts to ask for a better price. Since Playa del Carmen is home to a manufacturer of beautiful **women's pareos**, those sheer but colorful wraps that work as skirts or shawls or even tied tops. We always buy them here. The selection is impressive and the prices are the best around.

Dawn to Dusk

Most of Playa's daytime activities involve the water - the beaches are fabulous for swimming, snorkeling, or diving. There are numerous dive shops around. Try the **Tank Ha** (Ha means water in Mayan) dive shop at the Maya Bric Hotel (no phone). **Phocea Caribe** gets good marks as a PADI dive shop. Look for them on the beach Av. 5a, between 12 and 14 (www.playadelcarmen.com).

Talk to a local travel agent for one of the many organized tours that leave from Playa, or take public transportation to the several ecoparks nearby (see Field Trips section). Besides the main bus terminal and many taxis, car rentals are also available if you're off to Tulum, Aktun Chen, or any other local excursion. Take the ferry and explore Cozumel for the day. For local adventure tours try **Alltournative**, in Plaza Antigua, Playacar (☎ 9/873-2036, www.alltournative.com). They do climbing, rappelling, archeological and cultural trips, hiking, cenote snorkeling, etc. So much to see, so little time.

Golf is available in Playacar on an 18-hole course designed by Robert Von Hagge. **Beachcombers** could hike north and make a whole day of it, relaxing in one or two of the beachside restaurants along the way. Bring water, wear a hat, and much sunscreen.

After Dark

If you thought Playa was alive with people during the day, wait until you go out at night. Fifth Avenue is filled with beautiful people like you, strolling, shopping, eating, drinking, and people watching. It's the social center of town. Most dancing is in the sidewalk/rooftop bars and their music competes for your attention. Beachcombing at night is fun, the sand is lined with small restaurants lit by candles or lanterns.

For now, Playa hasn't decided what it wants to be by night, but no doubt the demand for a big nightclub and disco will bring one here sooner rather than later.

ADDITIONAL RECOMMENDATIONS

Last, but not least: want to go where every North American goes? Try the **Blue Parrot**, the kind of place Jimmy Buffet might write a song about. Very busy bawdy beach bar, bungalows, hotel rooms and villas at the end on Calle 12 (☎ 9/873-0083, www.blueparrot.com). For a special B&B hotel experience, try **Baal Nah Kah**, on Calle 12 between 5a and 1a. It has only five deluxe rooms (☎ 9/873-0040, www.mexicoholiday.com). The **Quinta Mija** (☎ 9/873-0111) is an interesting high-quality boutique hotel. Look for it on 5th Ave at 14 or on the Internet at www.mexicoholiday. com. It's a Turquoise Reef affiliate (see page 225), as is **Chichan Baal Kah** (☎ 9/873-0040, Calle 16 between 5 and 4, www.mexicoholiday.com) a romantic little apartment hotel with maid service and an appealing little private pool.

New hotels constantly spring up in the downtown north of the pier where Playa's beautiful beach eventually wanders off to the seclusion of Punta Bete. South of the ferry are some very luxurious resorts in a complex known as Playacar. The only real adventure there is trying to find a place you can afford. You can't miss the pink, colonial design, 188-room **Continental Plaza Playacar**, (in the US, ☎ 800/882-6684) next to the dock.

❓ Playa del Carmen A-Z

Airport

There is a small airport for light planes and charters out by Hwy 307. **Aeroferinco**, ☎ 9/873-1919, is one outfit that offers charter flights to Chichén Itzá and other locations.

ATM

There are two banks with ATMs downtown on Juárez. The Bancomer has an ATM.

Cenotes

South of Xcaret on 307 there is a series of gift shops and cenotes along the road, managed by local Maya families. Cenote Crystallino, Kantun-Chi and Cenote Azul all offer swimming. Azul and Crystallino are best for swimming, Kantun-Chi's cenotes are in four caves with a small Maya ruin at one. Wash off any sunscreen before swimming in any cenote; it damages the marine life.

Ferry Tickets

You can buy ferry tickets to Cozumel at several kiosks near the dock, all have the same price (about US $5), but try and get the fast boat (25 minutes). Be aware that sometimes the crossing is a bit choppy.

Language Schools

Learn Spanish at **El Estudiante Academy** (www.playaspanishschool.com) on Av. 15, between 2 and 4. Lessons run around US $8 per hour for two or US $6 per person for individual instruction.

Parking

Parking on the street in Playa is a pain. A secure public lot on Av. 10 at the corner of 2 offers overnight parking.

Police

The police (☎ 9/873-0291) set up a tourist help booth daily on Av. 5 near the central plaza.

Post Office

The post office is three blocks back from the beach on Av. Principal.

Tourist Information

The tourist office can be reached at ☎ 9/873-1001 or on the web at www.playadelcarmen.com.

Riviera Maya

Little drops of water,
Little grains of sand,
Make the mighty ocean
And the beauteous land
Julia A. Carney, Little Things, 1823-1908

The long coast from Cancún south to Tulum where the Sian Ka'an biosphere begins is known as the "Riviera Maya." Actually, the name is a misnomer; Mexico's Caribbean coastline is so much more beautiful than the Mediterranean Riviera. Beach bums and knowledgeable travelers alike agree that these are the best beaches in the world. We have already written about the most popular destinations along the Riviera Maya – Cancún, Isla Mujeres, Playa del Carmen, and Cozumel – so this section concludes with the more individual destinations on the coastline.

The Riviera Maya's beaches are paralleled by a fast four-lane highway, **Highway 307**. We begin our journey 36 km (22 miles) from Cancún at Puerto Morelos, a quiet seaside vacation village. After that we head south to further stops at Playa Secreto, Punta Maroma, and Punta Bete, past Akumal to our final end at Tulum on the Boca Paila Road. The sights and activities are easily accessible from anywhere along the coast, either by tour, rental car, and or even public bus.

Puerto Morelos

Puerto Morelos is the first town south of Cancún and the embarkation point for the car ferry to Cozumel island. Visitors who stay are more likely to be here for a month than a week and Americans and Canadians dominate the part-time population. The beaches are fine and the town is very low-key, a little like the older suburban development that it is. Fortunately, the high-volume building and tourism frenzy bypassed this location for Playa del Carmen and resorts farther south. Puerto Morelos offers a good quiet vacation only 30 minutes south of Cancún. The town is also home to a very active environmental group who successfully stopped one of the big hotel chains (whose Cancún properties we no longer include in this book) from bulldozing the mangroves to build yet another resort.

*Bookworms: stop by the large English-language bookstore on the main square in the center of town. It's called **Alma Libre Libros**; it's owned by gringos Jeanine and Paul.*

As with many Riviera Maya locales, snorkeling and diving are major activities here. You can swim out to the reef close to shore, or take a boat trip with any of the qualified suppliers in town.

An adventure provider that has taken Puerto Morelos by storm is **Goyo's Adventures** (☎ 9/871-0033) run by Goyo Morgan, a colorful character who has lived in the area since 1976. Despite his beach town location, Goyo's specialty is jungle hiking adventures – fascinating guided tours that include Maya ruins, chicle villages, hiking and cenote swimming. Regular trips leave Tuesday and Friday at 9 am.

Two major nearby attractions are Croco Cun Zoo crocodile farm preserve and the Jardín Botánico, a botanical garden featuring identification signs in English and Spanish, in a garden of epiphytes and orchids. These are back on Highway 307.

Best Places to Stay

Alive Price Scale – Accommodations
(per night/two people per room)
Prices do not include a 12% tax.

Inexpensive.	under US $40
Moderate.	US $40-$100
Expensive	US $101-$200
Deluxe.	US $201-$300
Super.	US $301-$400
Ultra	over US $400

OJO DE AGUA
Av. Javier Rojo Gomez, beachfront
☎/fax 9/871-0027
www.ojodeagua@pibil.finred.com.mx
Moderate

Ojo de Agua means "eye of the water," a phenomenon caused by underground water rising into a lagoon or shallow sea and causing a change of water color. This is a popular hotel, opened in 1970, and it gets many returning guests. The Ojo boasts a charming odd-shaped small swimming pool, a sundeck lined with flowers and a restaurant that overlooks the sea. The rooms are large with good-size closets and modern bathrooms. The 12 studios with fans and kitchenettes are very popular with families.

RANCHO LIBERTAD
beachfront, south of the car ferry
☎ 9/871-0181
www.rancholibertad.com
Moderate

Six duplex, palapa-roofed, octagonal-shaped caba-ñas are set back among the palms here on a broad, bright-white sand beach. The airy second-floor guest rooms cost more, but all the rooms have comfortable beds suspended from the ceiling and spacious bathrooms. A huge sand-floor, beachside palapa, with a tiled dining area and kitchen, serves as a common room for guests. The kitchen dishes up a big buffet breakfast (included in the room price) and guests can use the facility to store food or cook. The unusually large common room is like a giant screened-in sand box with such toys as a swing, stereo, lounge chairs and books to read. They offer dive instruction and the room price includes the use of snorkel gear and bike use. Don't bring the kids, it's adults only. Good karma.

HACIENDA MORELOS
beachfront
☎ 9/871-0015
Moderate

A block south of the main square is the sparkling clean Hacienda hotel, overlooking the water, where the upstairs rooms have an especially pleasing view of the Caribbean. Each fair-size room has a small kitchenette with refrigerator.

Johnny Cairo's restaurant downstairs offers fine ocean-view dining and specializes in seafood.

CABANAS PUERTO MORELOS
Av. Javier Rojo Gomez
☎/fax 9/871-0199
www.cancuncabanas.com
Moderate

Gringo owners Roger and Teresa offer three very attractive one-bedroom suites that they call cabañas, completely furnished with all the amenities North Americans are used to. A home away from home, the three downstairs suite/rooms have complete kitchens (plus a personal coffee brewer, a rarity in Mexico) and sleeping couches with either one king-size, one queen, or two twins.

Best Places to Eat

In addition to the places we list below, in Puerto Morelos enjoy **Big John's** for Austrian food and late night partying at the bar; **Bruno's** English fish and chips; **El Café's** vegetarian dishes; or **Tios** for Yucatecan/Mexican home cooking. We've noted if you need reservations. Most places you can just walk in and get a table.

Alive Price Scale – Restaurants
(per person, not including beverage)

Inexpensive . . . . less than US $6
Moderate. . . . . US $6-$13
Expensive . . . . over US $13

JOHNNY CAIRO'S
in Hotel Hacienda Morelos, beachfront
Moderate

John Gray and George Cairo worked as a team, front and back, for many Five Diamond award winning Ritz Carlton restaurants around the world. They went independent to open this place and their more fancy one in Playa del Carmen on 5th Ave between 12 and 14. They claim the best restaurant in Cancún is theirs – in Puerto Morelos. Contemporary American cuisine.

PELICANOS
beachfront, opposite the park
Moderate

Great locations, atmosphere, service and menu. You'll find it opposite the park, under a huge palapa dome roof, overlooking the beach. Ocean breezes keep it cool and comfortable. The restaurant serves up Mexican food, fresh fish and seafood at moderate prices.

POSADA AMOR
Av. Javier Rojo Gomez
Inexpensive

This family-run restaurant in front of the hotel of the same name is the favorite meeting and eating place for Canadians staying in Puerto Morelos. The service is impeccable, the food is very good and the prices are reasonable. Worth a stop for cheap eats.

Playa Secreto

Just south of Puerto Morelos is this secret little beach lined by Mediterranean styled condos and private homes. One of them is the secret, but not-so-little house, **Casa Secreto**, a bed & breakfast (near new Km marker 312, ☎ 9/874-4286, www.casadelsecreto.com). Doy Cooper from San Diego opened her magnificent home to welcome guests for overnight, weekly, or monthly stays. Most families rent the entire upstairs apartment of three separate bedrooms with three private baths, kitchen, dining and sitting rooms. Check out the painted ceilings, a Riviera does Michelangelo combo. Appealing, coordinated Mexican décor. A veranda overlooks the warm Caribbean and a small pool is available on the patio. Cable TV, phones, video library, and a children's playground, guarded by a woodcarving of Don Quixote. Moderately priced and a great bargain for a large family.

There is no sign along the highway for the **Maroma Hotel**, a luxurious, secluded 36-room get-away that attracts Hollywood entertainment types, rock stars and the rich and famous. Exclusivity is their selling point. The hotel can be found 51 km south of Cancún off Rt. 307 (☎ 9/872-8200, fax 9/872-8220, www.maroma.net). The magnificent 500-acre property on a one-mile, powder-white beach, offers spa services, gourmet dining, a large pool, and a resident artists program. Expensive, but then you knew that.

Riviera Maya

Punta Bete

This isn't a town, but rather a superb beach about three miles long, stretching north above Playa del Carmen. With the explosive growth of Playa there may someday be no distinction between it and Punta Bete, whose near-perfect beach is known as Xcalacoco. There are no phones here, it's the kind of place you just show up.

Best Places to Stay

Xcalacoco boasts a series of several inexpensive rustic camping and cabaña beachfront hotels that includes its first (1971) family campground and hotel, **Los Pinos**. Just in front of Los Pinos is **Coco's Cabañas** with five cute bungalows. A couple from the Lake Woebegone area, Darlene and Richard, own **Paradise Point**. The last small place in the row is **Bahia Xcalacoco** that offers two-bed units with a shared kitchen. All these are basic, but very serene.

CAPITAN LAFITTE
Km 62, Hwy. 307
☎ 800/538-6802; in Mexico, 9/873-0212
www.mexicoholiday.com; www.capitanlafitte.com
Expensive – All-Inclusive

This property sits north of Playa del Carmen and is accessed by a long white sand road from the highway. Immensely popular with vacationers for many years, Lafitte's posada quarters are located in duplex, triplex and quad buildings, spread out upon a broad wide beach with coconut palms.

Pleasing bedrooms, a playground, a beautiful beach and lots of activities (horseback riding is one of them) all contribute to a high rate of repeat patrons. Rooms are villas with red tile roofs and have private balconies, all with sea view.

KAI LUUM II
Km 62, Hwy. 307
☎ 800/538-6802
www.mexicoholiday.com
Expensive – All-Inclusive

When Hurricane Gilbert struck the Quintana Roo coast in 1988, it completely blew away Kai Luum I. That's because Kai Luum is an ecological concept hotel, whose bedrooms are comprised of comfortable camping tents on slightly raised platforms right on the beach. That's right, tents. Complete with netting and oil lamps, a stay at Kai Luum is an unforgettable experience. And you're not exactly roughing it. There are clean and large communal bathrooms and showers, a staff more than willing to help in any way, and a large palapa-covered dining room for their excellent meals (dining and recreational privileges shared with Capitán Lafitte's – see above). Fellow campers become friends. Enter Capitán Lafitte's arch and make a sharp right just before the Capitán's office, 50 meters down the beach.

The fame that Cozumel and the Mexican Caribbean has for incredible dive spots first spread from Akumal in 1958 when a group of ex-WW II

Riviera Maya

Mexican frogmen salvaged the Spanish galleon, *Mantanceros*, sunk against the Palancar Reef in 1741. They called their group CEDAM, the Club de Exploracíon y Deporte Acuáticos de Mexico. Before Cancún, Akumal (Mayan for "Land of Turtles") was the only resort along the Quintana Roo coast. Since then the shoreline has been built up to a point where condos, villas and hotels line the famous and formerly deserted Half Moon Bay beach. It's a fine place to stay if you're after the amenities of the Cancún hotel zone without the crowds. Several small boutique hotels and guest houses are available for vacationers and those who love to dive. It's 104 kilometers south from Cancún.

Our favorite spot at Akumal is **Yal-Ku**, a cenote and lagoon in a locally owned picnic park where the lagoon's fish-filled canals of emerald green and turquoise water provide wonderful snorkeling. It's at the north end of the road that loops Half Moon Bay in Akumal. US $6 entrance fee.

Best Places to Stay

Akumal doesn't have big high-rise hotels. It's accommodations are mostly in condominium hotels right on the beach and they are priced accordingly. Still, dollar for dollar these are good buys for what you get – wonderful beach, laid-back vacation, and immaculate lodgings. The best of them include **Hacienda de la Tortuga** (☎ 9/987-4451), which has 11 rooms and a restaurant; **La Sirena** and **La Iguana Condominiums** (☎ 612/295-5960, www.whitexplor@aol.com), luxurious one- , two- , and three-bedroom villas and condos; **Luna Azul** (www.luna-azul.com; no phone), which has eight units that can be rented as one- or two-bedroom apartments. All these have pools and are on the powdery white sand of Akumal's Half Moon Bay. If you really want to splurge, try the single vacation house, **Villa Nicte Há** (Water Lily) on the rocky coast. This three-bedroom vacation home was designed by the famous architectural firm of I.M. Pei (who designed the controversial glass entrance to the Louvre Museum in Paris). Furnished with Mexican antiques and original paintings the house was featured in Architectural Digest. By the week only and reserved far in advance. Call the above brokers for details.

Best Places to Eat

For us, the two best places to eat are not necessarily at any of the six or so restaurants in Akumal but at nearby beach hangouts (although we do breakfast at the charming Turtle Bay Café & Bakery). If you pass by **Playa Soliman**, you'll miss the kind of experience you came to Caribbean beaches for. Look for the sign on the highway, just a bit south of the Aktun Chen caves. Follow the sand road toward the beach and hang a left to **Oscar y Lalo's** restaurant cum laid-back hideaway. This shady palapa-covered beach-side restaurant offers cold beer and delicious seafood and Mexican dishes at very reasonable prices – please don't tell Jimmy Buffett about this beach, he'll only put it in a song and spoil it.

Riviera Maya

The second spot is the **Casa Cenote Restaurant**, near the **Tankah Cenote**, nine kilometers (5½ miles) south of Xel-Há. Perched on a rise above a gorgeous beach, the Casa serves up California-style pricey Mexican food. Before you come to the restaurant and unmarked cenote, there are a few houses scattered along the beach, one of which is a B&B, **Tankah Inn** (tankahdiveinn@ mailcity.com), managed by an American couple, Jim and Shelah.

Tulum, Punta Allen & Boca Paila Road

Just south of the Tulum ruins is Tulum Pueblo, once a sleepy little Maya village but now populated by Italians who fell in love with the area and set themselves up here. From Tulum Pueblo south the highway runs along the edge of the Sian Ka'an biosphere down to the state capital of Chetumal and the adjoining country of Belize, where it turns right across the peninsula, past many magnificent ruins, to Campeche. To the west the road leads to the ruins of Cobá and the land of the Maya. But to the east, beginning at the Tulum ruins, the coast curves southeast to form the narrow Punta Allen peninsula that serves as a barrier between land and sea. Along the road that hugs the beach are a myriad of small hotels – from rustic sand-floor cabañas to upscale boutique inns – that stretch even into the boundaries of the Sian Ka'an biosphere, a national park and protected reserve with limited access.

The road east is unmarked, but you'll find it opposite the western road to Cobá. Go east for two kilometers to where the road ends in a "T." Make a
right to find these hotels.

Best Places to Stay

Alive Price Scale — Accommodations
(per night/two people per room)
Prices do not include a 12% tax.

Inexpensive. . . . . under US $40
Moderate. . . . . US $40-$100
Expensive . . . . US $101-$200
Deluxe. . . . . US $201-$300
Super. . . . . US $301-$400
Ultra . . . . over US $400

ZAMAS CABANAS
Boca Paila Road
☎ 800/538-6802, fax in Mexico 9/871-2067
www.mexicoholiday.com or www.zamas.com
Moderate

Watch pelicans dive-bomb for fish in the surf at
this bend-in-the-road beachfront cabaña complex.
American owners, Susan Bohlken and Dan
McGettigan, bought a part of deserted paradise in
1986 and built beachfront bungalows. Across the
street from the beach, they recently added three
large palapa-roofed buildings that house two
suites in each. The hotel's restaurant, ¡Qué
Fresco! (How Fresh!) is well respected locally and,
not surprisingly, features fresh seafood and has

Riviera Maya

just put in a wood-burning pizza oven. Some of the beachfront cabañas share a bath and the ecological owners engage solar batteries for the lights.

★ DID YOU KNOW?

The name Zamá was the original name of the ruined city of Tulum, meaning "City of the Dawn."

MAYA TULUM
Boca Paila Road
☎ 888/515-4580
www.mayatulum.com
Expensive

This vacation retreat offers accommodations in three categories of deluxe and was formerly well known for years as "Osho Oasis," to beachcombing travelers. If the isolated seaside life isn't enough to soothe the wild beast in you, they offer yoga, meditation, massage, and a vegetarian restaurant. Very attractive cabañas and lovely communal areas.

RESTAURANT Y CABANAS ANA Y JOSE
Boca Paila Road
☎ 9/880-6022
www.tulumresorts.com

Extremely popular, Ana y José's is a landmark along the rough road to Punta Allen. It continues to be the standard by which other places are measured. Picturesque white stucco two-story buildings, set back from the stunning beach, house well-decorated rooms on both floors. Upstairs rooms, with their palapa roofs, are in higher demand. Ana and José offer an excellent, comfortable restaurant overlooking the water with inside or outside dining. The pool has a grotto at one end. Guided trips into the biosphere, led by a naturalist from the Amigos de Sian Ka'an, depart from here daily, except Friday and Sunday. You can sign up and pay in the restaurant. This trip leaves around 9 am and lasts about six hours. See details in the *Sian Ka'an Field Trip* section, page 268.

LAS RANITAS

Boca Paila Road
fax 9/873-0934
www.lasranitas.com

Everything about this former private home converted to villa hotel is appealing, from the visually stunning artwork and impeccable décor right down to the solar panels and recycling plant for water hidden under the tennis courts. Yannick, who with his wife Leïla, owns and operates this hidden gem, takes great pride in the ecological innovations incorporated into the construction. Suites are built in a half-moon shape with individual verandas or patios facing the sea and bathrooms with custom designed matching Mexican tile work.

★ DID YOU KNOW?

Las Ranitas' name is a play on the nickname the English have for the French, "Frogs." When you hear Yannick's accent you'll understand why. Where else would you find a bidet in Mexico? Reservations recommended.

Best Places to Eat

There are several good hotel restaurants along the Boca Paila Road, most notably the ones at Zamas, Piedra Escondida, Ana y José, Las Ranitas and Bananas. But Tulum Pueblo also boasts several good restaurants. If no phone number is listed, no reservations are needed.

Alive Price Scale – Restaurants
(per person, not including beverage)

Inexpensive . . . . less than US $6
Moderate. . . . . US $6-$13
Expensive . . . . over US $13

IL GIARDINO DI TONI Y SIMONE
Up a side street near where the concrete road divider begins.
Moderate

This is a lovely garden restaurant run by Toni and Carmela (Simone is Carmela's daughter) that features fine Italian cuisine. The large kitchen is behind stone walls and dining is under a palapa overhang on the porch, or you can eat under individual palapa umbrellas in the garden. Very welcome is their spotlessly clean bathroom. If you've just discovered the ruins nearby, this is a good place to celebrate the experience. Don't leave without having a homemade cappuccino.

DON CAFECITO
middle of town
Inexpensive

The most popular restaurant in the downtown is also the place for the best coffee and food. It opens early for breakfast, uncommon in Mexico, and fills the tables under the overhang and out on the front patio with hungry tourists, expatriates, and locals. Clean and cheap, we really liked it and went back often.

Field Trips

I shall be telling this with a sigh
Somewhere ages and ages hence:
Two roads diverged in a yellow wood and I –
I took the one less traveled by,
And that has made all the difference.
The Road Not Taken, Robert Frost, 1874-1963

What adds to Cancún's and Cozumel's attractiveness are the fabulous day-trips, either down the unbelievably beautiful coastline – known as the "Riviera Maya" – or into the peninsula's fascinating interior. The Yucatán's excellent roads and bus service allow you to easily enjoy the region on your own in a rental car or with a tour from a travel agency.

The natural water park attractions of **Xcaret** and **Tres Rios** are covered in this section – they're a popular Cancún diversion. Other sights that are sure to please include **Tulum**, a Post-Classic Maya ruin perched on a cliff over the turquoise sea; **Chichén Itzá**, an ancient Maya city abandoned and lost to the world until the mid-1800s, strewn with huge pyramids where human sacrifices were once held; **Valladolid**, near Chichén, one of the peninsula's most Spanish Colonial towns in the heart of Maya country; **Aktun Chen**, natural caves that contain a beautiful deep green cenote; and **Cobá**, a sprawling ruin deep in the jungle.

FEATURED FIELD TRIPS

The following recommended diversions are profiled in this chapter and are grouped as follows. We look at the water parks first, then skip around the Maya ruins and ecological attractions in the region. All sites are shown on the map on the opposite page.

The coast of Quintana Roo was the primary trade route for the Maya. Cozumel, Tulum and Xel-Há were their important trade stops.

Other sights worth considering are the **Rio Lagartos flamingo feeding area**, where huge flocks of bright pink birds gather, and **Sian Ka'an Biosphere**, a nature preserve south of Tulum. You'll find extensive details on many more adventures in our other Hunter Guide: **Adventure Guide to the Yucatán, Cancún & Cozumel**, available for purchase at bookstores nationwide or at www.hunterpublishing.com. In case you want to extend your time exploring (for example, staying for the night-time laser show at Chichén), we've included some hotels and restaurants to consider for overnight stays near the various destinations.

Don't be afraid to try these excursions on your own; it's easy and safe – just buy public bus tickets at the downtown Cancún station or in Playa del Carmen, if you're staying on Cozumel. However, guided tours are more convenient for most

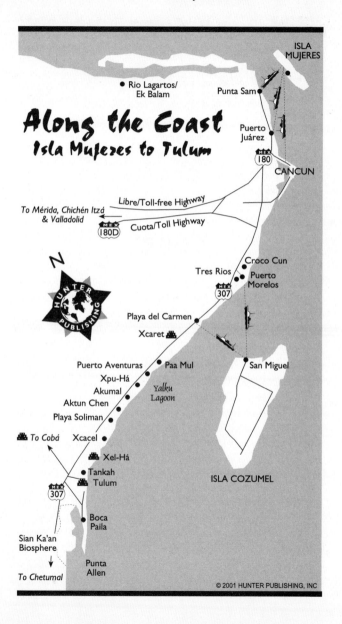

ISLA MUJERES

Rio Lagartos/
Ek Balam

Punta Sam

Along the Coast
Isla Mujeres to Tulum

Puerto
Juárez

MEX 180

CANCUN

Libre/Toll-free Highway

To Mérida, Chichén Itzá
& Valladolid

MEX 180D

Cuota/Toll Highway

Croco Cun

Tres Rios

Puerto
Morelos

MEX 307

N
HUNTER PUBLISHING

Playa del Carmen

Xcaret

San Miguel

Puerto Aventuras • Paa Mul

Xpu-Há

Akumal

Yalku
Lagoon

Aktun Chen

Playa Soliman

To Cobá   Xcacel

Xel-Há

ISLA COZUMEL

Tankah
Tulum

MEX 307

Boca
Paila

Sian Ka'an
Biosphere
↓
To Chetumal

Punta
Allen

© 2001 HUNTER PUBLISHING, INC

travelers and usually include a guide at the sight, lunch and a shopping stop.

Xcaret

This large-scale "eco-archeological" park – with walking and horseback riding trails, authentic Maya ruins, a recreation of a Maya village, two snorkeling rivers (one underground that runs through a sacred cave), as well as fabulous beaches with soft white sand – attracts busloads of water-lovers and fun-seekers. Dolphins perform in the lagoon and there's an aquarium and a zoo. Brightly painted buses leave from the Xcaret terminal building across from Plaza Caracol at 9 and 10 am every day. No reservations are needed, but aim to be there at least 30 minutes before departure. This is a full-day excursion.

Xcaret is a resort playground that combines Maya ruins with tranquil coves, inlets, grottos, natural wells and an underground river. Originally known as Polé, meaning "place of trade," it was the prehispanic port for Maya canoes to the sacred island of Cozumel. Excellent swimming (available with dolphins for US $50 extra), several good restaurants (crowded at lunchtime), snorkeling and sunbathing are here. There's a wild bird aviary, gift shops, a small museum, scale models of some of the Yucatán's more famous Maya ruins, and a botanical garden. You can horseback ride or cork off in a traditional string hammock under the shade of palm trees.

Colorful funky buses run from the hotel zone on the strip a few miles south of Playa and 45 miles (72 km) south of Cancún. Cruise ships docking at Calica often list Xcaret as the port of call. Buses and taxis run cruisers to the park. Xcaret has added a nighttime light show (starts at 5 pm) with festive dancing and folk activities all included in the admission price of about US $35 (under 11 years, US $20) for the day.

Bring your snorkel equipment or rent it at the park. There are two choices for river trips, one is the Maya river run and the other the underground river. The underground river is an interesting trip but not for the claustrophobic, especially not when it's crowded. The aboveground Maya river run, past a replica of a Maya village, is much less jammed and you'll see more fish. ☎ 9/883-3144.

Xel-Há

Five miles north of Tulum, Xel-Há is billed as the world's largest natural aquarium. Its blue-green lagoon, lined with coral caves and a sunken Maya altar, offers snorkeling and swimming within an attractive park-like setting. A snorkel and cool swim after visiting Tulum is their big selling point.

Mayan for "clear water," Xel-Há (SHELL-HA) is aptly named. The park is a series of interconnected clear-water lagoons that form a natural aquarium for angelfish, lobster, barracuda, parrot fish, French grunts and many others. Snorkeling and swimming are the big pastimes here, or you can drop into one of the comfortable Yucatecan hammocks strung in a sandy grove of coconut palms. The park features five restaurants, 11 shops, lockers, showers and changing rooms. ☎ 9/884-9422.

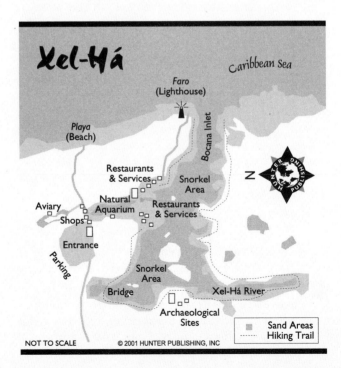

Xel-Há

Caribbean Sea

Faro (Lighthouse)

Playa (Beach)

Bocana Inlet

Restaurants & Services

Snorkel Area

N

Natural Aquarium

Restaurants & Services

Aviary

Shops

Entrance

Parking

Snorkel Area

Bridge

Xel-Há River

Archaeological Sites

☐ Sand Areas
---- Hiking Trail

NOT TO SCALE   © 2001 HUNTER PUBLISHING, INC

A few hundred feet before the inlet entrance are several small cenotes plus some diminutive Classic and Post-Classic Maya ruins with painted murals. A good walking path through the surrounding forest offers a close-up view of the typical vegetation, including bromeliads, orchids and ferns, while frigate birds swing by overhead.

General admission is about US $25. An all-inclusive plan covers the entrance charge, use of snorkeling gear, towel, locker, floats, life jackets, food and beverages in the five restaurants and *nevarias* (ice cream stores) and taxes and tips. Adults, US $49; children 4-12, US $34; under 4, free. Open year-round from 8:30 am-6 pm.

Tres Ríos Park

This entertainment and recreational park proclaims itself a "Tropical Reserve," because of its natural setting and activities in nature. Not as elaborate or established as Xcaret or Xel-Há, Tres Rios features a rather unusual ostrich petting and riding area, bicycle rides in the forest, snorkeling in a cenote or the beach, sea kayaking on the rivers or the ocean, swimming, horseback riding in the forest or on the beach, and fishing.

Opened late in 1999, Tres Rios will undoubtedly grow with its amenities and offerings, especially because it is the nearest of the nature theme parks to Cancún, just south of Puerto Morelos.

The all-inclusive entrance fee (including buffet lunch) in 2001 was about US $46. Prices including

Field Trips

transportation from Playa are slightly cheaper. A non-all-inclusive entrance fee (US $24) includes the use of canoes, kayaks, life vests, and bicycles.

Drive, catch a bus, or make arrangements with a travel agent in your hotel. They also offer a half-day excursion (10 am to 2 pm) including transportation from Cancún.

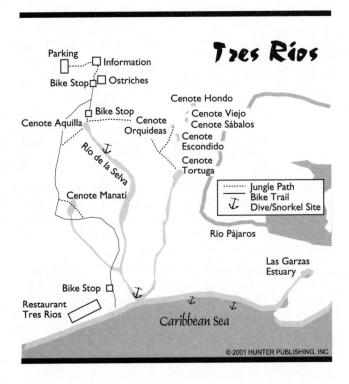

Tres Ríos

Parking
Information
Bike Stop
Ostriches

Cenote Hondo

Bike Stop
Cenote Orquideas
Cenote Viejo
Cenote Sábalos
Cenote Aquilla
Cenote Escondido

Río de la Selva
Cenote Tortuga

Cenote Manatí

.... Jungle Path
⚓ Bike Trail
⚓ Dive/Snorkel Site

Río Pájaros

Las Garzas Estuary

Bike Stop

Restaurant Tres Rios

Caribbean Sea

© 2001 HUNTER PUBLISHING, INC

Xpu-Há

The developers of Xpu-Há Ecopark (www.xpuha.com.mx), located south of Puerto Adventuras, boast that they created their slice of paradise "in harmony with nature." Any development, especially a recreational park that attracts many people, does environmental damage but Xpu-Há has made much effort to minimize its impact. Of the 91-plus acres in the park, nearly 87 are untouched and natural. The park sponsors a reforestation effort and raise-and-release projects. Entrance fee to the park includes everything – complete breakfast, beginning at the opening at 9 am, buffet lunch, served 12:30 until 5 pm, drinks until closing at 6 pm. The tropical beach is picture perfect and activities include snorkeling, intro to diving for novices, kayaking, hiking, and lazing in a hammock. There's also a zoo with an aviary, crocodile pen, and botanical garden. Admission is about US $40. Book an excursion here through a local travel agent in a hotel or downtown.

Aktun Chen

The caves and cenote Aktun Chen, near Playa, opened in 1999 and contain incredible underground caverns with plenty of stalactites and stalagmites and a beautiful emerald green cenote. Discovered by local workers, who used the caves for shelter in bad weather, the labyrinth caverns were un-desecrated by human hands.

The one-hour guided tour of the area is offered in Spanish or English. It covers 600 meters, about a half-mile, underground. It is a trip through fascinating caverns with plenty of dramatic icicle tips of slow-growing stalactites and stalagmites. The lighting is cleverly hidden so that it appears as natural as possible. In general, the caverns are large and open and not claustrophobic to most people, but the incredible natural cave walls are close enough that you can appreciate their delicacy. The tour climaxes at an amazingly beautiful shallow green cenote, so peaceful and still, with an *ojo de agua*, an eye of water. The tour exits at a different point so you and your group can eat or relax at the snack bar then walk back on a road through the jungle. This breathtaking natural wonderland underground is matched by what's above, an ecological preserve of native trees and animals (including deer, spider monkeys, badgers, wild boars, wild turkey, iguanas, and lots of birds). Hard to miss the sign on Route 307. Drive 3½ km up a bumpy dirt road. Admission around US $16, open 9 am to 5 pm, ☎ 9/850-4190 and on the web at www.aktunchen.com.

Tulum

Tulum, like Cancún, is actually two cities: the ancient abandoned Tulum ruins and Tulum Pueblo, a city 1¼ miles (2 km) south of the archeological zone. The Sian Ka'an Biosphere is accessed through Tulum Pueblo.

The **Gran Cenote** is not far outside Tulum Pueblo, 2½ miles (4 km) down the road west toward Cobá. A small admission fee (US $3) and a climb down some steep steps into an open limestone sinkhole finds the bright blue water of the Gran Cenote.

Cenotes exist only in the Yucatán. The word "cenote" is a corruption of the Mayan word for "well."

★ DID YOU KNOW?

A cenote is formed when underground water collapses the limestone overhead, creating a sinkhole or cave.

Where the water flows under the Gran Cenote's cave to an open area beyond makes a fabulous place for snorkeling. On the other side of the open area is a deep-water pool, where only the brave dive from the rock ledge above.

Another cenote worth a visit is **Cenote Crystal**, a short distance south of Tulum Pueblo on 307. This cool clear languid cenote, surrounded by trees, is great for swimming and snorkeling. It's a hot spot for cave divers because of the extensive network of underwater caves, including one that leads under the road to another cenote on the other side.

Do not wear suntan lotion when going into cenotes. It's very bad for the fish and pollutes the water.

Tulum Ruins

Civilization is a movement and not a condition, a voyage and not a harbor.

Arnold Toynbee, historian, 1889-1975

For a collection of old stone buildings, Tulum is a particularly impressive site. It sits perched high

Field Trips

on top of limestone cliffs that spill down to the turquoise waters of the Caribbean below. The first time we entered the modest walled city, it took our breath away. El Castillo, a big temple, is the site's largest structure and dominates the enclosure. The nearby Temple of the Descending God is accessible to climb and has a fabulous view from the top. You can't go inside but it's still a great place to visit. If there are not too many people around it's a wonderful feeling to sit in the sun on the temple's platform with the waves crashing below. Imagine what it must have been like to have been the first explorer to find this magical place.

★ TIP

If you time your visit for early morning or late afternoon there will be fewer crowds.

The books Incidents of Travel in Central America, Chiapas & Yucatán (1841) *and* Incidents of Travel in the Yucatán (1843), *by John Lloyd Stephens, are still in print.*

Tulum is not a particularly important city to archeologists. A Late Postclassic city, the buildings don't show the complex architectural style of those built in the Classic period. (By that time the building arts and stone-cutting skills of the Maya had degraded and much use was made of heavy stucco.) But what Tulum lacks in architectural style it more than makes up for in location. It is now the most visited archeological site in all of Mexico, with busloads of tourists coming from Cancún and the cruise ships docked at Cozumel, Calica or Playa. Even its first tourist, John Lloyd Stephens, American author and adventurer who toured the Yucatán in the early 1840s, was impressed:

Besides the deep and exciting interest of the ruins themselves, we had around us what we wanted at all the other places, the magnificence of nature.... We had found this one of the most interesting places we had seen in our whole exploration of ruins.

The walls on three sides enclosing the city may have been defensive as they average 18 feet thick and between nine and 15 feet high. Entrance is via one of the original five tunnels through the wall. Guides are available outside at the visitor's center that's complete with snack bars and good gift shops. A troop of brightly dressed Native American Los Olmecas Ototonacos de Veracruz perform ceremonial twirling dances hanging upside-down from a huge flagpole. Nothing to do with Tulum or the Maya, but entertaining and worth the US $1 they ask.

⚠ WARNING

A word of caution if you're driving a car. The parking lot has odd-angled low stone walls. If you're not careful, you can easily scrape the body of your car against them.

If you are serious about appreciating many of the Maya ruins in your journeys into the Yucatán, we highly recommend *An Archeological Guide to Mexico's Yucatán Peninsula*, by Joyce

Kelly (University of Oklahoma Press), available in paperback.

Day-trips from Cancún frequently include a swimming/snorkeling stop at Xel-Há after the hot sun at the Tulum ruins. It's a great idea and worth doing even if you're on your own. Xel-Há park is fairly close by, back up the road toward Playa.

 # Sian Ka'an Biosphere

People into eco-tourism really don't want things made too easy for them. They are generally travelers who eschew anything like mass tourism.

Barbara MacKinnon, one of the founders of
Amigos de Sian Ka'an

The **Amigos de Sian Ka'an** (Friends of Sian Ka'an) is a private ecological organization that aids in the management of a huge wilderness area set aside as a nature preserve in the south of Quintana Roo. Only a few tourists are allowed into the preserve daily and then only with an Amigos guide. (Those who need to use the coast road to reach Punta Allen are also permitted access.) Increasing awareness by Cancún-based tourists is encouraging los Amigos to begin putting together trips departing from Cancún. Check with a travel agent or the Amigos directly (☎ 9/884-9583) to see what's available. We went the old-fashioned way, by public bus to Tulum and taxi to the sandy beach departure point. Here is how it went for us:

Our Trip Into Sian Ka'an

The bus we catch for the wilderness area known as Sian Ka'an leaves the Cancún terminal at 6 am. By the time we reach Tulum Pueblo, the tourist contingent is down to the two of us and an American doctor who is kicking around Quintana Roo on a two-week vacation. At 9 am we catch a cab down the beautiful beach along the Boca Paila Road to Ana y José's cabañas, where our biologist guide, Manuel Galindo, greets us enthusiastically. "The Sian Ka'an Biosphere was set aside as a protected natural reserve in January 1986," he tells us. "Named from the Mayan, Ziyan Caán, or 'birth of the sky,' the biosphere was the first large-scale attempt by the government to actively safeguard the fragile ecology in one of Mexico's last undeveloped areas."

The unique reserve covers 1.3 million acres of land, savannas, salt marshes, beaches and lagoons (three of them). The protected area also includes 69 miles (110 km) of coral reef. Fewer than 1,000 people live in the zone, most of them lobster fishermen based in Punta Allen. Manuel drives us to Boca Paila while he tells us about the exceptional flora and fauna of the area that includes 1,200 different species of animals. We join with other tourists for a boat ride into two of the large lagoons. When we enter the twisting chan-

Field Trips

nels that connect the lagoons, the banks come alive with bird life – roseate spoonbills, blue and white herons, wood storks, kingfishers, diving cormorants and king vultures. We watch the banks, thickly lined with reed and mangrove roots, for any of the two species of crocodile, 12 kinds of snake, five types of iguana, wild pheasants, pelicans, flamingos, jungle cats, manatees, several kinds of marine turtles and Amazonian dolphins that make their home here.

Birdwatchers should pick up Barbara MacKinnon's book, *100 Common Birds of the Yucatán*, published by Amigos de Sian Ka'an and available in their office or at local bookstores.

After seeing some *ojos de agua* in the lake ("eyes of water" are circles of clear water created by underground springs), we re-enter the canal and dock at an overgrown Maya ruin, a Customs house that checked cargo and collected fees from trading canoes nearly 1,000 years ago. The highlight of the trip occurs when Manuel goes ahead in the boat while we jump in the strong current of the channel and float downstream, joking about the two types of crocodiles.

Trips into the biosphere run daily, except Fridays and Sundays, and are sponsored by the Amigos de Sian Ka'an, which works closely with the govern-

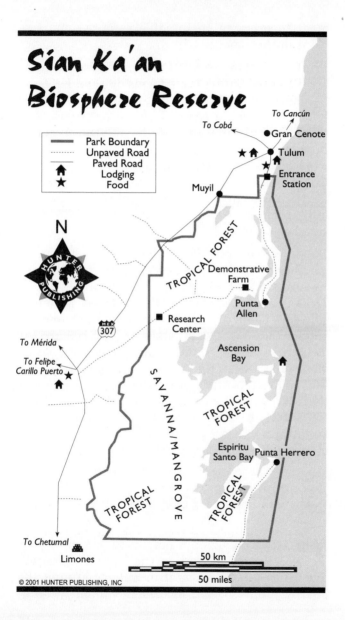

Sian Ka'an
Biosphere Reserve

Park Boundary
Unpaved Road
Paved Road
🏠 Lodging
★ Food

To Cancún
To Cobá
● Gran Cenote
★ 🏠 Tulum
★ Entrance
■ Station
Muyil ●

N

HUNTER PUBLISHING

TROPICAL FOREST

Demonstrative
Farm ■

Punta ●
Allen

307

■ Research
Center

Ascension
Bay 🏠

To Mérida

To Felipe
Carillo Puerto ★

🏠

SAVANNA/MANGROVE

TROPICAL
FOREST

Espiritu
Santo Bay Punta Herrero ●

TROPICAL
FOREST

TROPICAL
FOREST

To Chetumal

Limones

50 km

50 miles

© 2001 HUNTER PUBLISHING, INC

Field Trips

ment to promote sustainable resource management in the zone.

Trips (approximately US $50 per person) can be arranged by calling the Amigos de Sian Ka'an in Cancún at ☎ 9/884-9583. Their offices are in the Plaza America on Av. Cobá, upstairs rear. They sell books and gift items that benefit the preserve. Impulsive people can just show up for the 9 am trip by asking for Manuel or at least informing the Ana y José restaurant staff that you're there for the trip. You run a slight risk that the boat will be fully booked. Wear adequate insect repellent, sunglasses and a hat.

To aid in the ecological efforts here, become a member of los Amigos. Send a check in US funds to: Amigos De Sian Ka'an, Apartado Postal 770, 77500 Cancún, Quintana Roo, México. Membership fees begin at US $25 for individuals and US $50 for families. Donations over US $100 are tax deductible in the States; those checks should be made out to "Sian Ka'an Project of the FMDF" and sent to Friends of Mexican Development Foundation, 165 East 72nd Street Suite 1B, New York, NY 10021. Member benefits include a bilingual bulletin, a car sticker and various discounts for merchandise and ecological tours.

Cobá

The Maya civilization may have grown around Cobá due to its rare-in-the-Yucatán group of five lakes, scattered as if by chance around the nearby jungle. Cobá, meaning "ruffled waters," was mentioned in the *Chilam Balam de Chumayel*, a chronicle of Maya history told in Mayan, but written down in Spanish. Occupied from the Classic through the Post-Classic periods, it was a rival of Chichén Itzá during the latter's apex. The large site spreads out over a few miles but, in general, the ruins are not well preserved.

The most interesting of the structures are the massive Nohoch Mul temple and the Iglesia, a nine-tiered pyramid with broad steps. From the base of the tall Nohoch Mul pyramid, a *sacbé*, a sacred white road, runs some 62 miles (100 km) to the minor city of Yaxuná, near Chichén Itzá.

Cobá is also the place to see standing steles, carved with incredibly long date glyphs. Most are badly weathered. Climbing any of the structures takes you above the tree line, where a cooling breeze may be a welcome relief – the jungle is hot and humid during the day. The little town has improved itself on the east side of the lake near the bus station and several restaurants. The other side of the lake has the residential village without services, except for a small local crafts store and gasoline that is dispensed from steel drums.

Best Place to Stay & Eat

VILLAS ARQUEOLOGICAS
Cobá
☎/fax 9/874-2087
Moderate
40 rooms with air conditioning, pool, restaurant, tennis courts.

Field Trips

You might be able to use the Villas' pool if you buy a drink at their bar.

This is a near mirror-image of its sister hotels in Uxmal and Chichén. It sits on the lake a few minute's walk from the ruins. Intimate room are air conditioned and very comfortable. The restaurant bar is next to the large pool and is a welcome respite from exploring the ruins.

The sunset over the water and into the jungle is quite beautiful here. See our review of the Chichén Itzá property, page 285.

Nearby Sights

 Cobá can be included in your itinerary from either Tulum or Nuevo Xcan, a town halfway between Cancún and Valladolid on Highway 180. North of Cobá on the road to Nuevo Xcan is the **Reserva de Areania Mono**, a spider monkey reserve (no telephone). It was organized a number of years ago by Serapio Canul Tep, a Maya elder who realized the population of local monkeys was endangered by fellow villagers who hunted them for food. His efforts led to the reserve, now managed by local families from his town of Punta Laguna. A US $2 admission gets you a guide (in Spanish or Mayan) on paths into the thick jungle. In addition to spider monkeys, the reserve also has howler monkeys, cousins of the spider monkey. They can swell their larynx to form a natural amplifier, allowing their cry to be heard as far as five or six miles away. You may *Make sure to wear plenty of insect repellent if you travel to Lago Punta Laguna.* also see wild turkeys or deer on the path past a small Maya ruin to the cave where the monkey colony lives. Just down a dirt road is a large natural lake, Lago Punta Laguna.

Chichén Itzá

*I would rather live in a world where my life is
surrounded by mystery than live in a world so
small that mind could comprehend it.*

Mystery of Life, Harry Emerson Fosdick

The enigmatic ruins of Chichén Itzá ("Mouth of
the Well of the Itzás") have intrigued and baf-
fled archeologists and historians since they were
first described by Bishop de Landa in the late
16th century. Nineteenth-century books by author and adventurer John Lloyd Stephens and
British artist Frederick Catherwood, as well as
some by Augustus Le Plongeon and his wife, Alice, fueled imaginations about the mysterious civilization that simply seemed to have "disappeared" into the remote jungles of Mexico and Central America.

Today there is no living city. The closest town to
the ancient ceremonial center is Piste, 1¼ miles
(2 km) west. If you're looking to stay overnight
nearby to see the light show (in Spanish at 7 pm
and English at 8), or just spend more time at these
exceptional ruins, the better hotel choices include
three in the archeological zone itself and one just
outside.

Every resort travel agency hawks one-day tours of
the ruins. While it is possible to see the ruins in
one long day (open 8 am to 5 pm), you may prefer
to stay overnight – if only to get there early in the
day, before the crowds arrive, or late afternoon, as

shadows begin to fall and the sun's glow illuminates the magnificent restored structures.

The site occupies nearly four square miles (10 square km), and to fully appreciate it will take some time. Guides are available (try joining or forming a group) at the visitors center that's complete with bathrooms, gift shops (with surprisingly reasonable prices), a bookstore, museum and an excellent food court.

History

Time is a dressmaker specializing in alterations.
Face Toward The Spring, Faith Baldwin

 The social catastrophe in the ninth century that caused the demise of the southern Classic Maya cities resulted in Chichén Itzá's gradual rise to rule the northern Yucatán. It was believed to have been settled during the Late Classic period, based on the architectural similarities of the "old" part of the city, Chichén Viejo, to the "Puuc" area style. This part of Chichén was abandoned along with the rest of the Classical cities, but it was resettled by Chontal Maya, or Itzás, a seafaring tribe who invaded the northern Yucatán in the Early Post-Classic period. These people, whom the locals considered barbarians, were in turn culturally absorbed by the Yucatecan Maya. Prior to the Terminal Classic period, influences from central Mexico culture had already permeated Maya culture. One of those influences was the cult of Quetzalcóatl, the king/god whom the Maya called **Kukulcán**. The

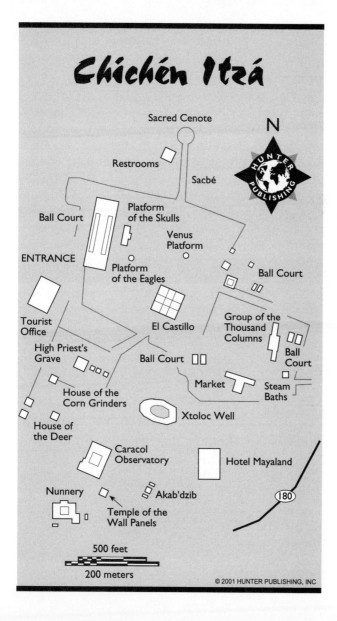

Chichén Itzá

Sacred Cenote

N

Restrooms

Sacbé

Ball Court

Platform of the Skulls

Venus Platform

ENTRANCE

Platform of the Eagles

Ball Court

Tourist Office

El Castillo

Group of the Thousand Columns

High Priest's Grave

Ball Court

Ball Court

House of the Corn Grinders

Market

Steam Baths

House of the Deer

Xtoloc Well

Caracol Observatory

Hotel Mayaland

Nunnery

Akab'dzib

Temple of the Wall Panels

180

500 feet

200 meters

© 2001 HUNTER PUBLISHING, INC

building boom over the 300 years of Chichén's dominance resulted in stunning architectural projects decorated with Chac rain god images and Kukulcán, the plumed serpent.

The eventual downfall of Chichén, in AD 1221, at the hands of a rival city-state, Mayapan, purportedly involved the kidnapping of the bride of the king of Izamal. Hunac Ceel, the ruler of Mayapan, engineered a plot whereby he pitched Izamal against Chichén, which resulted in the downfall of both. Montejo briefly tried to found a Spanish city here but, luckily for archeology, found local resistance too fierce.

The Ruins

The unrecorded past is none other than our old friend, the tree in the primeval forest, that fell without being heard.

Barbara Tuchman, quoted in *The New York Times*, March 8, 1964

El Castillo

The 82-foot-tall (25 meters) Temple of Kukulcán, known as El Castillo, the "Castle," dominates the view as it rises majestically in the apparent center of the ruins. Built before AD 800, the pyramid is a mute but eloquent statement of engineering genius and an elegant highlight of a mighty city that stretched at least 10 square miles (25 square km) beyond its wide central plazas. The view from the top is delightful and worth the steep climb.

The impressive structure you view covers a smaller, older one that can still be seen by entering a narrow stairway at the western edge of the north staircase (11 am to 1 pm and 4 to 5 pm). Inside, archeologists found a Chac Mool (a reclining statue that holds a bowl over its stomach, thought to be where hearts cut from sacrificial victims were offered to the gods) and a red jaguar altar with inlaid eyes of shimmering jade.

⚠ WARNING

It is often hot, crowded and humid inside. The interior is not recommended for claustrophobics.

The construction of this temple encompassed the engineering, mathematical and celestial reckoning abilities of the ancient Maya. In some ways it is the Maya calendar embodied in stone. There are 364 steps, plus a platform, which equal the 365 days of a year. The 52 panels on each side represent the 52-year cycle of the calendar round. Nine terraced levels on either side of the stairways total the 18-month Maya solar calendar. El Castillo's axis are so perfectly aligned that the shadows of the rounded terraces fall on the side of the northern staircase where they form the image of an undulating serpent. During the Spring Equinox (approximately March 21 each year) the serpent appears to be slithering down the stairs, while in the fall (September 21) it reverses and climbs the pyramid. The clever optical illusionists who built it also made the edifice seem taller than it really is. You'll wonder how such diminutive people as the Maya could climb such tall steps. Coming down is more difficult than going up. Even using the rope aid, you may have to walk down almost sideways. Some speculate that the steps were designed this way to ensure that you never turn your back on the temple of Kukulcán that crowns the pyramid's top.

Ballcourt & Vicinity

The largest and best-preserved ballcourt in all Mesoamerica is located here, just northwest of Kukulcán's pyramid. This is one of nine ballcourts built in the city, emphasizing the importance of the ceremonial game the Maya called **Pok-Ta-Pok**. The game was a religious rite more than a recreational game. Carvings on both sides of the walls show scenes of players dressed in heavy padding (they struck the ball with their hips and body, never their hands or feet). The object was to get the leather ball through one of two carved stone rings placed high at the center of opposite walls. A carved relief also shows a player holding the head of another player kneeling next to him, blood spurting out of the lifeless body.

Experts disagree on whether it was the winner or the loser who was sacrificed.

The site's fantastic acoustics allow you stand at the Temple of the Bearded Man and, speaking in normal tones, your voice will be heard clearly over 500 feet away at the southern wall. Above the southeast corner of the court is the Temple of the Jaguars with serpent columns and carved panels. Inside the temple are polychrome bas-reliefs recounting a battle with a Maya village, a vault in good condition and a sculpture of a jaguar, possibly a throne.

Located to the right of the ballcourt is the **Temple of the Skulls**, where rows of skulls are carved into a stone platform. Here, heads of sacrificial victims were put on a pole for display. Eagles tear the hearts from the bodies in another V-for-violence-rated carving. The platform due north of El Castillo is the Temple of Venus. Rather than a voluptuous woman in a diaphanous gown, the Maya depicted her as a feathered monster with a man's head in its mouth. Hmmm. This structure is also named Chac Mool, because his image was discovered buried inside.

The sacred cenote, **Cenote of Sacrifice**, is a hike (about a fifth of a mile long) up an original *sacbé* to the north. Two hundred feet across and 115 feet deep, the well was used for ceremonial purposes, not for drinking. To this end, the Maya paid tribute to Chac with gifts of various artifacts and sacrificial victims. Bones of 50 children, men and women have been discovered here. Original dredging was done in the late 1800s and early 1900s by American Edward Thompson, who owned the Hacienda Chichén. He sent a huge cache to the Peabody Museum at Harvard University, much of which is still on display. The National Geographic Society and CEDAM, the Mexican diving association, pulled thousands more pieces from the well in the 1960s.

Group of a Thousand Columns

The complex east of the pyramid is named after the many rows of columns, once roofed over, that form a colonnade around the courtyard. Almost Greek or Roman in appearance, the imposing

Temple of the Warriors, a huge three-tiered platform with a temple on top, approached by a staircase on the west, dominates the surrounding buildings. There is a large colonnade of stone pillars carved with figures of warriors at its base and a reclining Chac in the temple at the top. Columns wrapped with carvings of serpents served to hold up the roof, now long gone. The temple was built over an earlier one, the inner temple with pillars sculpted in bas-relief that retain much of their color. Murals are painted on the walls. The courtyard to the south contains the **Steam Bath** (No. 2; under restoration), believed to be a Maya ceremonial sweathouse, and a platform at the south end known as the **Market**. Neither of these is in good condition.

South Chichén

The trail south from the El Castillo pyramid leads to an area often less crowded with tourists. The first structure you come to is the Ossuary, or **Grave of the High Priest**, now being actively restored. A similar design to El Castillo – on a less significant scale – this pyramidal base covers a natural grotto cave in which bones of a man were found. A small temple farther down the trail is the **Red House**, or Chichán-Chob, meaning "small holes," probably referring to the latticework in the roof comb. With a pleasing view of the other structures, this building is in the Puuc Late Classic style, dated by a glyph at about AD 869.

The trail then leads to **El Caracol**, one of the most fascinating structures on site. The name means "snail" or "conch" in Spanish, alluding to the spiral staircase found inside (off limits). The round structure, the only one of its kind at Chichén, is the celestial observatory once used by the Maya to check the heavens. The slits in the dome and walls aligned with certain stars. Chac masks over its four doors face the cardinal directions. The cenote up a path to the northeast leads to Chichén's former water supply, the Cenote Xtoloc, "Iguana." Due south is the **Temple of Sculptured Panels**, a good spot for photos of El Caracol.

The Nunnery, or Las Monjas, is next, an impressive 210 feet long (62 meters), 105 feet wide (31 meters) and more than 50 feet high (15 meters). The resemblance of the myriad rooms to European convents gave it its name. A doorway in the Annex next to it forms the open monster mouth associated with the Chenes architectural style. Near the Annex is the tiny **La Iglesia**, whose upper facade and roof comb are a riot of Chac masks and animal gods – *bacabs*. Another building, down a dusty foot trail east of the Nunnery, is the plain Akab-Dzib, **Obscure Writing**, named for some undeciphered hieroglyphics on its lintel.

Old Chichén

A third section of the ruins lies scattered in the brush. It is connected by trails south of the Hacienda Chichén hotel.

Unless you fancy yourself an explorer, it's probably best to hire a guide to see these structures. Wear slacks and insect repellent; take water and a hat.

The most noteworthy of these ruins is the Temple of Three Lintels, dated AD 879, in the Classic Puuc style.

Grutas De Balankanche (side-trip)

The caverns of Balankanche, 3.7 miles (6 km) east of Chichén's ruins, were a center for the worship of the gods Chac, Tlaloc and Kukulcán during the 10th and 11th centuries. Artifacts, sculpture and pottery are found at the crowning attraction of the caves – a thick stalagmite which the Maya believed to be the trunk of a Ceiba tree that led to the underworld. Open from 9 am to 4 pm. Guided tours are the only way to see the caves (relatively large and open). Spanish-language tours are at 9 and noon; there's a French one at 10 am; English-language tours are at 11 am, and 1 and 3 pm. If you get here early, hang out in the cool, inviting botanical gardens, with flora identification signs in English and Spanish. Admission: US $4.

Best Places to Stay

Is forbidden to steal towels, please.
If you are not person to do such
Is please not to read notice.
sign in Tokyo hotel, 1969

There are three major hotels in the hotel zone (close to the ruins) and one just outside the hotel zone on the Mérida Libre. All of them are excellent and make for a comfortable stay.

Alive Price Scale — Accommodations
(per night/two people per room)

Prices do not include a 12% tax.

Inexpensive.............. under US $40
Moderate................. US $40-$100
Expensive............... US $101-$200
Deluxe.................. US $201-$300
Super................... US $301-$400
Ultra .... over US $400

The most historical is **Hacienda Chichén** (☎ 800/624-8451, in Mexico 9/924-8844, www.yucatanadventure.com.mx, Moderate/Expensive) where part of the main house was built using stones from the ruins. We really like its cottage bedrooms in a natural setting. The **Villas Arqueológicas** (☎ 800/258-2633, in Mexico 9/851-0034, Moderate/Expensive) is a Club Med property, without all the Club Med gimmickry. Not all-inclusive. Originally built for archaeologists working on the ruins, comfortable and intimate. The queen of the hotel zone is the **Mayaland** (☎ 800/235-4079, in Mexico 9/887-0870, fax 9/884-2201, www.mayaland.com, Expensive/Deluxe) the largest of the Mayaland chain of luxury resorts. Located with a view of the ruins at the back pedestrian entrance. Very impressive property.

Stones from the ruins are visible in the Hacienda's interior west wall.

Outside the hotel zone, a few kilometers away is the **Dolores Alba Chichén** (Km 122 on Hwy 180, ☎ 9/928-5650, www.doloresalba.com, Inexpensive/Moderate). This hotel is very agreeable

Field Trips

and has a wonderful faux-natural swimming pool and restaurant. A good buy. Across the street is a private park with swimming cenote, Ik-Kil (US $5).

___

Queen Móo & The Egyptian Sphinx

An investigation into the history of archeology in the Yucatán will eventually lead you to Augustus and Alice Le Plongeon, referred to as either crackpots or important contributors to the understanding of the lost Maya.

In 1873, Augustus and his young wife landed in the Yucatán to study and document Maya civilization using glass plate photography. He and Alice first stirred up controversy when, in an effort to protect Uxmal from looters, he placed an advertisement in a Mérida newspaper claiming to have set dynamite booby-traps around the ruins. It was to prevent destruction, Alice later explained to the *New York World*, "not at the hand of Indians, who stand in awe of the effigies of the ancient rulers of the country, but the very administrator who is destroying these monuments, by order of the master, to use the stones in the building of his farmhouse."

Although it temporarily stopped the plundering of Uxmal's stones, the ploy blew up in the face of the Le Plongeons when it became a false but oft-repeated story that he had used dynamite to excavate buildings at Uxmal and Chichén Itzá.

But the nail in the coffin of the Le Plongeons' credibility came from their own ill-conceived speculations of Maya history. Augustus and Alice believed the Maya to be descendants of the Atlantis civilization. In their re-creation of the story, Queen Móo, leader of the Maya and builder of some of Chichén's marvels, traveled to Egypt where she was welcomed as the god Isis. Unfortunately for the Le Plongeons, they were attacked in professional circles by jealous archeologists who ridiculed both the conclusions they reached as well as them personally. Lost in the insults from critics was the Le Plongeons' ground-breaking work and professional methods of excavation – as good as, if not better than, their trained contemporaries – and the important find of Chac Mool at Chichén Itzá.

He and his wife could report only what they actually found, but it was impossible to be in the presence of so many wonders without doing a little wondering themselves.

Manly Hall, writing about the Le Plongeons in *Horizon* magazine, 1948

A very readable and sympathetic book about the Le Plongeons is ***A Dream of Maya***, by Lawrence Desmond and Phyllis Messenger, published by the University of New Mexico Press.

Valladolid

*Tradition does not mean that the living are dead,
it means that the dead are living.*
Harold Macmillan, British prime minister,
quoted 18 December, 1958

Valladolid, like a small gem in a broad gold setting, rests almost in the center of the Yucatán
Peninsula, 100 miles (160 km) from Cancún and
about the same distance from Mérida. It's a Colonial town (pop. 70,000) often overlooked in the
rush of tourists heading to nearby Chichén Itzá.
It's a great place to spend one night, or more if
you're exploring the Chichén Itzá and Ek Balam
ruins or the surrounding countryside.

Tour buses to Chichén stop briefly in Valladolid –
for a quick shopping trip under the green trees
that line the plaza. Maya women sell *huipiles*,
hammocks, jewelry and handicrafts there.
Harried tourists then re-board the bus, eager to
arrive at the Maya ruins before the day gets too
hot. Yet, pleasant, provincial Valladolid (pro-
nounced "buy-a-doe-LEED" is not a city to be hurried. Its rhythm and old-world style need to be
savored, absorbed in time. Many European tourists stay overnight here as a base for their
Chichén Itzá visit.

*If you're not go-
ing on to Mérida,
Valladolid is a
good place to buy
hand-knotted
hammocks, the
most comfortable
ones in the world.*

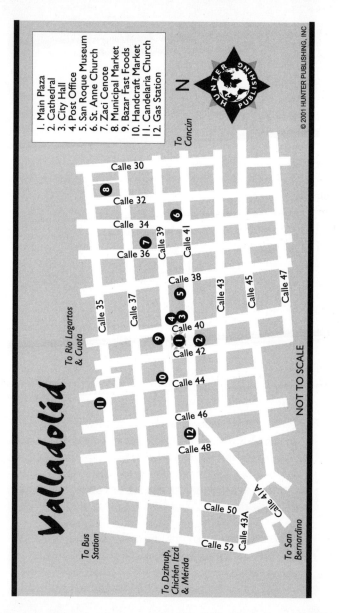

Valladolid

Legend:
1. Main Plaza
2. Cathedral
3. City Hall
4. Post Office
5. San Roque Museum
6. St. Anne Church
7. Zaci Cenote
8. Municipal Market
9. Bazar Fast Foods
10. Handcraft Market
11. Candelaria Church
12. Gas Station

N

To Cancún

To Rio Lagartos & Cuota

To Bus Station

To Dzitnup, Chichén Itzá & Mérida

To San Bernardino

Calle 30
Calle 32
Calle 34
Calle 36
Calle 35
Calle 37
Calle 39
Calle 41
Calle 38
Calle 40
Calle 42
Calle 44
Calle 46
Calle 48
Calle 50
Calle 52
Calle 43
Calle 45
Calle 47
Calle 43A
Calle 41A

NOT TO SCALE

© 2001 HUNTER PUBLISHING, INC

Field Trips

Finding Your Way

To reach Valladolid from Cancún, follow either the fast toll road (Cuota) to the Valladolid exit, or take the free but slow road called Mérida Libre, accessed from downtown Cancún (Av. Lopez Portillo). For us it has the great advantage of letting you see the "real" Yucatán, and we've had a special adventure every time we've been on it. The road is always interesting, wandering through villages passed by time, but it does require some patience. *Topes* (speed bumps) guard each village from speeding cars and make for a slow journey. However, there's more to life than driving fast, especially in Mexico. Private homes along the way sell handicrafts, gifts and bottles of honey. First-class public buses depart frequently from the Cancún bus station at the Av. Tulum and Av. Uxmal circle.

A new road connects Cobá to Chemax, the town just east of Valladolid, which makes it a more direct run from Tulum and the Riviera Maya coast.

Chichén Itzá is about a 30-45 minute drive west from Valladolid. Ek Balam and the flamingos at Rio Lagartos are due north.

Best Places to Stay

There are several good hotels. On the square, moderately priced **El Meson del Marquéz** (☎ 9/856-2073) is the best in town. El Meson was originally the ancestral family

Colonial home of its owner, Mario Escalante Ruiz. It features pleasing rooms, a wonderful restaurant, and a pool. Also on the square is the **Maria de la Luz** (☎/fax 9/856-2071), with comfortable rooms and a very good street-front restaurant next to its garden pool. We also like the **Hotel Zací**, (☎ 9/856-2167) on a side street, Calle 44. It is inexpensive, very pretty and very quiet. The newest entry is **Quinta Real** (Calle 40 at 27, ☎ 9/856-2924, quintareal@mexico.com), a luxury hotel built on the outskirts of town in late 2000.

Best Places to Eat

The very best places to eat are in the hotels, **El Meson** (the most romantic and highest quality) and the **Maria de la Luz** (a sentimental favorite). In addition, there are several engaging small restaurants around the square, all serving inexpensive and tasty Mexican fare. In the open building next to El Meson, on a corner across from the main square, is **El Bazar**, a non-bizarre collection of family-owned eateries and shops. It's the most fun place to eat in town, featuring about a dozen little market-style *loncherias* that open early and close late. It's inexpensive and our favorite place for breakfast or lunch when we're on the move. You'll have innumerable choices of where to sit and what to eat. As the babble of languages overheard attests, everybody eats here – tourists and residents – sooner or later.

If you have the stomach for it, this is the place to try *mondongo*, a Yucatecan haggis-like sausage dish made from cow stomach. Those that try it

Field Trips

(and it's very popular) say it has a strong taste and smooth texture. Dinner usually features a simple *comida corrida*, "daily special," that will fill you up without cleaning out your purse.

Don't miss the *panaderia* **La Especial**, a clean and delicious bakery on Calle 41. Jorge Canul owns it, along with the one in Tizimín, and it has been a family business since 1916. Be sure to try their *pan cubano*, a sweet bread that is as velvet as pound cake and just as delicious. A cousin, Eduardo Canul, owns La Especial bakery in Bakersfield, California. Say *hola* for us.

Sightseeing

 Finding your way around Valladolid is very straightforward. The city is compact, with its roads laid out in the typical Colonial grid of mostly one-way streets. Odd-numbered streets run east and west, those with even numbers run north and south. Most of the attractions are close to the main plaza. The free highway, Mérida Libre, becomes Calle 39 through town heading west, and Calle 41 heading east.

The main sights include the magnificent baroque **San Servacio Cathedral**, on the square in town. It is not the original one consecrated on March 24, 1545. That one (called San Gervacio) was torn down in 1706 by the order of Obispo Reyes Rios, who had it rebuilt facing north as a "punishment" to the unknown criminals who stole from the altar of the original church. Their mark of shame means that the entrance door does not face east, as do most other Colonial churches in the Yucatán.

The **central plaza** is especially pleasant in Valladolid. At its heart is a water fountain with a painted statue of a Maya woman pouring water from a clay jug. The circular brick walk that surrounds it is lined with iron bench seats and romantic *confidenciales* for sitting and relaxing (or getting your shoes shined!). The park's trees fill at dusk with hundreds of birds whose combined calls drown out the sounds of traffic. In the evening, wrought iron lanterns glow yellow under the shadow of the cathedral that presides over the strolling lovers, candy vendors, shoe-shine men and mothers with their children, in awe of the tall *touristas*.

The Church of San Bernardino de Siena and the Ex-Convent of Sisal are a religious complex at the corner of Calles 41A and 49 in the Sisal section of Valladolid. The complex is often considered to be the most beautiful of the Colonial period.

Cenote Zací, the ancient Maya city water source, is located on Calle 36 between 39 and 37. The dramatic large open hole has terraced stone steps down to its somber water coated by a floating film of green vegetation. The owners have built a cool, shady park around the cenote that contains long stone walls, a life-size Chac Mool statue (great for photos) and a welcoming lunch café. Unless you're eating, there's a small admission charge.

The **municipal *mercado*** in Valladolid (Calles 37 and 32) is one of our sentimental favorites. It's the town meeting place for *Vallísoletaños* and plenty of country folk from the surrounding Maya vil-

Field Trips

The mercado *is a good place to buy hot chile powder, honey, fruits and vegetables and plastic shopping bags.*

lages. Open daily, but Sunday is the big market day (best in the morning). Produce and food dominate the eastern and center stalls. The inside meat market, a staple of village *mercados*, is not the kind of place to take your vegetarian friends. Clothes and sundry crafts fill the rest.

Cenote X-Keken

A beautiful and truly unique cenote is Cenote X-Keken (ISH ka-KEN). It's one mile (2 km) west of Valladolid, toward Chichén Itzá, then another one mile south, toward the village of Dzitnup. X-Keken is best visited early or late in the day (open from 8 am to 5 pm), when there are fewer people and no tour buses. Entrance (US $2) requires climbing down some steep steps carved into the stone – there's a rope to assist you – until the passage opens into a huge underground cavern filled with turquoise blue water. Across the road is another cavern cenote called **Samula**.

Bring a bathing suit (but no suntan lotion) to X-Keken, a magical cenote in an underground cave.

Río Lagartos & Ek Balam

Writers and travelers are mesmerized alike by knowing of their destinations.
Eudora Welty speech at Harvard, 1984

The road north from Valladolid, Highway 296, passes over the toll road from Cancún to

Mérida. It's a broad, flat and straight run to Tizimín, a Colonial city in the center of Yucatán's cattle country, then directly up to Río Lagartos, a working fishing village inside the Río Lagartos National Park.

In the agricultural countryside, you'll be surprised by the number of windmills on metal towers with vanes advertising their manufacturer, Aeromotors Chicago. American galvanized metal windmills were introduced to the Yucatán by Edward Thompson in 1887, when he imported and extolled the virtues of the lightweight wind-driven pumps for water. By 1903 there were over 1,200 windmills in the capital of Mérida alone. Wells then averaged 30 feet deep and were hand-dug through limestone.

The newly opened ruin at **Ek Balam** ("Black Jaguar") is the first stop along the way, six miles (10 km) north of the Cuota. Follow the sign on the right toward the villages of Santa Rita and Hunukú. Up until late in 1998, archeologists believed this large site was a Post Classic agricultural center, with very attractive buildings. Then they began uncovering the mountain that sat at the north end of the ceremonial courtyard. The archeologists always knew it was a pyramid, overgrown with trees and covered by dirt and rubble, but were unprepared for the fabulous condition of stucco friezes and Puuc decorations they found on the pyramid's sides. The Maya who abandoned the site long before the Conquest had built stone walls in front of the decorations and filled them with dirt. That effort preserved those beautiful carvings for a thousand years – and more are being discovered as work proceeds. Larger than El

Castillo at Chichén Itzá, the views of the surrounding dry jungle from Ek Balam are breathtaking. From here you can see the tallest
structure at Cobá – nearly 48 km (30 miles) away.
Two tall hills that are other buildings flank the
newly excavated pyramid so you can see just what
archeologists face when they begin work.

The road to the fishing port of Río Lagartos has finally been upgraded from a rutted *sacbé* to actual
pavement and is now fine and fast – 33 miles
(53 km) or 30 minutes from Tizimín. Named for
the alligator river that no longer contains any alli-
gators, the Lagartos River is really an inlet to the
Caribbean that opens into a huge estuary-lagoon
east of town. The lagoon is home to tens of thousands of pink flamingos who breed in cone-shaped
mud nests. The perfect combination of shallow
water and salt in the mud flats accounts for the
brilliant pink and salmon colors of these gawky
but graceful birds. Boat trips out to see them feeding are a big attraction for visitors here.

When they recognized the importance of the flamingo colonies, the Mexican government set aside
118,000 acres in 1979 as a national park to protect the land and the 212 species of native and mi-
gratory birds. During the summer months, April
through August, the flamingo colony breeds, and
tourist access to their breeding area, at the far
eastern part of the lagoon, is strictly forbidden.
But the areas where they feed are accessible year-
round and, even during the winter months, huge
flocks blanket the shallow mud flats in a coat of
pink and white.

Don't be put off when you enter Río Lagartos (some dilapidated housing rests in the mangrove swamp south of town); the community itself is quite quaint and appealing. As you pull into the riverfront, hawkers may approach you and ask if you want to see the flamingos. These young entrepreneurs are legitimate, but make sure to check the price quoted with the cooperative kiosk along the *malecón*.

Another attraction of Río Lagartos is a fabulously photogenic brilliant blue cenote, **Cenote Chiquilá**. It's a cool relaxing swim or snorkel and a great place to camp for free (no facilities) or have a picnic. Located less than a mile out of town, follow the waterfront to the right (east), past the summer homes that dot the harbor, along the dirt road to a palapa-roofed, open-sided shed. Worth the walk. It's a fixed price.

Flamingos

Flocks of flamingos dine at several locations along the estuary and lagoon and prices for boat rides out to view them depend on how far you travel. Boats are available on the *malecón* from the fisherman's cooperative. The lagoon begins to widen east of the wooden bridge over the river and it's about 30 minutes to the first feeding spot, Yoluk or Yolv'i (about US $25). This trip takes about two hours total and can include another smaller colony nearby, Najochin. Adding the Chiquilá colony boosts the price to US $30. The next option is about 3½ hours total for a trip to the larger colony of San Fernando (US $40-$50). Still larger is the colony at Punta Meco, a 4½-hour round trip for about US $75. On all the trips, the guide will point out the white mountain visible on the barrier peninsula. That's a mountain of salt at Las Coloradas. Salt has been mined there by the Maya for over 2,000 years!

Best Places to Stay & Eat

If you're hungry while in Río Lagartos, try informal **La Isla Contoy** (Calle 19), where seafood is the specialty. In fact, fishing boats tie up in front of the dining area. Free tourist information, fishing trip or flamingo tour arrangements. We also recommend **Los Negritos** (Calle 10), which lacks the waterfront ambiance, but has plenty of really delicious food. They offer a *comida casera*, a daily non-fish special. Otherwise they serve fresh fish (try the *mojo de ajo* – a filet broiled in garlic butter) and a ceviche appetizer with every drink.

Mexicans love to eat mayonnaise (mayonesa) on their lobster. If you're not sure you do, ask for it on the side.

A wonderful place to stay overnight is in the next door village to the east of San Felipe at the **Hotel San Felipe de Jesus** ☎ 9/862-2027. The village harbor here is the prettiest we know of in Mexico, and at night is alive with lights from shrimp fishermen, bobbing in their boats.

Authors' Farewell

One must never miss an opportunity of quoting things by others, which are always more interesting than those one thinks up oneself.
Marcel Proust, 1871-1922

No matter where you go, or what you do, we hope you enjoy yourselves in Mexico as much as we have. We've tried to organize and evaluate the amenities and attractions of this fabulous land in a way that you'll find useful. And we hope to provide both seasoned and first-time visitors with new things to see and do in a destination we're sure you'll want to return to again and again. *¡Hasta la vista!*

Say goodnight, Gracie.
George Burns

Appendix

Days of the Week

Sunday . . . . domingo
Monday . . . . lunes
Tuesday . . . . martes
Wednesday . . . . miercoles
Thursday . . . . jueves
Friday . . . . viernes
Saturday . . . . sabado

Months of the Year

January . . . . enero
February . . . . febrero
March . . . . marzo
April . . . . abril
May . . . . mayo
June . . . . junio
July . . . . julio
August . . . . agosto
September . . . . septiembre
October . . . . octubre
November . . . . noviembre
December . . . . diciembre

Numbers

one . . . . uno
two . . . . dos
three . . . . tres
four . . . . cuatro
five . . . . cinco

six. . . . . seis
seven. . . . . siete
eight . . . . ocho
nine . . . . nueve
ten . . . . diez
eleven . . . . once
twelve . . . . doce
thirteen . . . . trece
fourteen . . . . catorce
fifteen . . . . quince
sixteen . . . . cieciséis
seventeen . . . . diecisiete
eighteen . . . . dieciocho
nineteen . . . . diecinueve
twenty . . . . veinte
twenty-one . . . . vientiuno
twenty-two . . . . vientidos
thirty. . . . . treinta
forty. . . . . cuarenta
fifty. . . . . cincuenta
sixty. . . . . sesenta
seventy. . . . . setenta
eighty . . . . ochenta
ninety . . . . noventa
one hundred. . . . . ciento
one hundred and one . . . . ciento uno
five hundred. . . . . quinientos
one thousand . . . . mil
one thousand and one. . . . . mil uno
two thousand. . . . . dos mil
one million. . . . . un millón
one billion . . . . mil millones
first . . . . primero
second. . . . . segundo
third . . . . tercero
last. . . . . último

Conversation

How are you?. . . . . ¿Como esta usted?
Well, thanks. And you? . . . . Bien, gracias. ¿Y usted?
Good morning. . . . . Buenas dias.

Good afternoon. Buenas tardas.
Good evening/night.. . . . . Buenas noches.
Goodbye. . . . . Adios.
Glad to meet you. . . . . Mucho gusto de conocerle.
Thank you. . . . . Gracias.
Please. . . . . Por favor.
You're welcome. . . . . De nada/con mucho gusto.
Pardon me. . . . . Perdoneme.
I'm sorry. . . . . Lo siento.
What is your name?. . . . . ¿Como se llama usted?
My name is... . . . . Me llamo...
I don't know. . . . . No se.
I'm thirsty. . . . . Tengo sed.
I'm hungry. . . . . Tengo hambre.
I'm an American. . . . . Soy norteamericano/a.
Where can I find...? . . . . ¿Donde puedo encontar...?
What is this? . . . . ¿Que es esto?
Do you speak English? . . . . ¿Habla usted ingles?
I speak/understand . . . . Hablo/entiendo unpoco
... a little Spanish. . . . . Español.
Is there anyone. . . . . ¿Hay alguien aqui que
here who speaks English?   habla ingles?
I don't understand. No entiendo.
Please repeat. . . . . Repita por favor.

Telling Time

What time is it? . . . . ¿Que hora es?
It's... . . . . Son las...
... five o'clock. . . . . .cinco.
... ten past eight. . . . . ocho y diez.
... quarter past six. . . . . seis y cuarto.
... half past five. cinco y media.
Last night. . . . . Anoche.
This morning. . . . . Esta mañana.
At noon. . . . . A mediodia.
In the evening. . . . . En la noche.
At night. . . . . De noche.
At midnight. . . . . A medianoche.
Tomorrow . . . . Mañana.

Directions

Which way is...?	¿En que direccion queda...?
Take me to... please.	Lleveme a... por favor.
Turn right.	De vuelta a la derecha.
Turn left.	De vuelta a la isquierda.
How far is it to...?	¿A que distancia estamos de...?
Is this the road to...?	¿Es este el camino a...?
Is it...	¿Es...
... near?	... cerca?
... far?	... lejos?
... north?	... norte?
... south?	... sur?
... east?	... este?
... west?	... oeste?
Please point.	Indiqueme por favor.
Please direct me to...	Hagame favor de decirme donde esta...
... a telephone.	el telephono.
... a bathroom	el excusado.
... a post office	el correo.
... a bank	el banco.
... a police station.	la comisaria.

Accommodations

Where is a hotel, pension?	¿Donde hay hotel/pensión?
I'm looking for a hotel that's...	Estoy buscando un hotel...
... good.	... bueno.
... cheap.	... barato.
... nearby.	... cercano.
... clean.	... limpio.
Do you have available rooms?	¿Hay habitacioes libres?
Where are the bathrooms?	¿Donde están los baños?
I would like a...	Quisiera un...
... single room.	... cuarto sencillo.
... room with a bath.	... cuarto con baño.
... double room.	... cuarto doble.
May I see it?	¿Puedo verlo?
What's the cost?	¿Cuanto cuesta?
It's too expensive!	¡Es demasiado caro!

Index